LEGENDARY LOCALS

OF

THE BIG BEND AND DAVIS MOUNTAINS

TEXAS

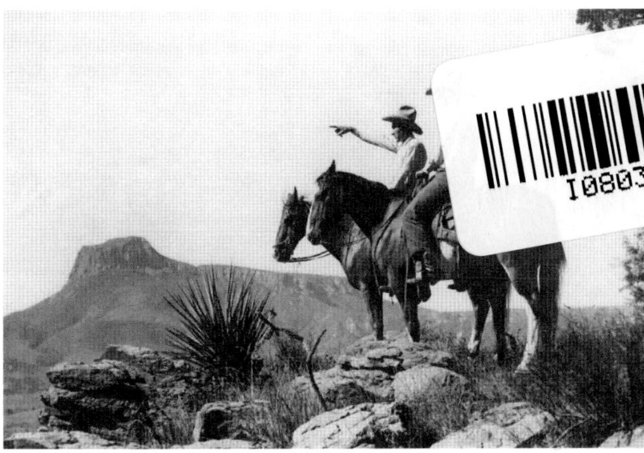

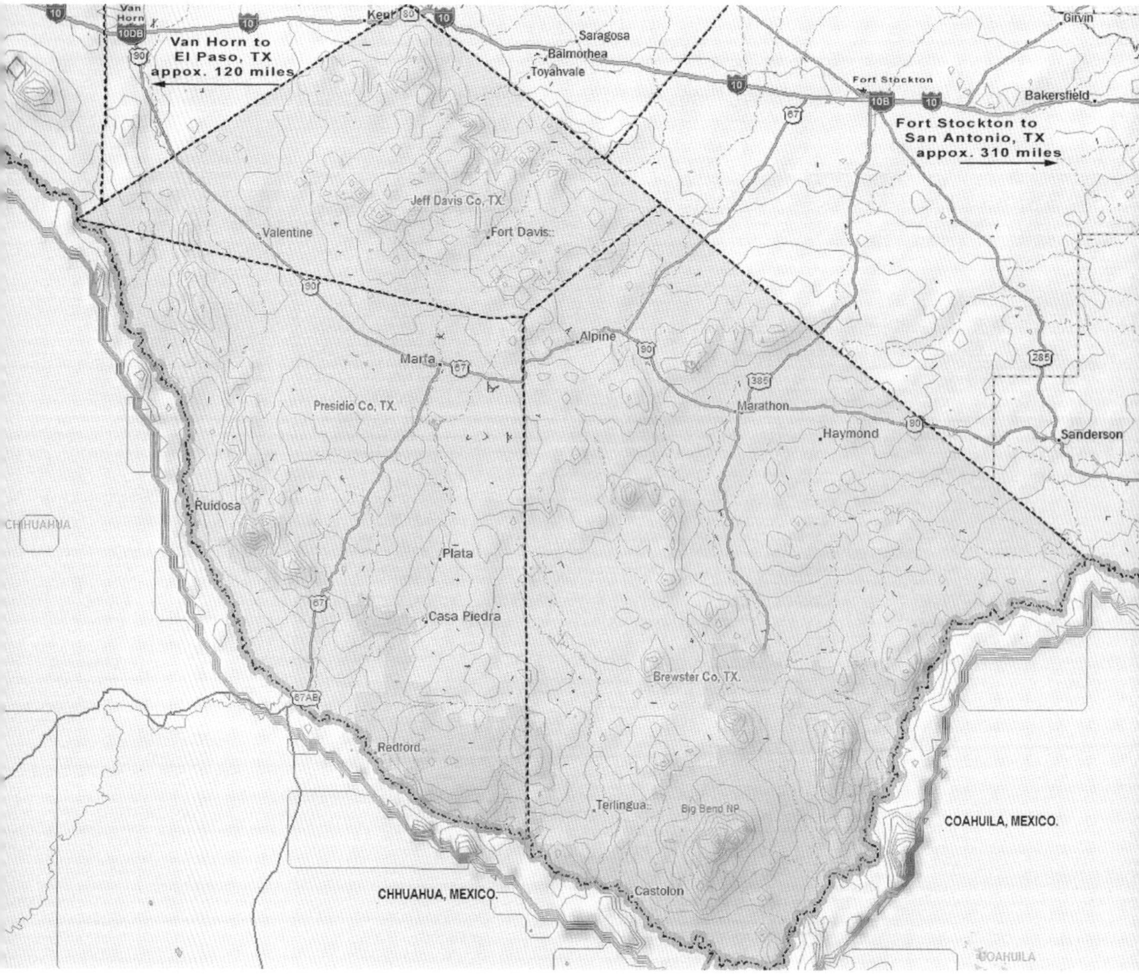

Big Bend and Davis Mountains Map

Brewster, Jeff Davis, and Presidio Counties encompass more than 12,000 square miles and have a population of less than 20,000. (Courtesy of Big Bend Telephone Company.)

Page 2: Cowboys at Cathedral Mountain

Cowboys Dom Adams and Pete Crawford are pictured near Cathedral Mountain. (Courtesy of Archives of the Big Bend, Bryan Wildenthal Memorial Library, Sul Ross State University, Alpine, Texas.)

LEGENDARY LOCALS

OF

THE BIG BEND AND DAVIS MOUNTAINS

TEXAS

JIM GLENDINNING

LEGENDARY LOCALS

ISBN 978-1-4671-0054-0

Legendary Locals is an imprint of Arcadia Publishing
Charleston, South Carolina

Printed in the United States of America

Library of Congress Control Number: 2012947241

For all general information, please contact Arcadia Publishing:
Telephone 843-853-2070
Fax 843-853-0044
E-mail sales@arcadiapublishing.com
For customer service and orders:
Toll-Free 1-888-313-2665

Visit us on the Internet at www.arcadiapublishing.com

Dedication
To the people of the Big Bend and Davis Mountains—easy folks to live with.

On the Front Cover: Clockwise from top left: Judy Majers, itinerant free spirit (Photograph by James H. Evans; see page 121), Gilberto Luna, early farmer (Courtesy of Archives of the Big Bend, Bryan Wildenthal Memorial Library, Sul Ross State University; see page 11), Victorio, Indian chieftain (Courtesy of Anthropological Archives, Smithsonian Institution; see page 116), Chata Sada, border businesswoman (Courtesy of Archives of the Big Bend, Bryan Wildenthal Memorial Library, Sul Ross State University; see page 15), Chisos Mining Company (Courtesy of Archives of the Big Bend, Bryan Wildenthal Memorial Library, Sul Ross State University; see page 83), Felix Valenzuela, constable killed while on duty (Courtesy of Archives of the Big Bend, Bryan Wildenthal Memorial Library, Sul Ross State University; see page 112), Ross Maxwell, first superintendent of Big Bend National Park (Photograph by Blair Pittman; see page 107), Cynta de Narvaez, historian and community activist (Photograph by Sue Rife, Rife Photography; see page 118).

On the Back Cover: From left to right:
George Vose, still flying at age 91 (Photograph by Harlan Gardner; see page 119), Shella Condino (second from the right), Presidio teacher with her students (Photograph by Shella Condino; see page 46).

CONTENTS

ACKNOWLEDGMENTS

The challenge of getting a fair and balanced mix of people from three counties (12,000 square miles) over the span of 150 years was considerable. Fortunately, when it comes to history and also when it comes to opinions, the folks here are close to the former and not slow with the latter.

I was immensely helped in choosing names by the following authors, librarians, historians, and longtime residents: Glenn Justice, Larry Francell, Donna Smith, Lonn Taylor, Mary Willams, Lucy Jacobson, Travis Roberts, Bill Ivey, and others. Some, like Larry Francell, Dr. Martin Terry, and David Lewis, read through something I had written and made suggestions. The staff at the Museum of the Big Bend had a meeting and made a list of recommended names.

When it came to choosing photographs, the staff at the Archives of the Big Bend at the Brian Wildenthal Memorial Library at Sul Ross State University (SRSU) were outstanding. The archives are the major repository of Big Bend historical data, possessing numerous bequeathed collections including those of the West Texas Historical and Scientific Society. The archives contributed 52 images, which appear on those pages without credit acknowledgments. Thank you, Melleta Bell, Jerri Garza, B.J. Gallego, and Michael Howard, for always being helpful and thoughtful.

Other pictures came from Fort Davis National Historic Site, the Museum of the Big Bend, the *Big Bend Sentinel*, the Museum of Marfa and Presidio County, and photographers James Evans and Dan Klepper. Single images came from the relevant organizations featured in the book, from family members, or from persons who had known the subject. Julia West drove to Shafter to sort through photographs of the late Amparo Fuentes for me to choose from.

What struck me often when I talked with local people about the book was their belief that we live in an area of rich history and that historical memories need to be preserved while the participants are still living. Maybe this book will help to do that. Finally, thanks go to Bailey Moyers for enhancing photographs and to Dorothy Angrist for proofreading.

INTRODUCTION

Texas, larger than France, stretches 878 interstate miles from east to west. Three quarters of the way across Texas, moving to the west, is the Big Bend and Davis Mountains region that contains three counties, including Brewster County, Texas's largest.

The name "Big Bend" was coined in 1849 by Lt. William H.C. Whiting, who headed a military expedition mapping the area. He found that the Rio Grande, which follows a southeasterly course toward the Gulf of Mexico, suddenly turns northeast. He named the immediate area "Big Bend," and the name stuck. It later (1944) became a national park and, today, is often referred to in a wider regional context. The Davis Mountains in Jeff Davis County, to the north of the Big Bend, were named after Jefferson Davis, leader of the Confederacy.

The Big Bend terrain of desert, mountain, and river canyon is rugged and remote, while the Davis Mountains present a somewhat gentler appearance. Both form the northernmost part of the Chihuahuan Desert, the second largest of North America's four deserts, which stretches south into Mexico. The highest mountains in the southern part of the region are the Chisos Mountains in Big Bend National Park, which rise to 7,832 feet. Low rainfall and scorching summer temperatures add to the difficulties of making a living in this sort of place.

The first white man to discover the region was a shipwrecked Spanish explorer, Cabeza de Vaca, who passed through the area on foot in 1535 with three exhausted companions. Their epic seven-year journey finally ended when they met some of their compatriots near Culiacan in Sinaloa, Mexico. De Vaca reported in his journal meeting some Indians, called Jumanos, cultivating the rich soil along the Rio Grande near today's Presidio.

From 1581, the next outsiders to pass through the region were on Spanish expeditions, soldiers accompanied by priests, seeking gold in the lands to the north of the existing frontier of New Spain. They called the whole region *despoblado* or "uninhabited" due to the absence of people, with the exception of the Jumanos whom they too encountered and reported on favorably.

Other Indian tribes had a history in the region. The Comanche, peerless horsemen, raided south into Mexico each year, crossing the Rio Grande at easy fording places, like Lajitas, and leaving wide tracks of their passage for many years. Mescalero Indians, fleeing their reservations, caused some years of trouble for the settlers and travelers on the westward routes. Despite the inspired leadership of Victorio, they were gradually denied access to watering places and were driven south into Mexico where they were surrounded and captured by Mexican troops at Tres Castillos, Chihuahua, in 1880.

The Treaty of Guadalupe Hidalgo in 1848 ended the Mexican-American War. In 1854, a military fort, named Fort Davis was established to protect citizens against Indian attacks. Settlers, homesteaders, and speculators started to arrive by mid-century. With the coming of the railroad in 1882, the numbers increased dramatically.

By the turn of the century, the rangeland was fenced, and county boundaries were formed. Within 20 years, a teacher's training college was to start in Alpine, later to become Sul Ross State University. After the death of Indian chief Victorio, Fort Davis closed down (1895), but Fort D.A. Russell in Marfa would later open with responsibilities for border protection.

Ranching became the dominant industry and, despite droughts, would continue. The area was rich in mineral despots and various mines (mercury, lead, silver, and fluorspar) would start up, and some would last for 40 years or more. The Chisos Mining Company in Terlingua became the second largest producer of cinnabar (mercury) in the world during World War I. Other mines gradually closed due to exhaustion of ore or market conditions. Against the trend, however, one local silver mine in Shafter reopened in 2012—124 years after it first started.

The Mexican Revolution (1910–1920) had a profound impact on life along the southern edge of the region. In January 1914, a whole army of Mexican federal troops and dependents (a total of more than 4,000 people) fled Ojinaga at the sight of Pancho Villa's approaching cavalry across the Rio Grande to the safety of Texas. They walked to Marfa and later boarded trains for El Paso and repatriation to Mexico. Local attacks by Mexican bandits across the Rio Grande were commonplace, and caused retaliation by US cavalry patrols and Texas rangers.

World War II caused the arrival of thousands of trainee airmen at Marfa Army Airfield, which had five runways. When Hispanic veterans returned home, they were a driving force in changing the law regarding equal opportunity. Today, citizens of Mexican ancestry form a clear majority of the population in the tri-county region, with Hispanics prominent in business, education, and public service.

By the late 1900s, two new forces were in place. Tourism was now an important part of the region's economy, with more than 300,000 annual visitors to the Big Bend National Park, and more to the other parks and sites in the region. The region's towns, particularly Marfa, were changing too, with the arrival of a different sort of newcomer. Some younger, some retirees, often working from computers, they came with new skills and interests—a second wave of immigrants 100 years after the first settlers.

The region remains difficult to reach without a long drive. Commercial air service into Alpine failed in the 2000s, and the nearest commercial airport is 155 miles northeast in Midland. Three-times weekly train service on the New Orleans–to–Los Angeles route is a useful option but not much taken advantage of. The residents, proud of their border history, relish the title of Alpine's radio station, KVLF, founded in 1947; the VLF means Voice of the Last Frontier. They seem to be happy with their relative isolation in a desert and mountain setting, living mainly in nine different communities, each one quite different. Less than 20,000 people live in just over 12,000 square miles.

CHAPTER ONE

Pioneers

It was not until the 19th century, after the end of the Mexican-American War, that settlers arrived with the intention of staying. Some, like Milton Faver and Alfred Gage, came and established ranching empires. Faver acquired water sources and let his herds of cattle and sheep (later numbering over 10,000 head) graze on unfenced rangeland. Others, like the Langford family, came to homestead and hoped that the dry desert air would cure a health condition. One arrived from Europe off a boat in Galveston. One or two arrived to spread the gospel. Many crossed the border from Mexico.

What they all found was a vast area of desert and mountain, almost without people. The Spaniards called the region *despoblado,* or "uninhabited." There were few Native Americans around except for the descendants of a peaceful, sedentary group called Jumanos farming along the Rio Grande. It was a harsh terrain with extreme temperatures, but in places, long grass grew, as yet ungrazed, and scattered here and there were springs of water.

The single-mindedness and fortitude of these early ranchers who arrived from elsewhere in Texas, sometimes herding their livestock on a trek lasting weeks, is memorable. Their determination to make a new life and raise a family is recorded in a few books, like *Beneath the Window, Early Ranch Life in Big Bend Country.* Those not in ranching, started businesses in the growing townships or ancillary services like freighting.

Settlements, later townships, grew up along the railroad, which arrived in 1882, often where there was a water source to supply the steam locomotives. They also formed where there was a military fort (Fort Davis), which had been established to protect settlers and westbound travelers against Indian attacks. It also grew where there was a geographic feature, such as a river crossing (Presidio). A trading post would be established, a bar would follow, a barber would hang up a sign, and soon a community would exist.

In these communities, a social structure soon evolved, prompted by the natural leadership and ambition of some of the citizens. The supreme confidence of the early leaders is nowhere more evident than in the huge, ornate courthouses they put up, towering over the few existing town buildings. They made a clear statement—the town's inhabitants were there to stay.

When the railroad arrived, the pace of settlement accelerated. Building materials could be shipped in, and cattle could be shipped out, saving the long overland cattle drives, which previously were the means of getting cattle to market. Meanwhile, attacks by Indian tribes had largely ceased upon the death of Victorio in 1880. This was still a lawless place and violence was commonplace, but gradually a sense of order was taking hold.

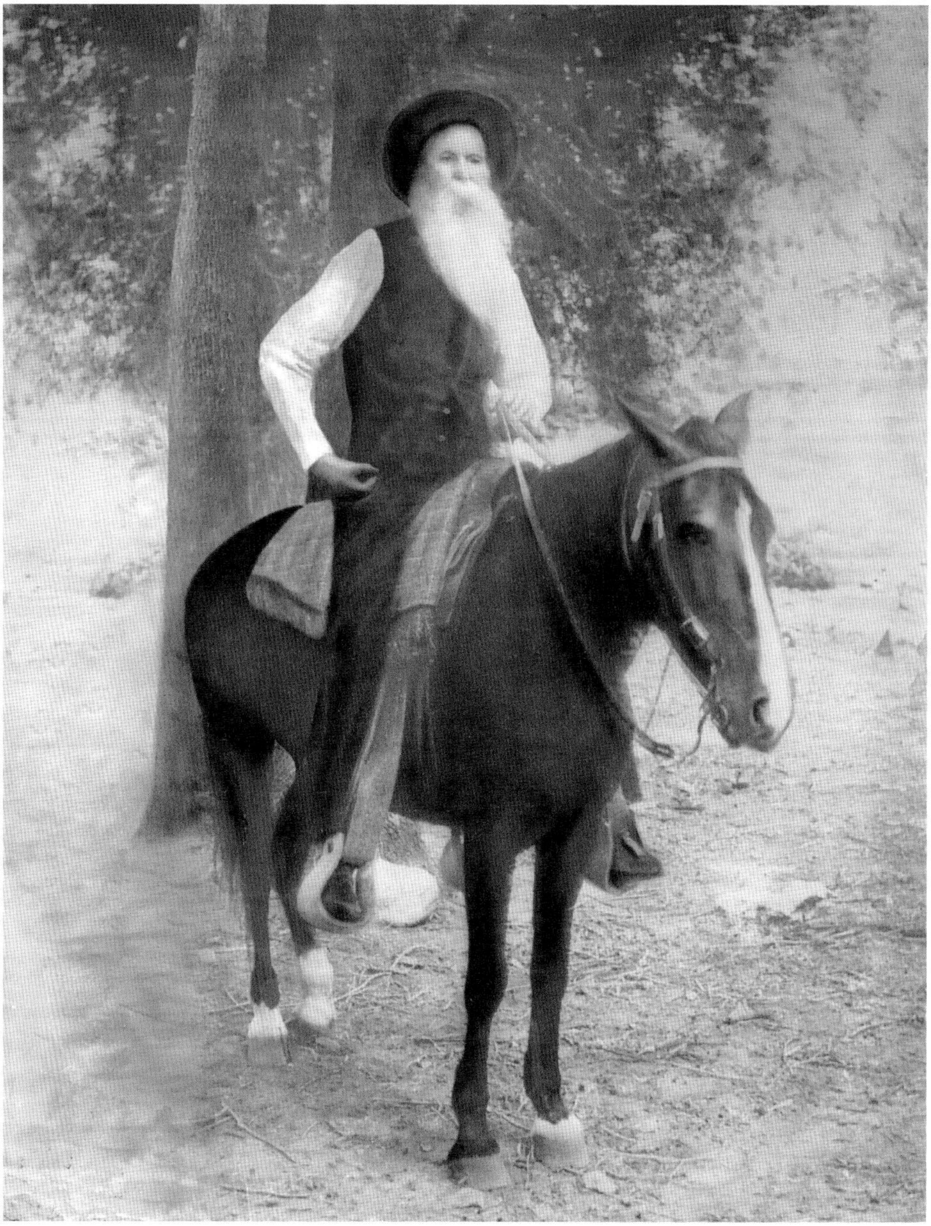

Milton Faver

Born in the United States around 1822, Milton Faver moved to Chihuahua, Mexico, and established himself as a freighter, subsequently opening a general store in Ojinaga. Anticipating business potential with the Fort Davis garrison, he acquired land on Cibolo Creek near present-day Shafter. He bought land only around springs, where he watered his expanding cattle herds, which grew to upwards of 10,000 head, grazing on unfenced rangeland. He built forts at these sites to protect against Indian attacks and moved into one of them (El Fortin de Cibolo) in 1858, with his Mexican wife, Francisca, and son. With the reestablishment of Fort Davis in 1867, Faver grew rich supplying the troops with meat and brandy made from his peach orchards. Small in stature, an autocrat and individualist, he preferred speaking Spanish. He died in 1889 and is buried at his ranch.

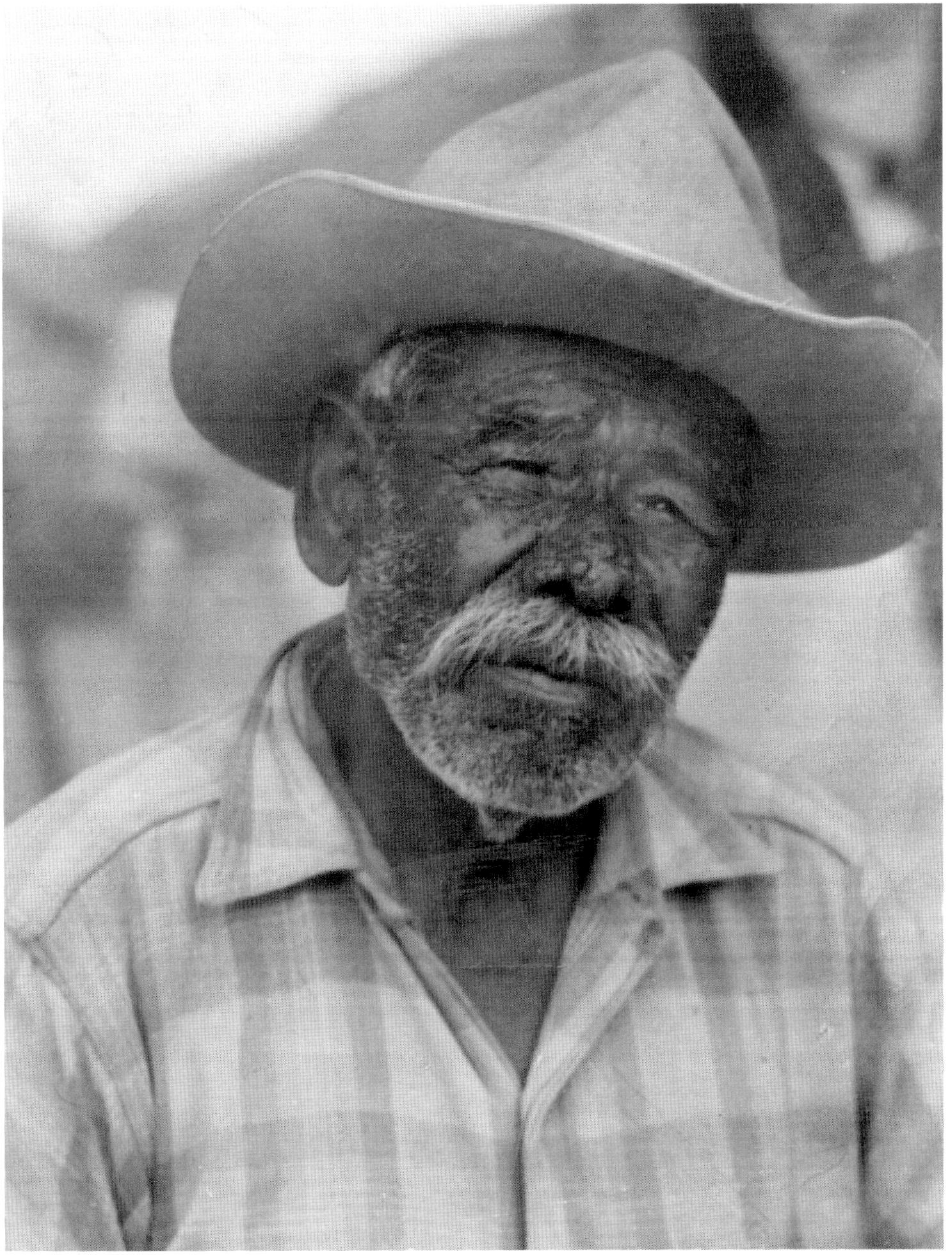

Gilberto Luna

Visitors to Big Bend National Park who take the dirt road from the Maverick Junction entrance to Santa Elena Canyon will pass a long, low structure halfway along the route. This hut, or jacal, made out of sticks, stones, and earth, was the home of Gilberto Luna, a venerable ancient who lived, reportedly, to the age of 108. Half Mexican, half American Indian, and tough as nails, Luna made his living by freighting and selling produce to the miners at the Terlingua mine. He farmed on Alamo Creek, which produced enough seasonal water to grow vegetables; he also kept a herd of goats. He had several wives on both sides of the border, who bore him countless children. How they all fit into his truncated house, barely four feet high, is anyone's guess.

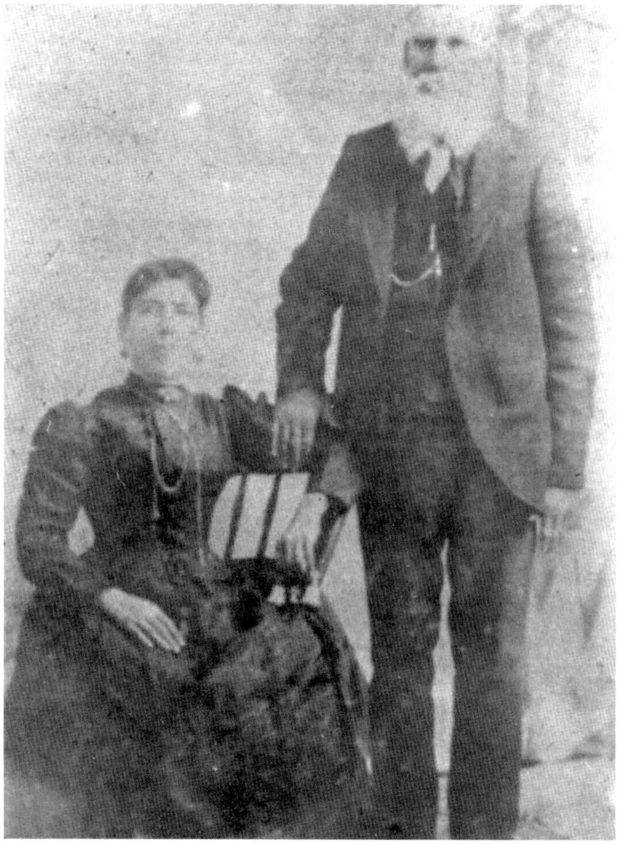

Ben Leaton

The well-dressed, bearded figure standing next to his wife is Ben Leaton, whose name adorns today's Texas State Historic Site near Presidio. Nothing is known of his origins or personal life. Mystery surrounds his brief and controversial time at Presidio, also the manner of his death and even his place of burial. He was murdered, according to a report from someone living in the fort, by farmworkers. Another report, from local historian Luis Armendariz, says he died in San Antonio in 1851 of natural causes.

Before coming to Presidio, Leaton had been employed as a bounty hunter by one J.J. Johnson, who had a contract with Chihuahua government to provide Indian scalps. Coming to Presidio at this time offered a business opportunity. Following the end of the Mexican-American war, Presidio, a key border crossing point on the San Antonio-to-Chihuahua trail, looked set for growth and profit.

He arrived in Presidio in 1848 with Juana Pedrasa, whom he later married. Using his wife's name, he took possession of land owned by Juan Bustillos, which contained a small trading post and a house. There was already a small fort on this land, one of a string of forts built by the Spanish along the Rio Grande.

Leaton greatly expanded this structure, adding 47 rooms around a compound built of thick adobe walls, and entered through immense wooden doors. Leaton's trading post and fort was the only safe place for travelers to stay and the only supply station, and he charged appropriately. He was a hospitable host, impressing all government or military visitors who arrived at the fort. He also farmed extensively on the surrounding floodplain, at one time owning 3,840 acres.

After he died, the story got complicated. His wife married Edward Hall, who obtained a mortgage on the fort. Unable to meet the payments, he was gunned down by assassins hired by the mortgage holder, who in turn was later gunned down in retaliation. Such is the bloody legacy of Ben Leaton, a name that is attached to the fort. (Courtesy of Junior Historians, Marfa Public Library.)

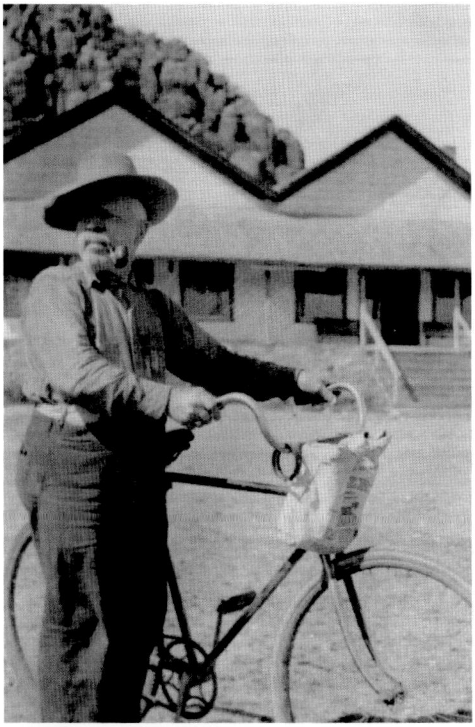

Nick Mersfelder
Born in Bavaria in 1858, the youngest of four children, Nick Mersfelder was apprenticed at age 14 to a barber in his new home, Cincinnati, Ohio. By 1881, he had his own barbershop in Austin, Texas, but closed it to serve for one year with the Texas Rangers.

By the late 1980s he was in Fort Davis. Elected as justice of the peace, he proclaimed "I'm the law!" He taught violin, became an early photographer, bought the first automobile in Fort Davis, and made good money as a moneylender. He resumed his barber trade. Thanks to the goats, chickens, dogs, and cats in his malodorous barbershop, many customers went home to wash after their haircut. His barbershop, cleaned up, is now the Fort Davis museum. Mersfelder died in the Pecos hospital in 1939. (Both, courtesy of Fort Davis Historical Society/ Overland Trail Museum.)

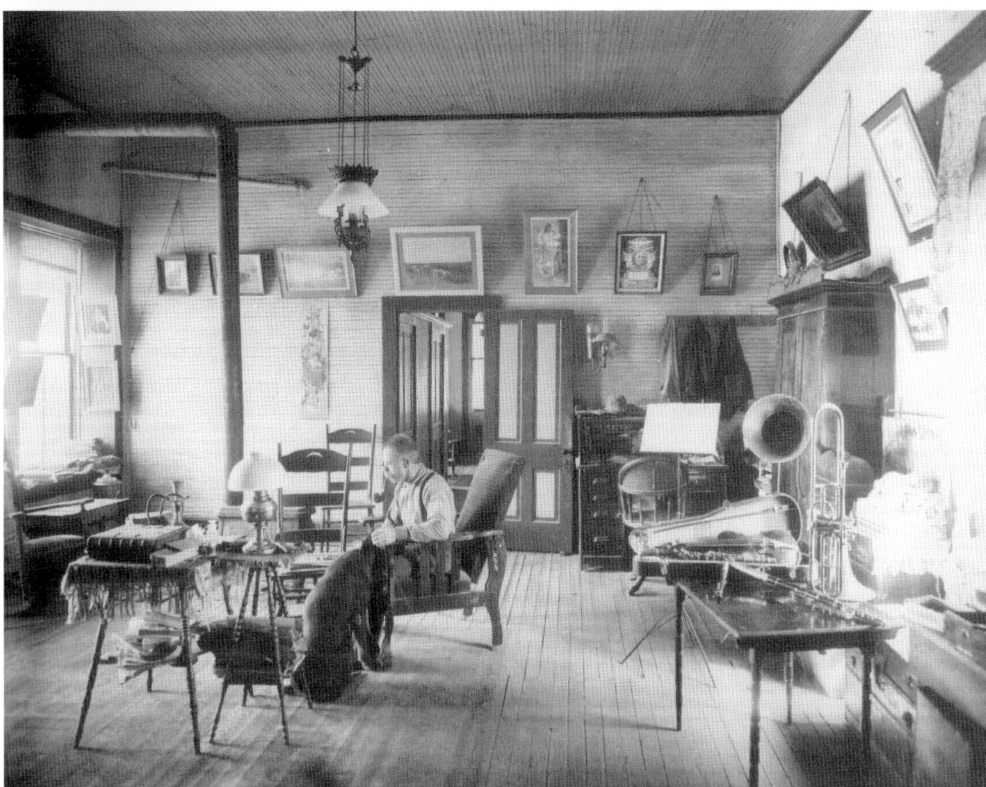

Diedrick Dutchover

Diedrick Dutchover witnessed a murder in his hometown of Antwerp, Belgium. To prevent him giving evidence, he was shanghaied aboard a ship. Eventually landing in Galveston and speaking no English, he was named "Dutchallover," since that was how he appeared (he had bright red hair). The name stuck and was abbreviated to Dutchover.

He arrived in Fort Davis in 1848, and was employed by Skillman as a stagecoach driver, worked as a freighter, and had a farm in Limpia Canyon. He married Refugia "Cora" Salcido in 1862, and they raised 10 children. He was appointed Constable at Fort Davis in 1867. He continued to farm successfully until he died, at age 85, in 1904. He and Cora are buried in Fort Davis's pioneer cemetery. He has countless descendants in the area, many in the restaurant business. (Courtesy of National Park Service, Fort Davis National Historic Site.)

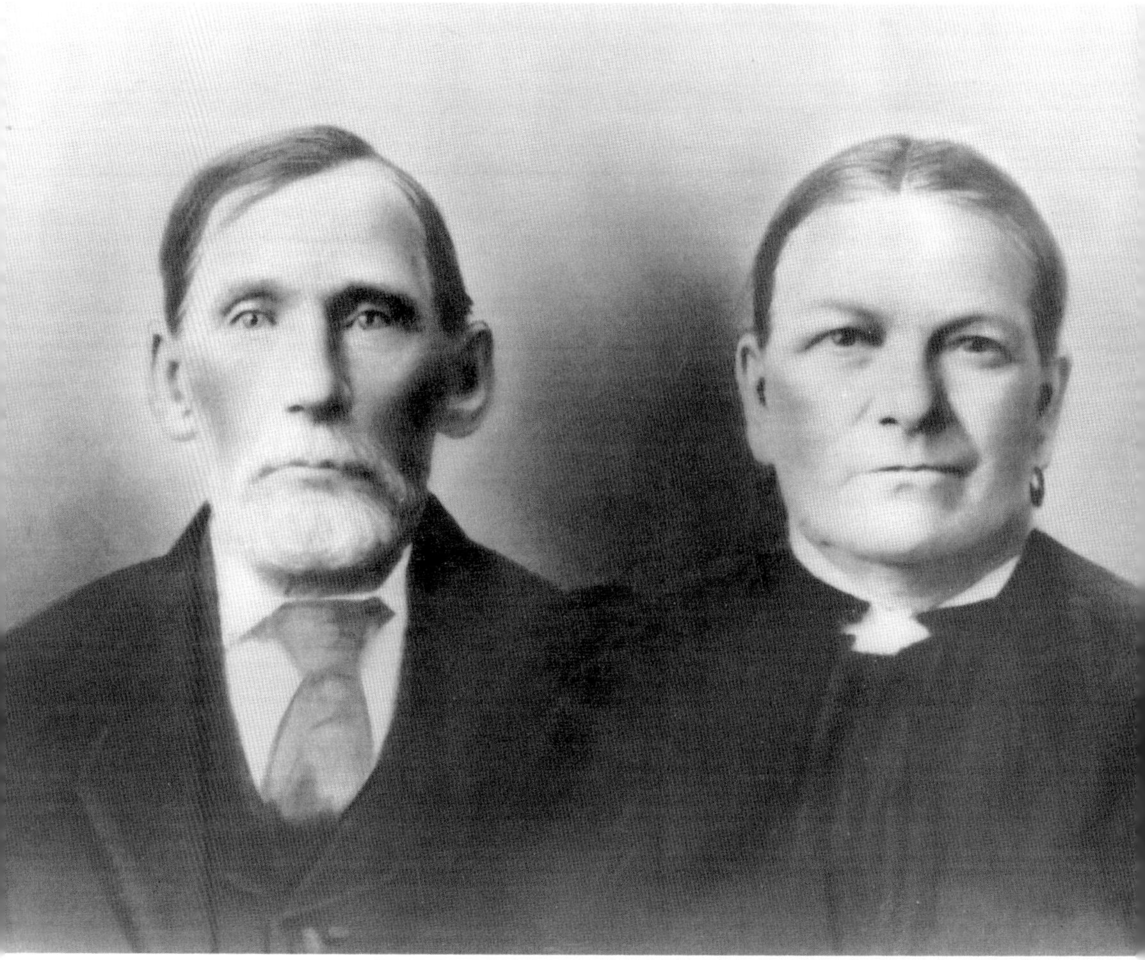

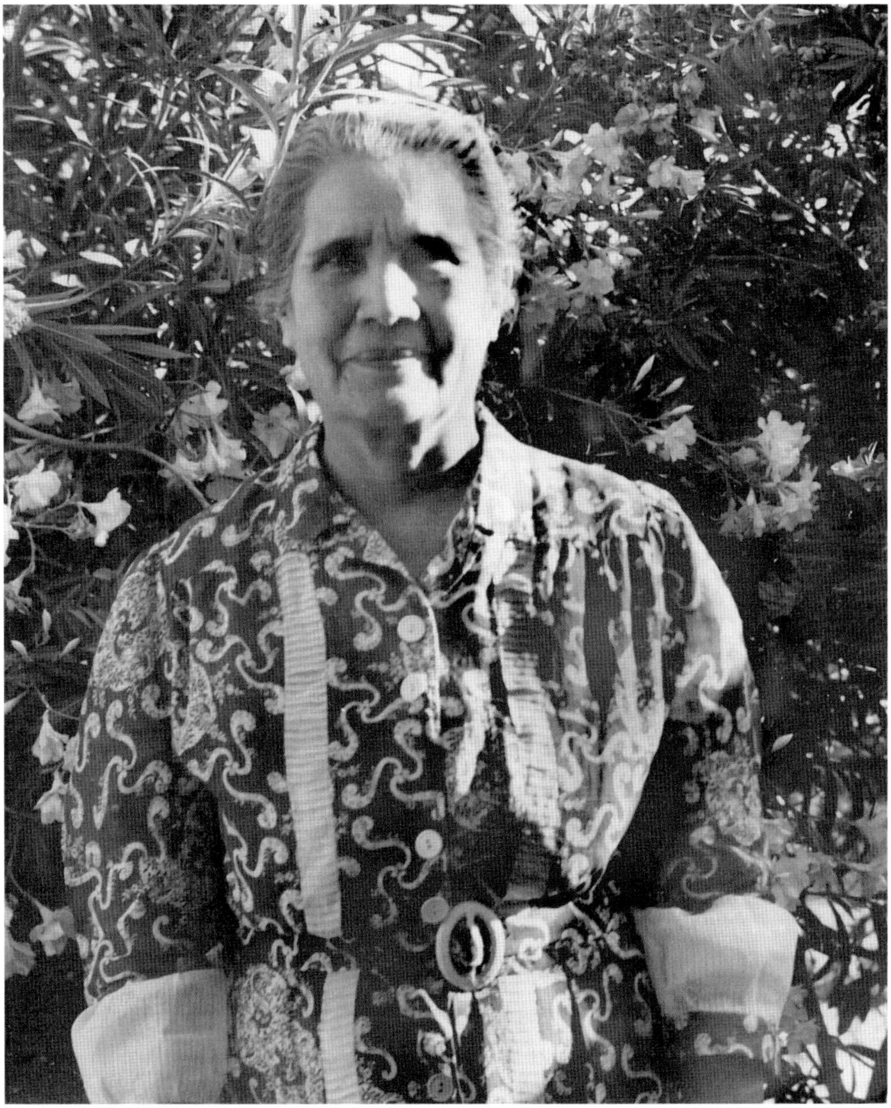

Chata Sada

Chata was born in Mexico in 1884 and married Juan Sada, who owned a silver mine in the Sierra del Carmen in Coahuila, in 1901. They operated a trading post and saloon in Boquillas, Mexico, and in 1926 got an immigrant visa to move across the Rio Grande to Boquillas, Texas.

In Boquillas, Texas, they built an adobe house and established a store and café, which became known as Chata's Place. In addition to cooking her renowned enchiladas, she acted as midwife, teacher, and judge in local community matters. She added rooms to rent, and Chata's Place became a community center, with live piano music and a blind Mexican fiddler.

Vivacious and charming in company, she also had a regal bearing, which commanded respect, not always easily obtained along the turbulent border. She worked hard tending her well-stocked garden and looking after her goats, in addition to minding the store and cooking meals.

They had no children, but Chata adopted local children at various times. When Juan died, she moved to Del Rio but returned to Boquillas, Texas, when the Big Bend National Park, which now owned the land, honored her at an event. She died in Del Rio, Texas, in 1973.

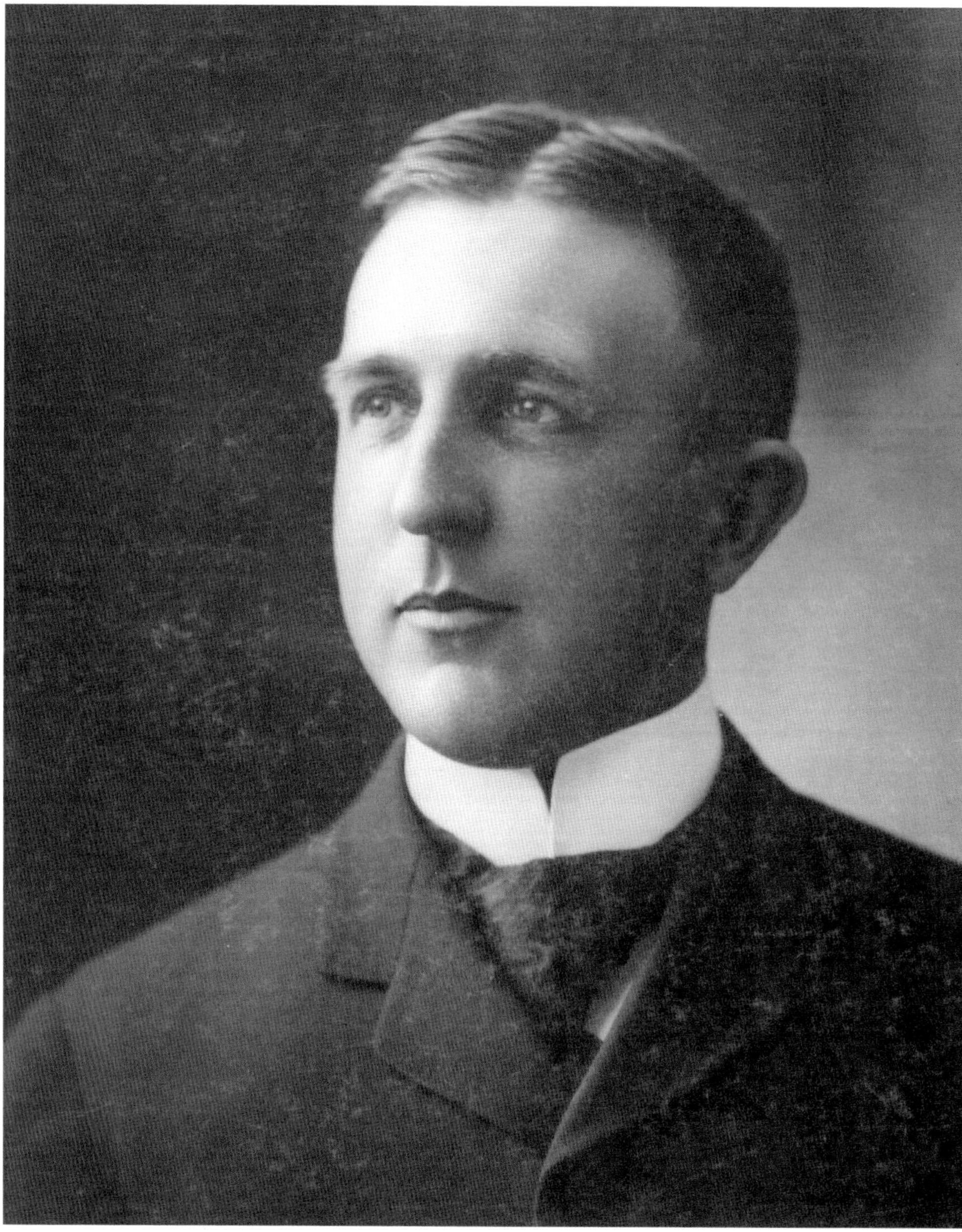

Alfred Gage

Alfred Gage, age 19, arrived in Marathon, Texas, in 1881 from Vermont, encouraged by the news of opportunities from his brother already there. For 30 years, through good times and bad, he managed the Gage family's ranching business, finally gaining controlling interest and meanwhile continuing to add land holdings. He grew to be one of the largest landowners and stockmen in Texas. In 1927, seeing a lack of suitable hotel lodging in Marathon for his visiting business colleagues, Gage built the Gage Hotel. He married Ida Swan, and they had two daughters. Alfred S. Gage died in 1928 after an appendicitis operation. His holdings totaled 500,000 acres. Today, his descendants still ranch under the name Paisano Cattle Company, and his hotel, upgraded and expanded, is the center of Marathon's tourism industry.

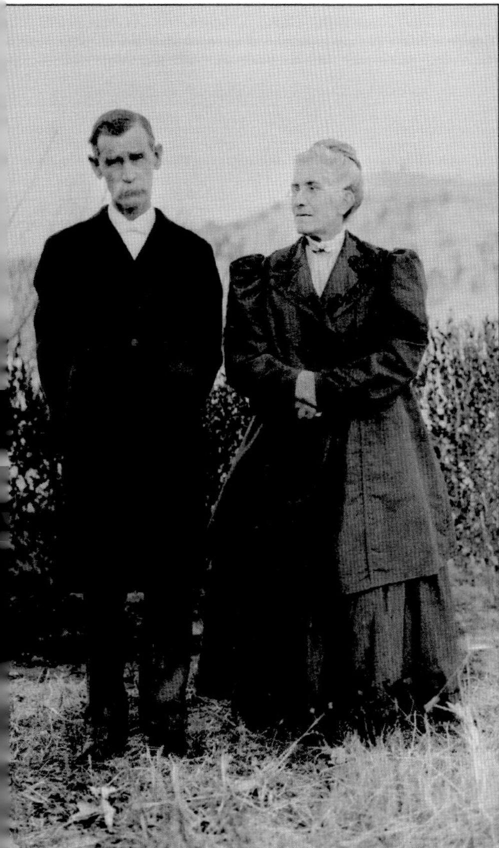

W.L. Bloys

Born in Tennessee in 1847, W.L. Bloys, licensed to preach in the Presbyterian Church, married schoolteacher Isabelle Yeck. Due to Bloy's ill health, the couple moved to the drier air of Fort Davis due to Bloys's ill health, arriving in a winter snowstorm in February 1888.

Responding to a request by residents for a camp meeting, he organized the first meeting in October 1890 at Skillman Grove west of Fort Davis and stated, "Every denomination will be welcome here." There under an oak tree, standing on a coffee box, he preached three sermons in two days—and Bloys Encampment, which today attracts up to 2,500 people each summer, was born.

He also organized the building in 1904–1905 of the First Presbyterian Church in Fort Davis. He died at his home next to the church in 1917. (Below, author's collection.)

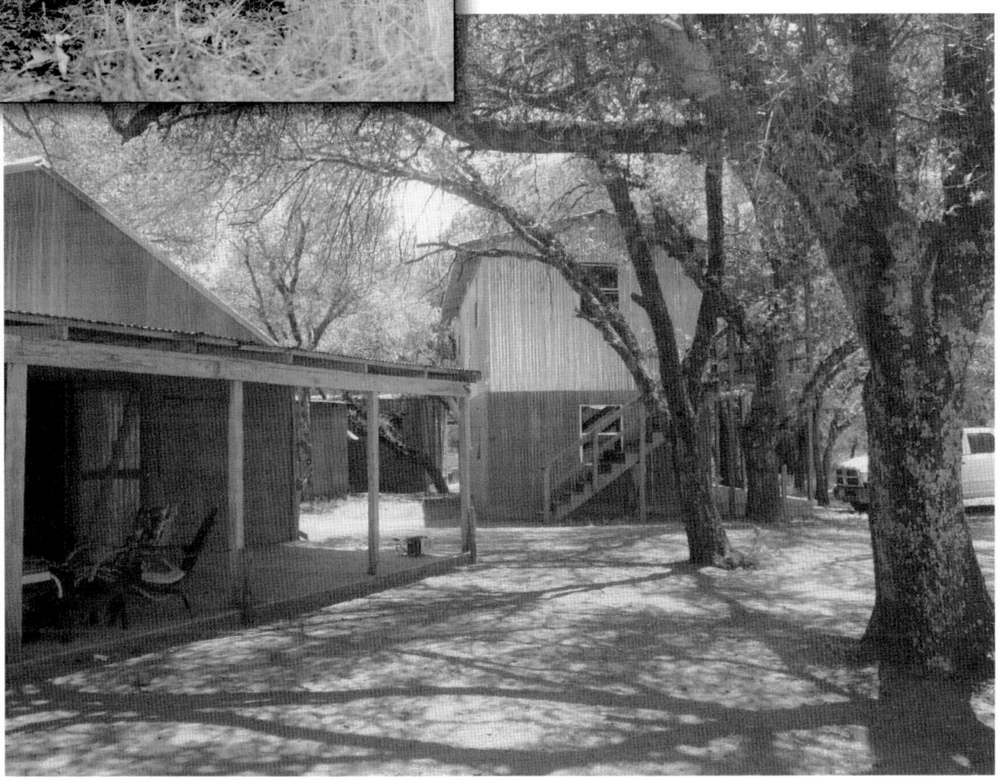

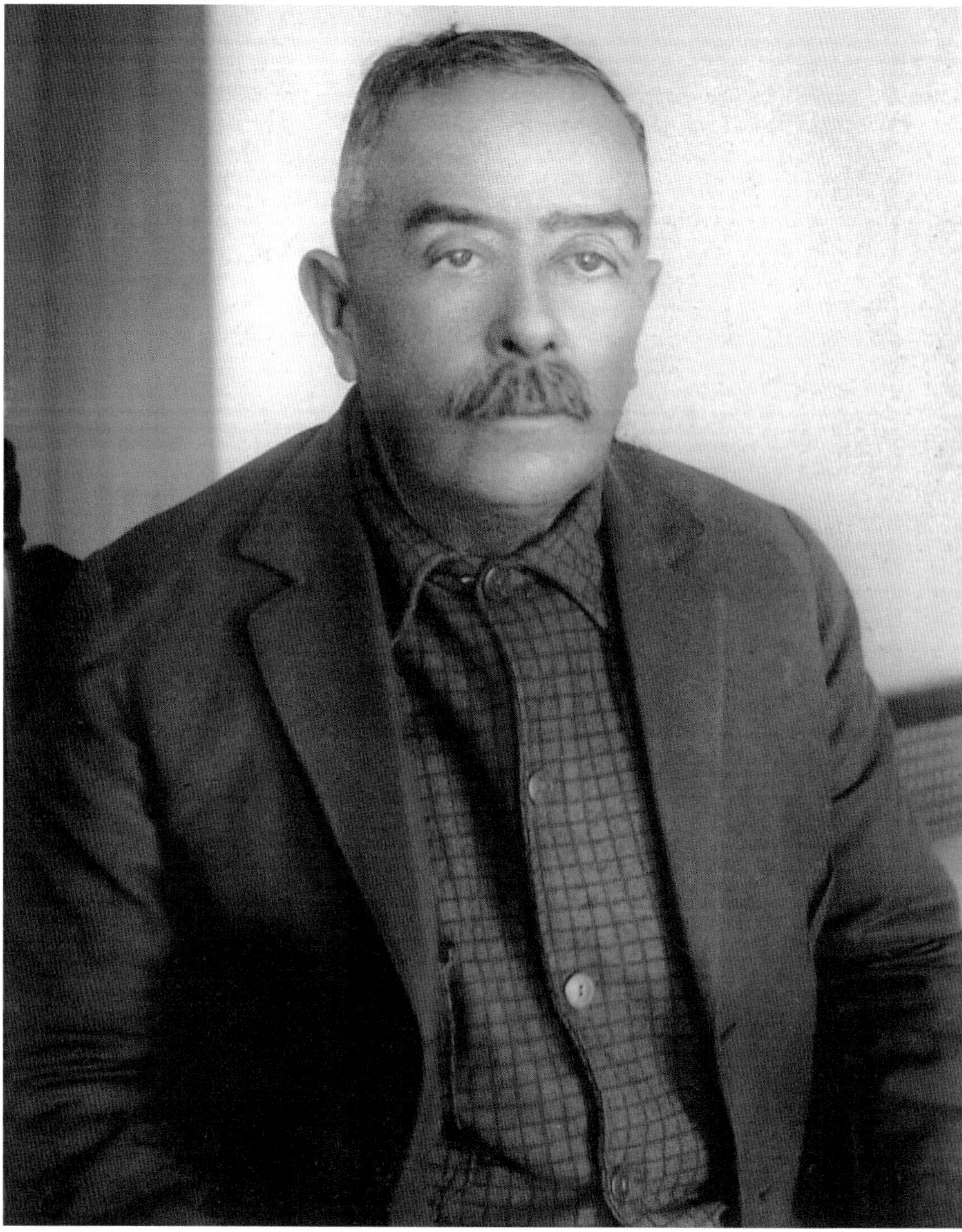

Federico Villalba

The life of Federico Villalba (1858–1933) offers the rare story of a successful Mexican immigrant to Big Bend during a time of violence and change. In 1880, Villalba crossed into Texas at Lajitas and established a ranch at Burro Mesa. There, he married Maria Navarrette de Cortez, by whom he had three children. This was the first wave of Mexican settlers. The second came 15 years later. The Big Bend was a lawless place, particularly so for Mexicans who had to contend with prejudice and hatred of some Anglos. But Villalba succeeded. He built up his herd of sheep and goats, discovered cinnabar (mercury), opened a store at Study Butte, and became a successful businessman. His story is told in *Federico Villalba's Texas*, by Juan Casas.

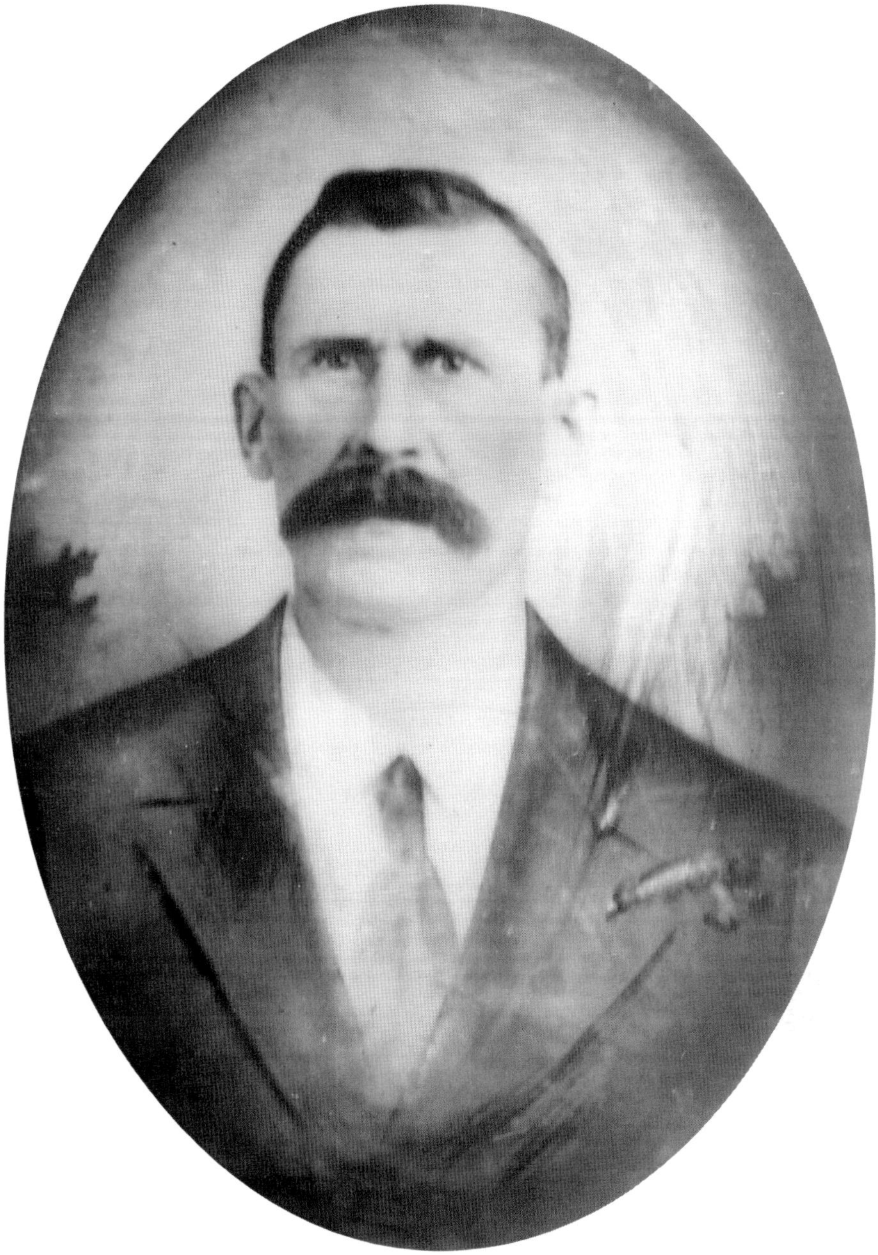

Joseph McGuirk

Joseph McGuirk, a native of Ireland, arrived in Lajitas in 1899 and soon became the dominant personality in the area. He farmed along the riverbanks, using a pump to irrigate his fields, opened a store/saloon, and acted as a mine prospector. Since Lajitas (Spanish for "flat rocks") was an important crossing point from Mexico, and there was always cross-border traffic, the store flourished.

McGuirk married Josefa Navarro, and they had three children. He had a genuine affection for Mexican Americans and contributed to the community by donating land for a church and building a school. However, he tired of the continuing violence along the border due to the revolution in Mexico and moved to New Mexico. He died in 1922.

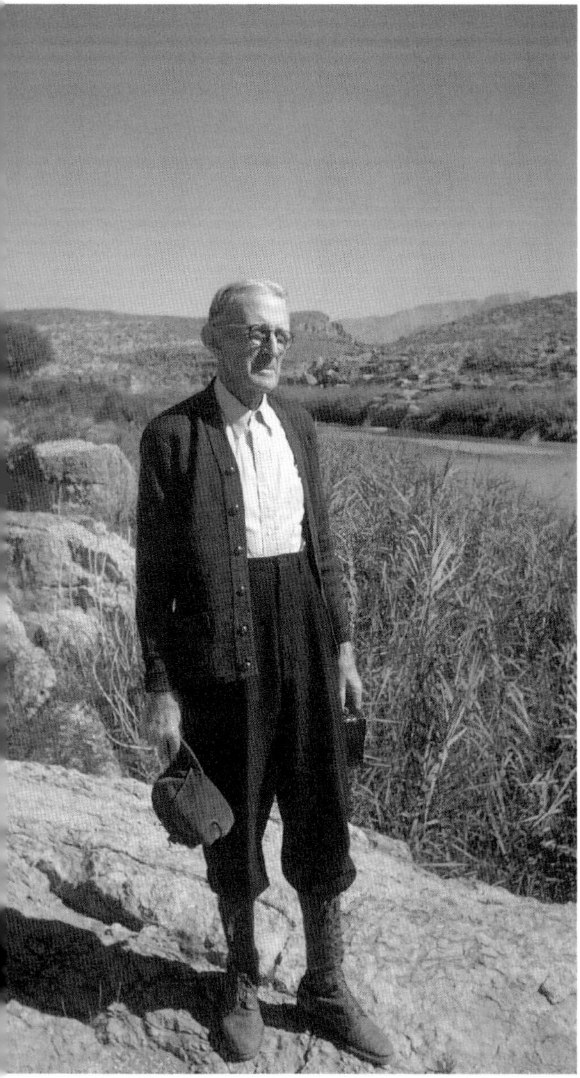

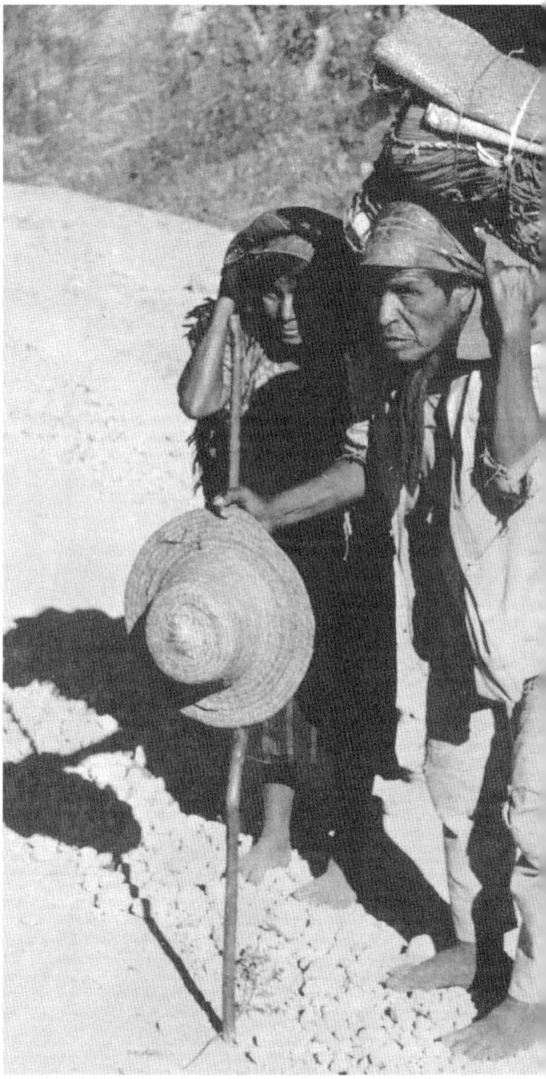

The Langford Family

In 1909, heading south from Alpine with all their worldly possessions piled on a wagon, the Langford family was heading for the Rio Grande, to homestead at a place called Hot Springs. The head of the family, Joe (top left), was hoping that the high, dry climate would help his precarious health. With him were his pregnant wife, Bessie, their18-month-old daughter, Lovie, and their female collie dog, Tex. At Hot Springs, they built cabins and developed a tourist business for those seeking to improve their health from the hot water that gushed from the ground. They stayed there until the dangers of the Mexican Revolution caused them to move temporarily to El Paso. In his book *Big Bend, A Homesteader's Story,* Langford paints a memorable picture of becoming acquainted with his neighbors at a time of change, such as the Mexican wax gatherers pictured here. (Images above from *Big Bend, A Homesteader's Story,* by J.O. Langford, UT Press.)

CHAPTER TWO

Ranchers and Cowboys

The first large-scale rancher in the region was cattle baron Milton Faver. He ran thousands of cattle over a large area of Presidio County in the 1850s when the land was unfenced. He realized he had to guard against Indian attacks, so he built forts where he found water. He sold his beef to the military garrison at Fort Davis and later diversified into the cultivation of peaches.

In the late 1800s, ambitious men like Alfred Gage and Herbert Lee Kokernot arrived and set about acquiring large tracts of rangeland. Their descendants today, owners of the Gage-Holland and 06 ranches, are the beneficiaries of their farsighted and hardworking enterprise. Smaller family ranchers also moved in, including Lizzie Crosson, who survived in a male-dominated culture by reason of being equally tough and hardworking. These pioneers and other ranching families, like the Means, started experimenting with crossbreeding their indigenous herds with imported Hereford, Angus, and later Limousin breeds to improve the yield.

The cowboys tended the cattle herds, and were especially active during seasonal activities like branding and roundups. Much of their time was taken up with less appealing work such as mending fences. The romantic aura of the cowboy lasted however and was (still is) pictured in movies, some of which were made in the Big Bend and Davis Mountains region. The movie *Giant,* filmed near Marfa in 1955, contained a message of racial tolerance, unusual for the times.

The cowboy tradition came from Mexico. The Spanish brought horses and cattle to the New World, and soon large cattle herds developed, especially in the northern states like Chihuahua. In Candelaria on the Rio Grande, a descendant of this tradition, Sergio Peña, works cattle on the United States side of the border, as a legal immigrant (see later in this chapter).

Cowboy traditions and skills are still being nurtured, thanks to the Range Animal Science department at Sul Ross State University in Alpine. Here, the cowboys of tomorrow are being trained and, in the adjacent rodeo arena, home of the National Intercollegiate Rodeo Association, they practice their skills. But will there be work for tomorrow's cowboy?

Ranchers have held on tenaciously to their family lands, believing they have a special responsibility. Despite repeated droughts and varying market conditions and the interference by the federal government, as they see it, they are still making a living but not easily. A few have sold out to a new breed of recreational rancher, and some have embraced tourism to increase revenue. Hunting leases can provide useful income. But for most, the annual cycle of ranch activity continues the same as before, always with the hope of rain.

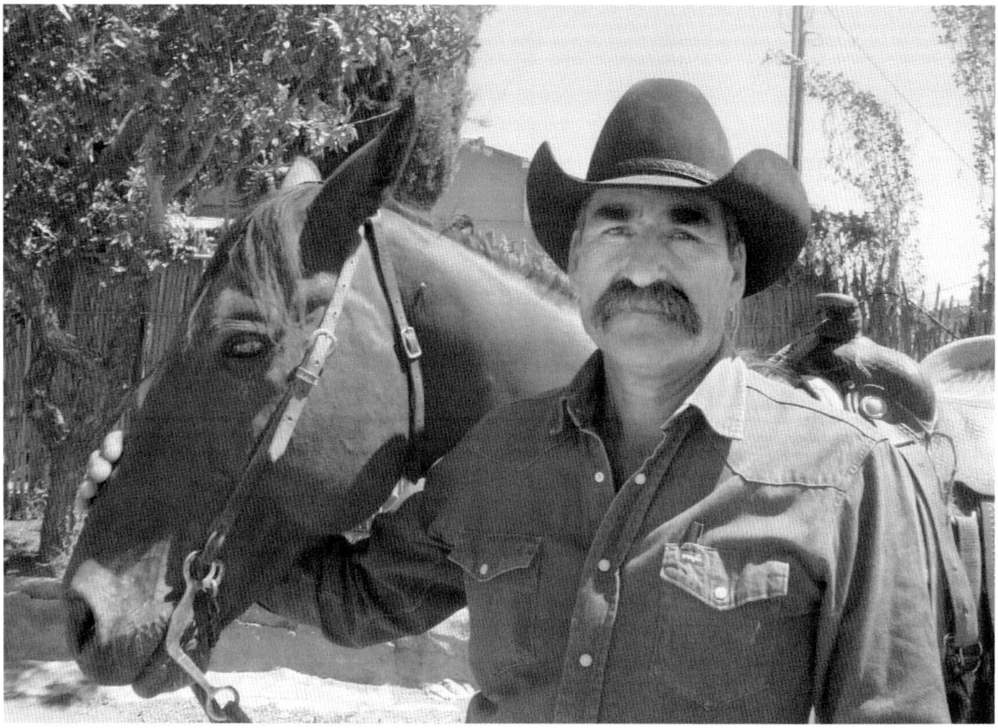

Sergio Peña

Texan cowboys acquired their skills and traditions from Mexican cowboys (vaqueros) 200 years ago. In the remote border village of Candelaria, Sergio Peña works as a ranch manager, speaking only a few words of English. In addition to working livestock, he possesses the skills of an expert horse trainer and demonstrates his skills outside the compound where he lives with his wife, Dominga. Trim at age 59, neatly dressed in denim and wearing a black hat, Sergio is with his eight-year-old gelding Alma Grande (Big Soul). On this day, he rode him around a courtyard of the compound, moving him round and round in tighter circles, using his body to give instructions. The horse slowed down, went gently down on his knees, then lay flat on the ground with neck extended. As seen here, Sergio, still in the saddle, leans forward to pat him affectionately; Alma Grande's ears twitched, showing he recognized the gesture. (Both, author's collection.)

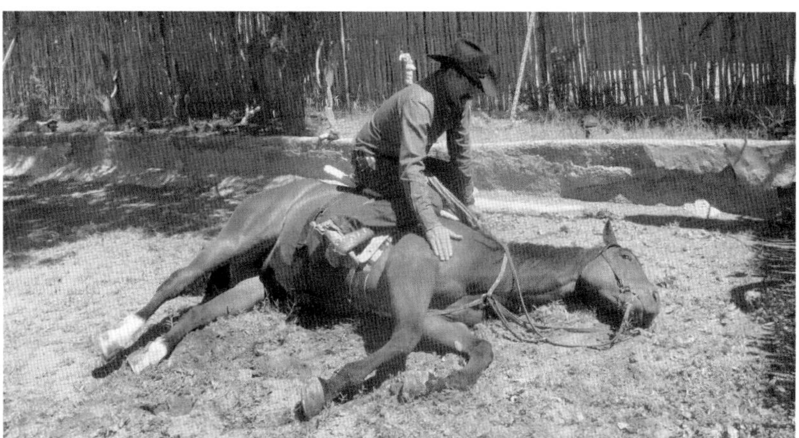

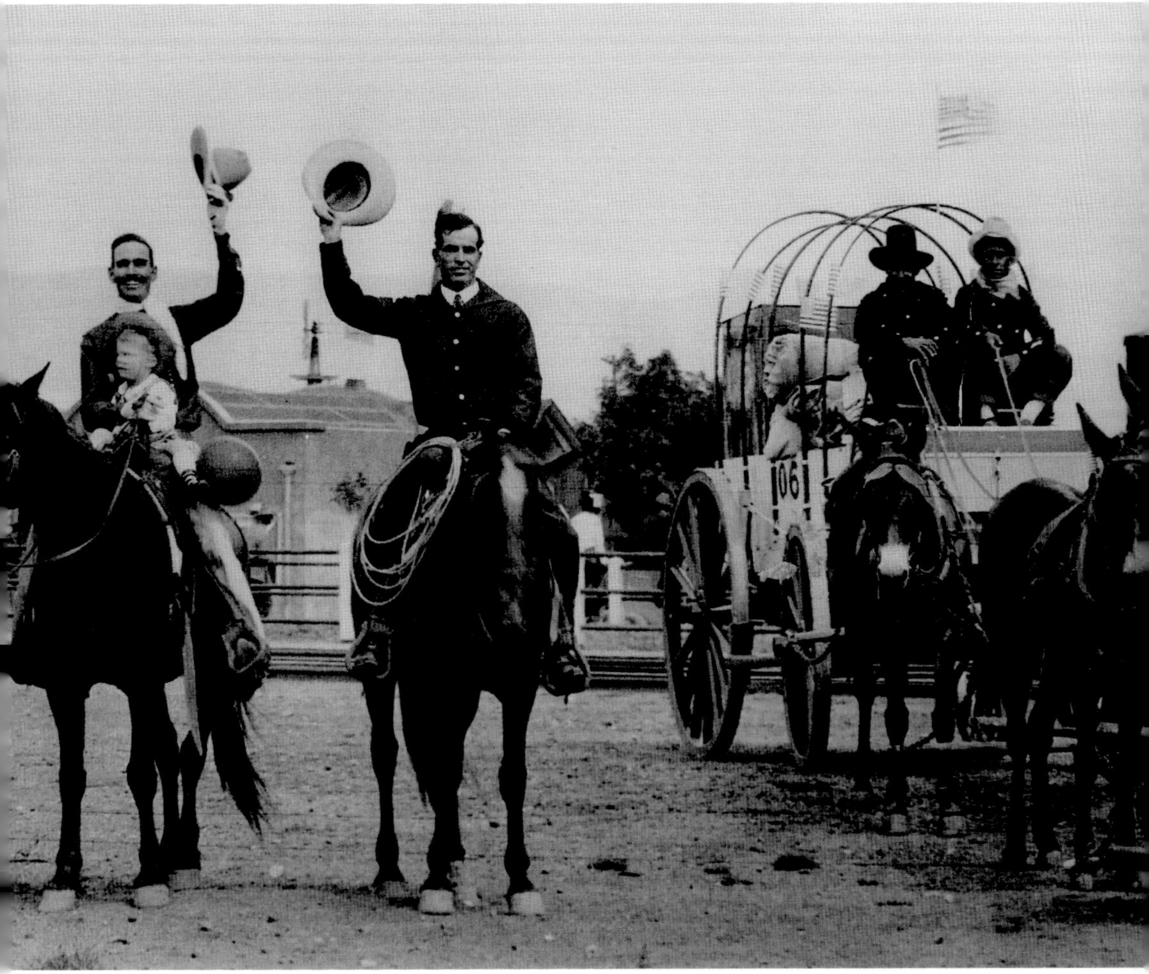

Herbert L. Kokernot Jr.

By any standards, Herbert L. Kokernot Jr. was an exceptional man. Representing six generations of ranchers of the vast 06 ranch, he was a man of the land, although he almost always wore a tie. As a public servant, he served for 62 years as county commissioner of Jeff Davis County and was on numerous bank, university, and association boards.

He gained widest recognition by launching a semiprofessional baseball team in Alpine, called the Alpine Cowboys, and building a marvelous 1,200-seat baseball field that cost $1.5 million. Naturally a jolly personality, he was never happier than when watching the Alpine Cowboys, who gave back to "Mr. Herbert," as they called him, by winning a dozen regional titles and were runners-up in a national championship during 1947–1958.

It was his philanthropic desire to help young people have a chance to get ahead that endeared him most to the community. Over eight years, he endowed 77 baseball scholarships to Sul Ross State University. Born in 1900, he ranched all his life and was a founding member of Paisano Baptist Encampment. He married Golda Rixon of Alpine in 1921, and they had one daughter, Mary Ann, shown here on a horse (left) with her father at a parade. He died in a Fort Worth hospital in 1987 after an exemplary life as a philanthropist, rancher, and baseball promoter.

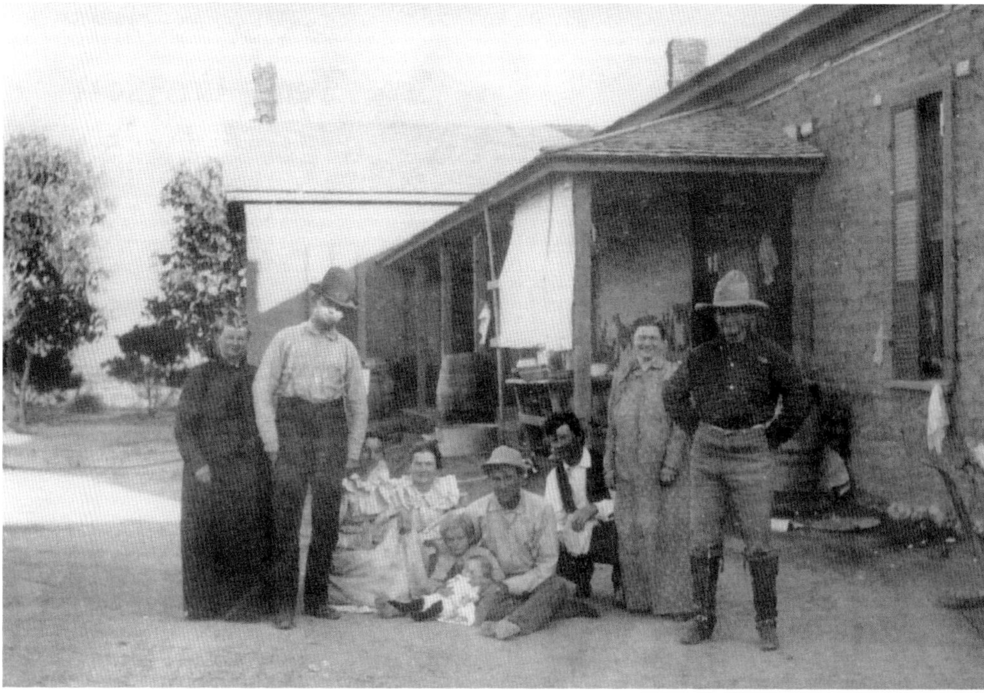

George Crosson

George Crosson, born in Ireland in 1812, arrived in Big Bend in 1861. He acquired 10,600 acres south of Alpine, which became the Crosson Ranch. In 1866, he met Lizzie Healey, who had also been born in Ireland (in 1842), and married her. They had six children. In 1885, Crosson died, leaving Lizzie responsible for running the ranch. Nothing daunted, she not only took to ranch management but also expanded the ranch. She introduced Durham half-breeds and registered Hereford bulls. She used the family (five of her six children are seen in this photograph) to provide the labor and proved in the ranching world, which was still largely male dominated, that a woman could succeed. She died in 1924.

Apache Adams (OPPOSITE PAGE)

He broke his first colt when he was only 10 years old. Today, his four-year-old grandson can keep him company for up to eight hours in the saddle. There must be something special in those Apache Adams genes. Adams believes his love of horses was inherited from his father.

His father specialized in raising and trading horses. Adams recalls the many times he helped gather and drive horses to the stock pens in Marathon to sell to area ranchers.

He also raised goats. In earlier days, goats were the most profitable stock to carry and, as with sheep, they were slower and harder work to handle. Predators, principally mountain lions and coyotes, were one reason the family quit the goat business.

In 1964, Adams sold his interest in the family ranch and headed for Houston. He attended horseshoeing school and later became an instructor before starting his own business. In 1974, he returned to West Texas and bought a ranch south of Alpine. Later, he moved with his wife, Joy, to Fort Stockton where he continues to raise cattle. At age 75, he attends Cowboy Poetry Gatherings including Alpine's, where he won the Heritage Award in 2009. (Top, courtesy of the Adams Family; bottom, photograph by Don Cadden.)

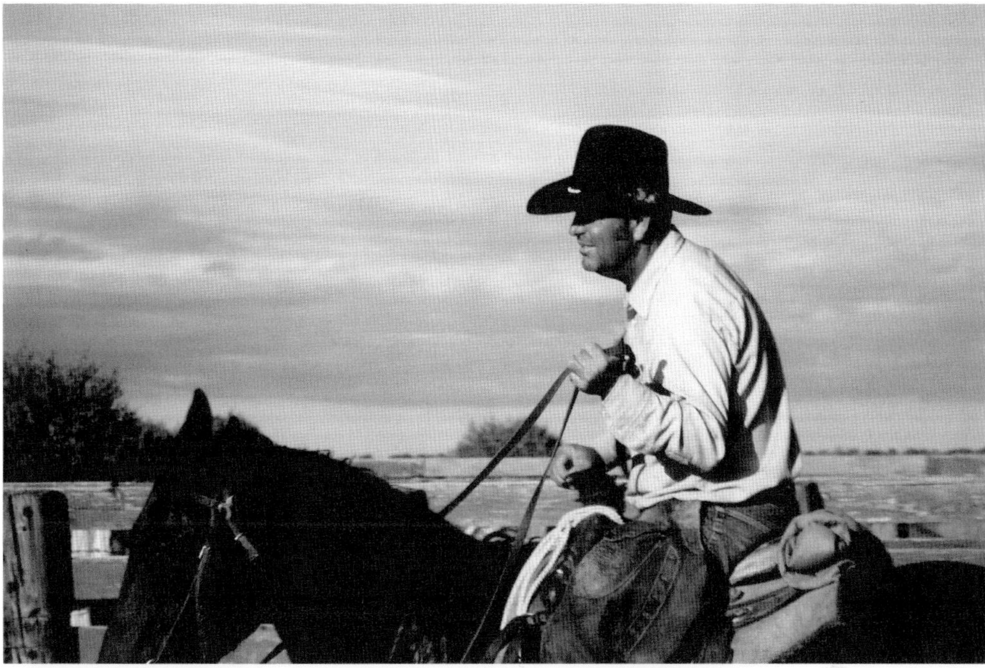

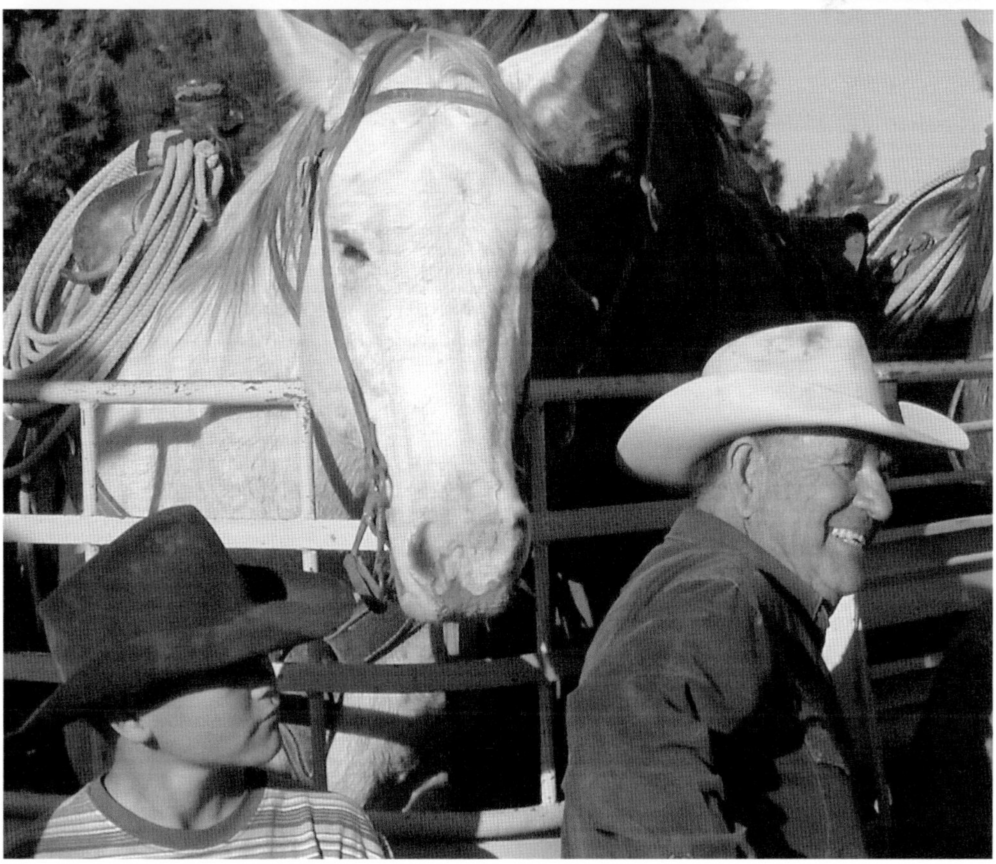

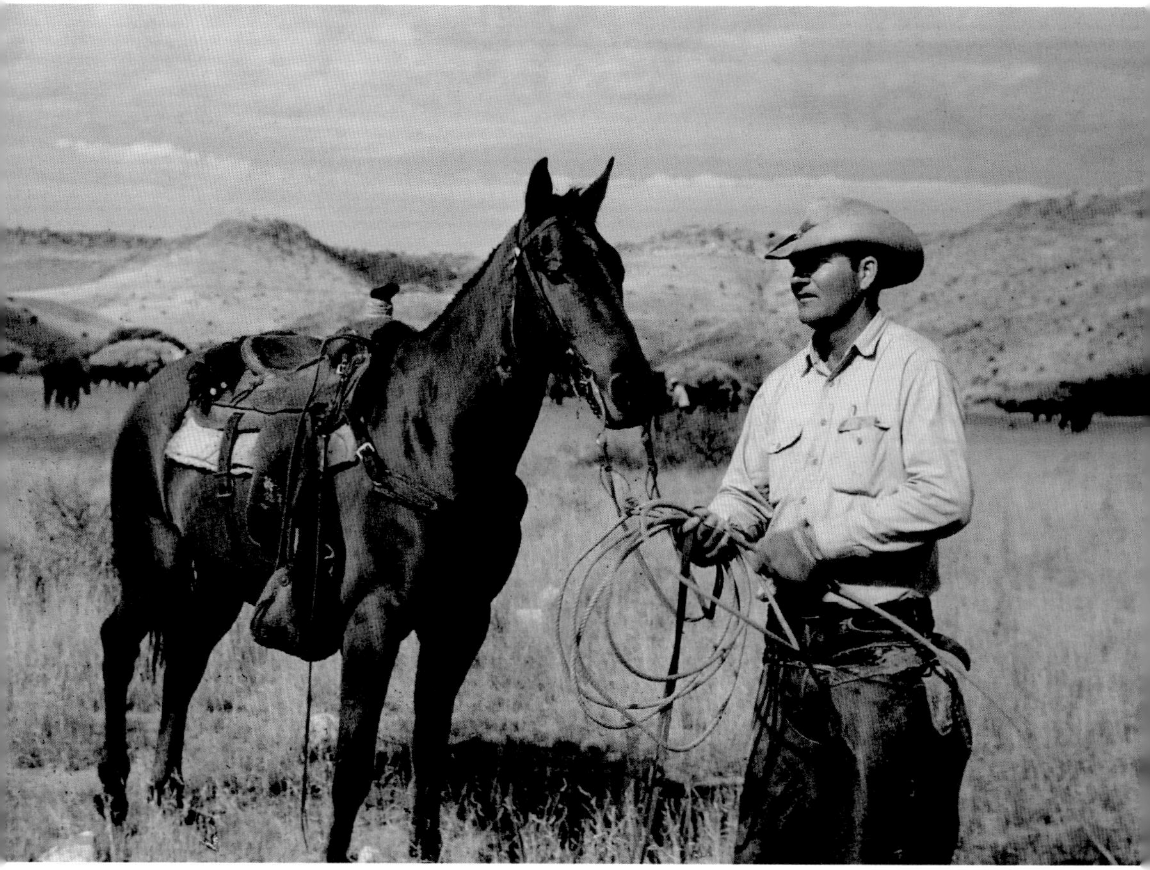

Ted Gray
At age 15, Ted Gray decided he wanted to be a cowboy. In those Depression days, the pay for a working cowboy was $30 a month. He learned how to break broncs, fight screwworms, fix fence lines, and live with droughts. For 23 years, he worked on local ranches, learning the ropes, as he advanced from cowboy to wagon boss. Many years later, he was able to buy land, stock it with livestock, and become a rancher. Finally, he was able to retire to a "house on the hill" in Alpine and became a bank stockholder. He wrote a memoir called *Shades of the West*. Even in his later years, he presented a straight back and slim appearance, maybe breaking into courteous conversation with a tourist in Alpine's coffee shop to sell him a copy of his book.

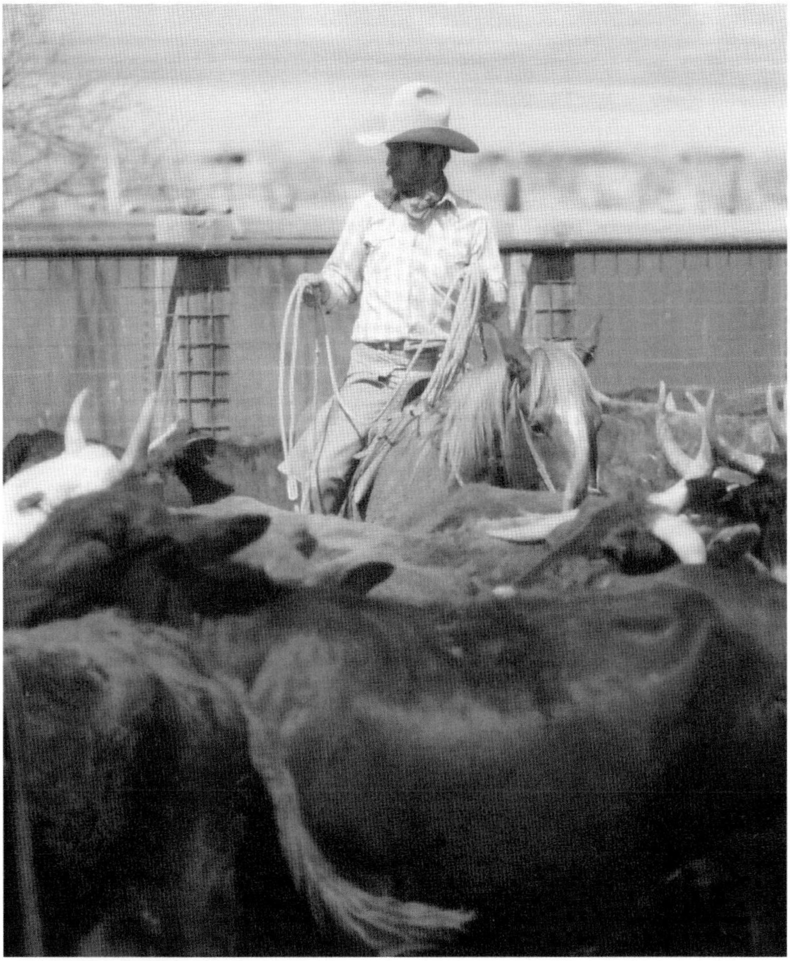

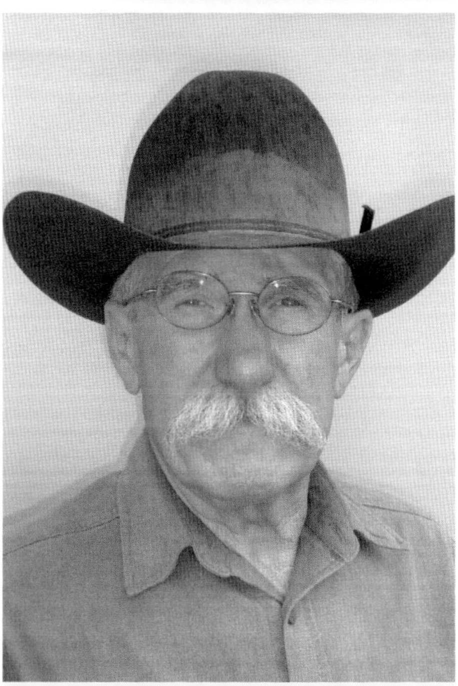

Joel Nelson

Wearing his trademark black hat and sporting a fine mustache, Joel Nelson looks ready for the stage. He has performed on many stages over the years and won a National Heritage Foundation Fellowship in 2009, the first cowboy poet so honored.

The cowboy's work has shaped his life and given meaning to his poetry writing. In the 1970s, he learned the cowboy's trade near Alpine. In the 1980s he acquired life-changing skills from master horse trainer Ray Hunt. In the late 1980s, he started to perform his own verse at Cowboy Poetry Gatherings, including Alpine's, which he helped to start.

Today, he runs Corriente cattle on properties around Alpine. He performs cowboy poetry when asked. A quiet and courteous external demeanor conceals the passion of poetry in his soul. (Above, photograph by Barney Nelson; left, author's collection.)

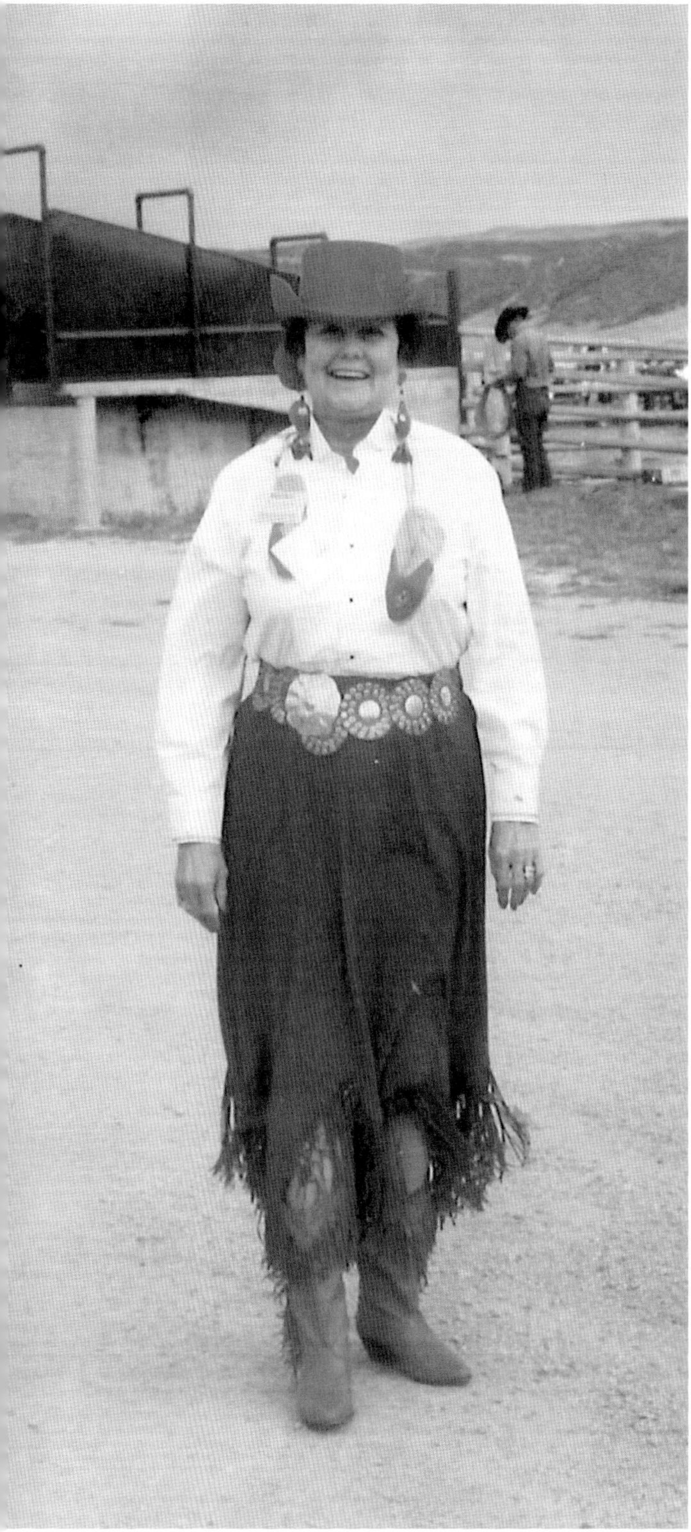

Becky Terry

Becky Terry talks of the early years of her marriage to King Terry when they worked like "galley slaves," running three different ranches in three different counties and learning ranch chores like vaccinating, branding, and rounding up. Little did she know that a later career awaited her as an international beef ambassador, which would take her much further afield than West Texas.

Growing up in Alpine, she taught English and was athletics director at the high school, going on to Sul Ross to obtain a bachelor's (1955) in biology and history and a master's (1959) in biology. She met King Terry in 1948, and they married the following year, a marriage that lasted 62 years until King's death in 2011.

While King minded the ranch, Becky launched forth in a career as spokesperson for the beef industry. After 40 years in various offices of West of the Pecos Cattle Women and Texas Cattle Women, she was elected in 1993 president of the American Cattle Women's Association.

As the figurehead of a national body, her life was one constant round of conventions, cook-offs, workshops, award ceremonies, and international events. She also wrote articles for newspapers and magazines. Then there were seminars, receptions, and parades to attend. In 1993, she was away from home 283 days.

In 2012, she was awarded the Texas Cattle Women's Lifetime Achievement Award. Her mantra of "be interested, be well informed, believe in what you are doing, and above all, love agriculture" had paid off. She had the presence for an ambassador's role: great charm, a generosity of spirit, West Texas vigor, and a throaty cowgirl's laugh. The beef industry was well served in her capable hands. (Courtesy of Becky Terry.)

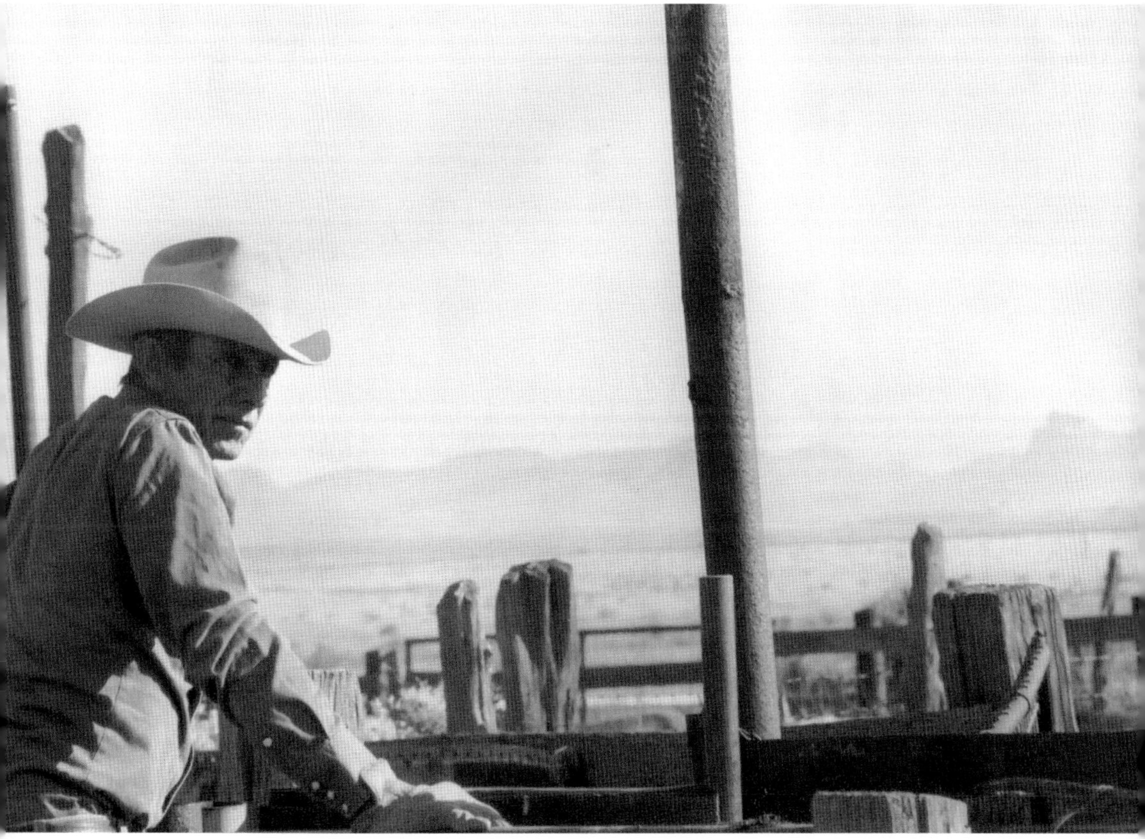

Ike Roberts

Billy Gene Roberts grew up on the Roberts Ranch near Marathon, Texas, one of three sons and one daughter of Travis Roberts Sr., a cattleman, himself the son of a cattleman. He was nicknamed Ike, a name that has been adopted formally in his family. He went to Marathon High School and then got a degree in business studies at Sul Ross, while starting ranch work to pay the fees.

Ike Roberts worked at the Catto-Gage widespread ranch near Marathon for 48 years as cowboy and then cattleman. As ranch manager, his responsibility was for the overall livestock supervision including vaccination, branding, and annual roundup. This was a management job but involved nonstop, hands-on work on the range, as his lined face and calloused hands bear witness. He is a man of the land, and the land is dear to him. He was awarded Texas's most prestigious Soil and Water Preservation Award at a ceremony in San Antonio in 2011.

In 1967, Roberts married Sue Brindley, a lively English woman who was working in Marathon as an au pair. They have three children—Joey, Sally, and Tim—who work, respectively, as a park ranger, a goat cheese maker, and in the oil field. There is a country modesty, interspersed with dry wit, about Roberts when he talks about his role in the cattle business. He finally got to slow down upon retirement in 2003, but the work ethic is truly ingrained, and he serves on various boards connected with ranching or conservation. He takes time off, however, to spoil his grandchildren when they visit. (Photograph by Jonathon Grammer.)

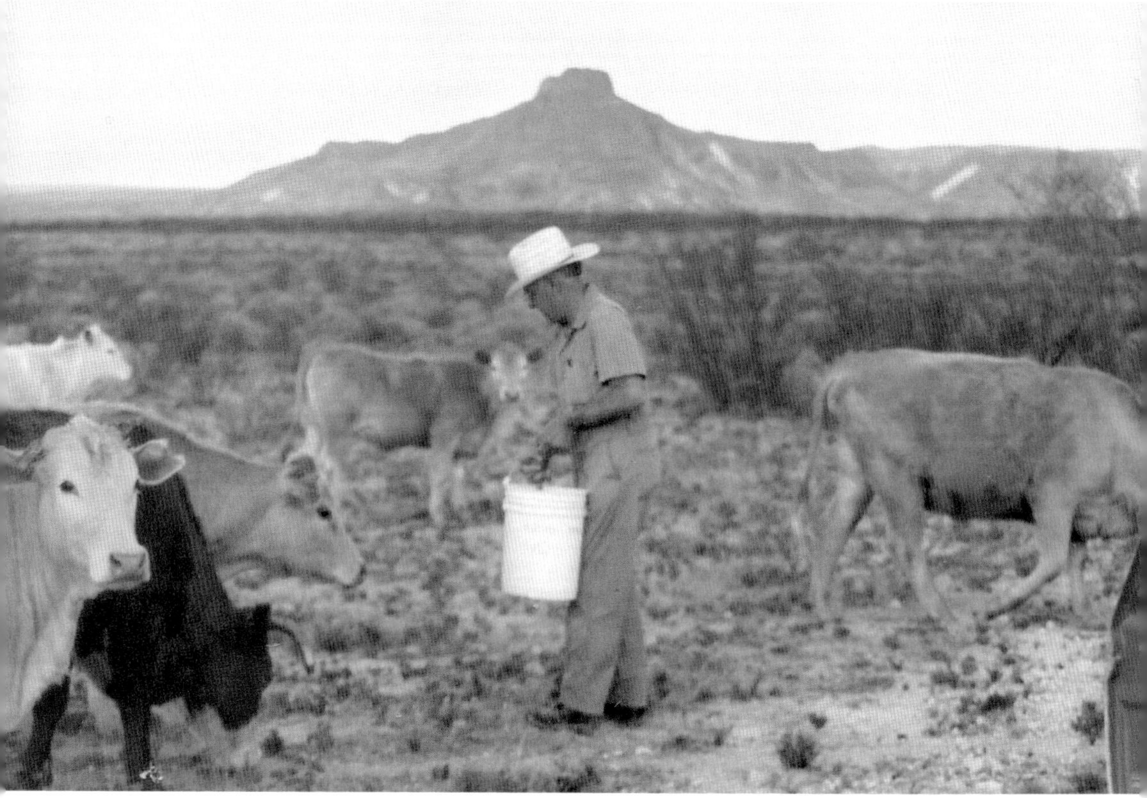

Armando Vasquez

Born in 1925, Armando Vasquez grew up in La Plata, 37 miles southeast of Marfa, at a time when the community numbered 100 persons. As a young boy, he witnessed government inspectors slaughter cows too weak to survive the 1930s drought.

The 1940s were better in terms of rain and work. But in 1943, he was scooped up into the US Army; he survived the experience of being in tanks for two years (notwithstanding, the inferior armament of the US Sherman tanks). After the war he moved into Marfa, learning the mechanic's trade. By 1954, he was ready to start up on his own in what he calls, "a chicken coop." Meanwhile, he got married, had children, and played in his own band known as Mando's Group.

In the 1990s, he sold his building to an artist couple, part of a wave of newcomers arriving in Marfa. This left him more time to visit the family property at La Plata and tend the cattle, which he still maintains there today. He believes in accepting change and feels the newcomers have brought life to Marfa. He promoted the Marfa Lights as a tourist attraction long before a Viewing Center was built. At 87, he looks to the future as much as to the past. (Both, courtesy of Armando Vasquez.)

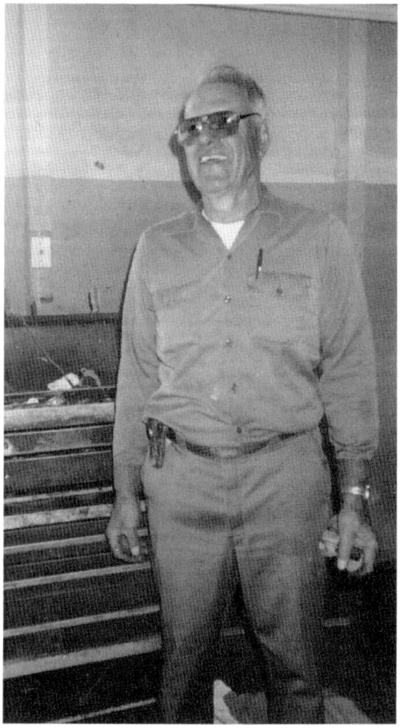

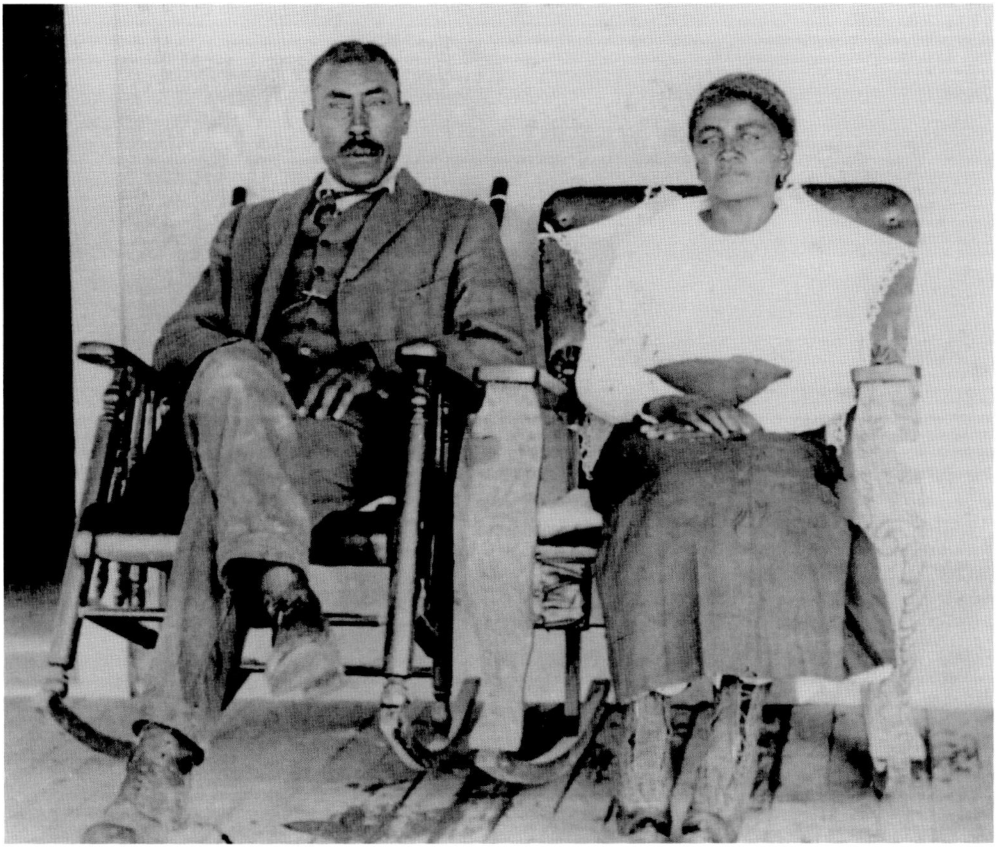

Monroe Payne

Monroe Payne, a black Seminole cowboy, arrived in Brewster County in 1904. A descendant of black slaves, mixed with Seminole Indians, Monroe had been hired by the US Army as a scout against Apache and Comanches. Kicked out by the Army when they were of no more use, the scouts took employment where they found it. Monroe Payne and his brother John, who arrived 10 years later, were natural horsemen and gained wide recognition for their cowboy skills. Monroe was foreman of the Butrill Ranch near Big Bend National Park for a number of years, before coming to Marathon. There, he bought property, ran a freight business, and was engaged in other enterprises. He possessed a great natural dignity that earned him respect, which, in those days, was not easy for a person of color. Monroe Payne died in 1952.

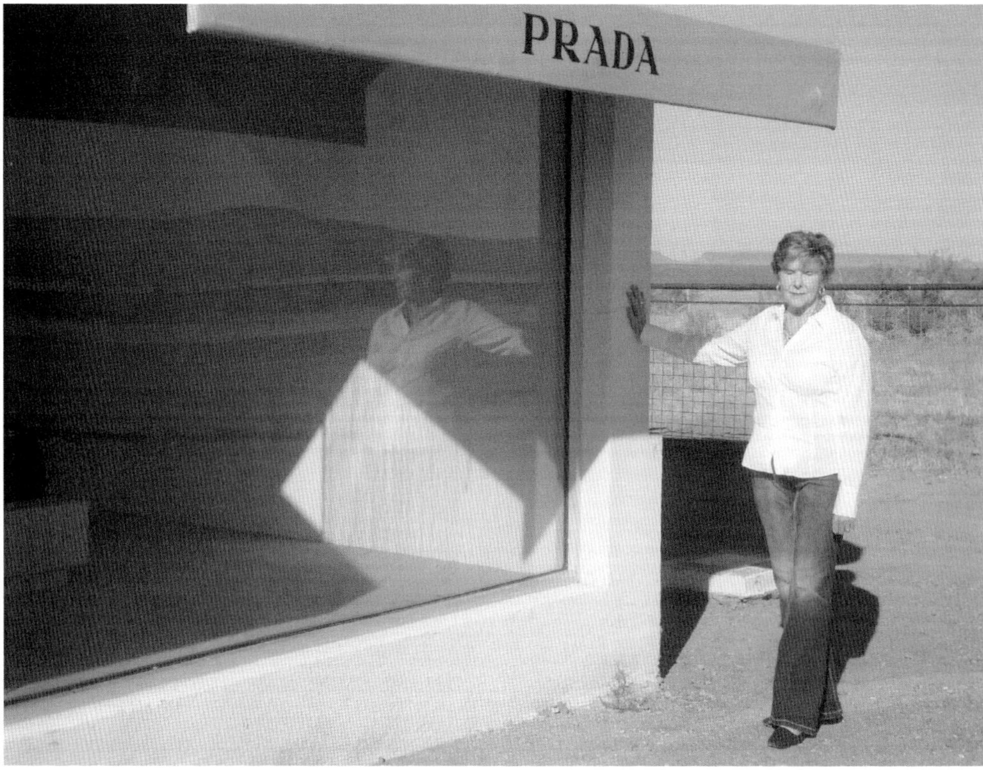

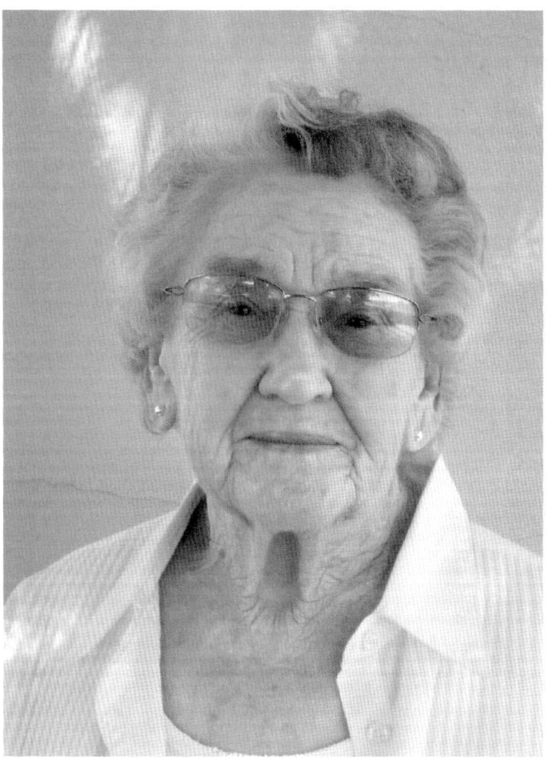

Smokey Hall and Ruth Means

The town of Valentine has only eight high school students. The population has shrunk to 134 persons. There is no general store. In the 1950s, when trains stopped here, it was a bustling small township. The lives of two residents illustrate the changing times.

Smokey Hall, the daughter of Walter Brown, a longtime rancher and trucker, lives here and works on the Internet as a land agent for an out-of-state oil company. She donated a small parcel of the family land to a new Marfa art installation, Prada Marfa.

Ruth Means (87), the widow of legendary rancher Alfred Means, who died in 2011, lives on the Y-6 ranch. Her son Bodie runs the ranch, which is leased back from a new owner. Fortified by the memory of a 62-year marriage, this gracious lady relishes the memories of ranch life. (Both, author's collection.)

CHAPTER THREE

Teachers and Coaches

The importance of education was widely recognized from the earliest days of settlement in the Big Bend and Davis Mountains region. Mrs. M.B. Anderson tells how she found 75 students waiting in her classroom on her first day of class in Fort Davis. When the school was too far from the ranch, children were homeschooled; homeschooling exists on a voluntary basis today.

For Hispanic families, the desire for an education, even during times of institutional segregation, was particularly strong. Amparo Fuentes, who had crossed from Mexico while the Mexican Revolution started, attended many summer school sessions at Sul Ross so that she could graduate as a teacher. Finally, she was certified and started on her teaching career at age 40, working for 25 years.

Around the same period, Lucia Madrid, teaching in Redford on the Mexican border, saw a woeful lack of books for her students. After school, she would drive 120 miles round-trip to Marfa to pick up a small number of books to bring back to her students. Dissatisfied with this situation, she started a local library that grew and grew, a venture that gained her national recognition.

At the university level, Sul Ross State University has been vital for the development of the region. In addition to dedicated teachers in other faculties, SRSU's strength lies in the following departments that focus on the region's assets: range animal science, geology, and botany. Prof. Barton Warnock's influence in spreading an interest in desert plants and wildflowers to another generation of students was huge.

Time and again, old-timers in the region have been heard extolling the importance of education in advancing a career or fulfilling individual potential. Armando Vasquez, like many Hispanic men who served in the war and got an education via the GI Bill at war's end, said, "Get an education; it's something they can't take away from you."

Sul Ross recently spent $110 million on the physical plant, expanding capacity and bringing it up to standards common elsewhere. Maybe this will prevent future attempts to close it down. But dropout figures are high and must be addressed, or there may be further efforts to close the place down.

Listening to 78-year-old Laverne Avery, still teaching in Marathon, making light of her age by describing her first grade students' surprise that she could get down on the floor with them, is to watch a motivated person whose value to the community is priceless.

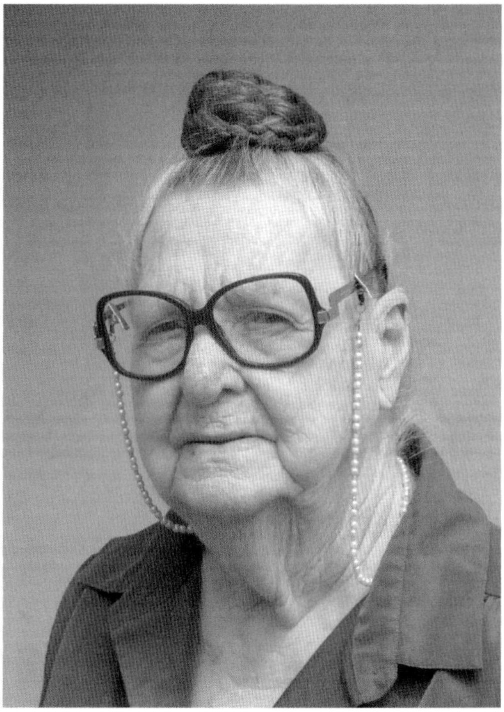

Johnnie Chambers

In August 1988, the two-room schoolhouse in the hamlet of Candelaria on the Rio Grande in far West Texas was closed by order of the local school authorities. Citing financial reasons, the officials stated that students would be bused daily from this remote corner of Texas to Presidio—54 miles distant. The principal-teacher, Johnnie Chambers, was offered a teaching position in Presidio but declined. Now, 25 years on, Johnnie reflects on the rewards of teaching on the border. She states, "There was total cooperation from students' families; if I called a meeting, everyone turned up." She taught anywhere from 20 to 40 students, from preschool to the eighth grade, for 27 years before the doors closed on the school, which achieved numerous awards and qualified as an Exceptional School of Texas. She even paid the phone bill herself. (Right, author's collection; below, courtesy of Johnnie Chambers.)

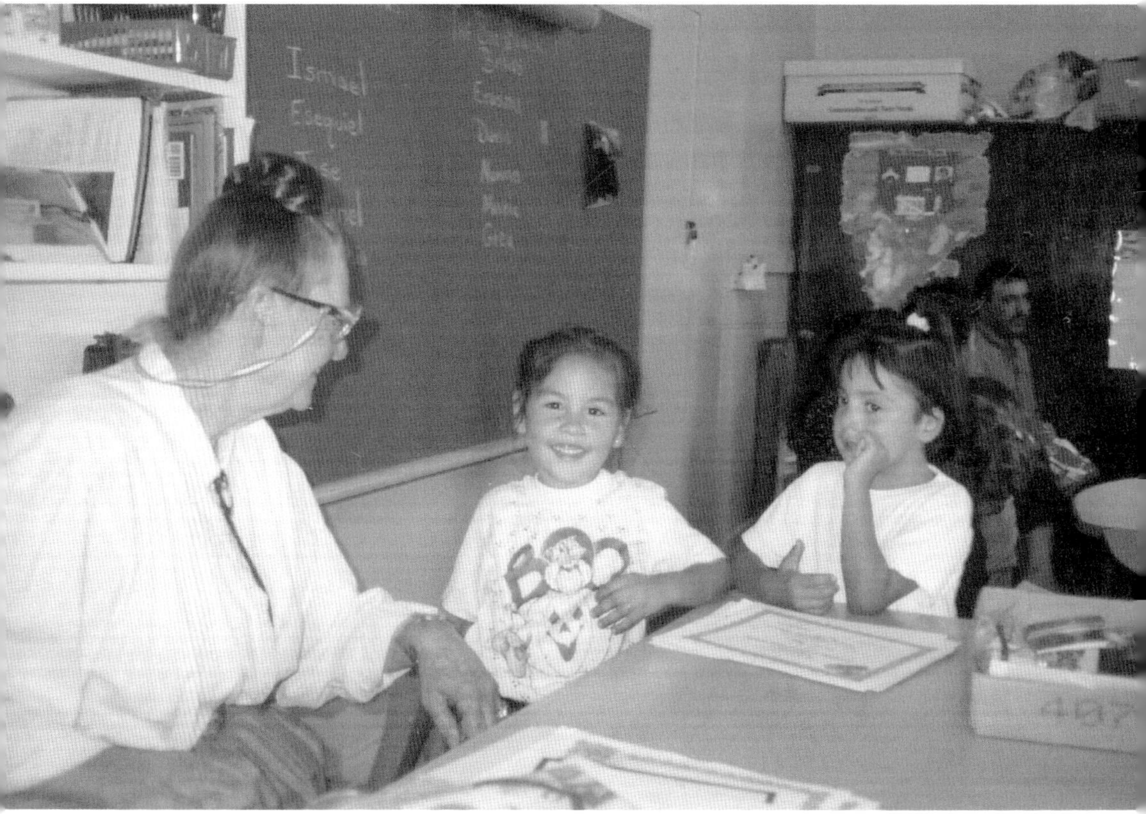

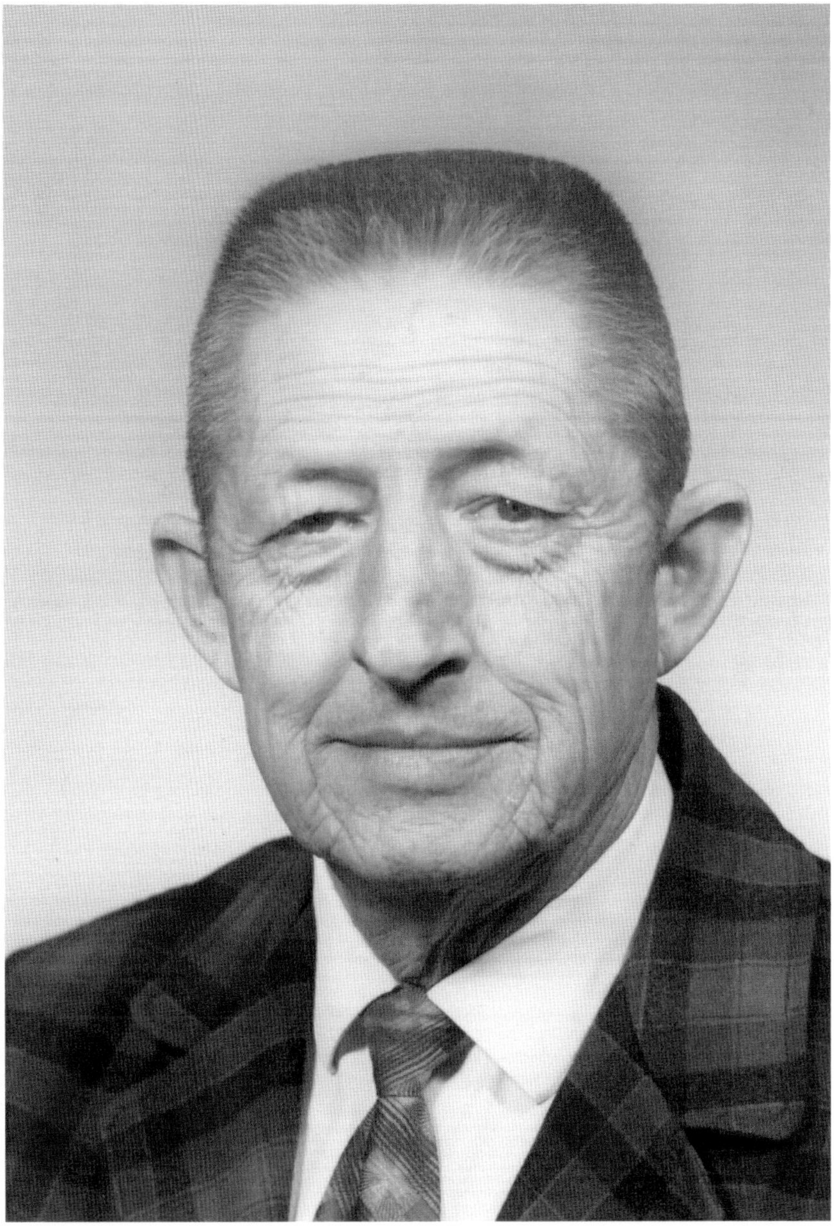

Everett E. Turner

Everett E. Turner gained his doctorate in animal production at the University of Wyoming before coming to Alpine. He joined the Sul Ross State University (SRSU) faculty in 1948, after briefly teaching vocational agriculture at Alpine High School. During his 28-year tenure at SRSU, he was instrumental in the formation of the National Intercollegiate Rodeo Association (NIRA) and was the sponsor of several SRSU teams that went on to win national titles.

NIRA, now in its 67th year, uses the arena at the SRSU Turner Range Animal Science Center, named after Professor Emeritus Turner. Here, the cowboys of tomorrow study for degrees in animal science and natural resource management, and tourists and Alpine residents can watch top-quality rodeo.

Turner's wife, LaNelle, bore two sons and two daughters. Turner retired in 1976 and died in 1992.

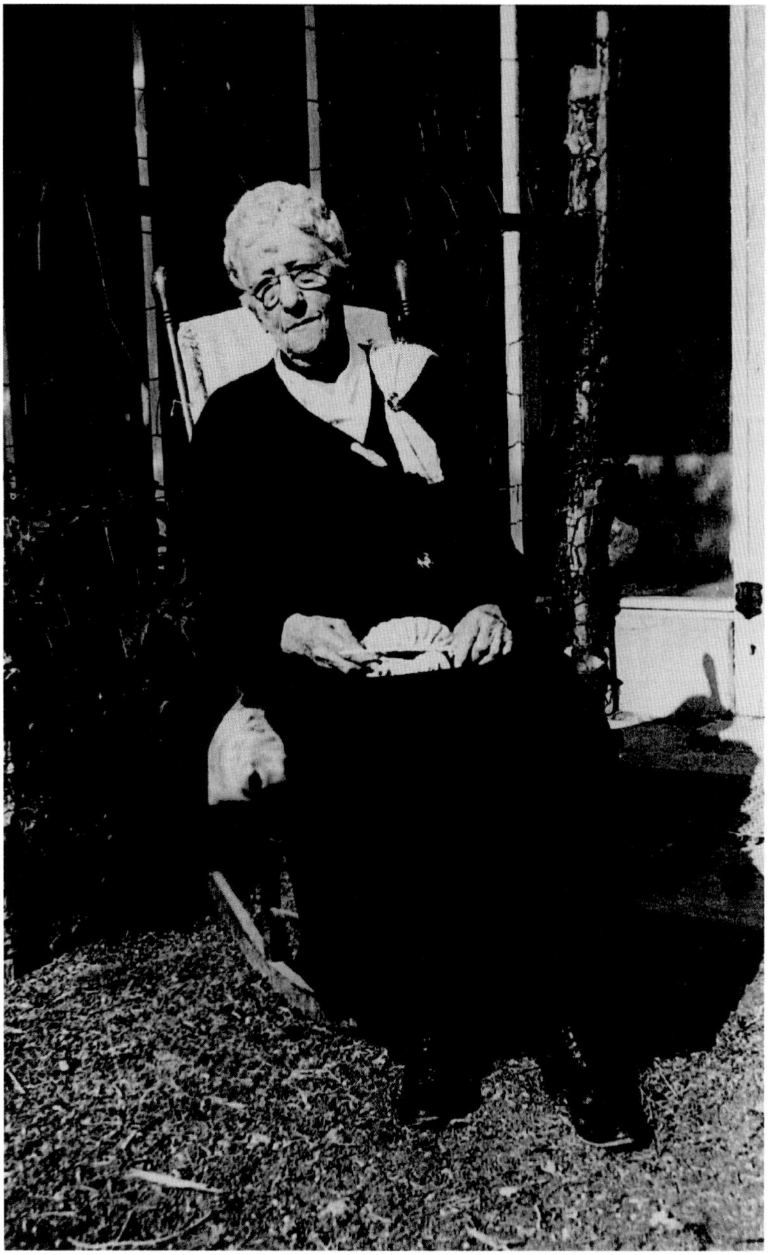

Mattie B. Anderson

Mattie B. Anderson came to Fort Davis in 1883, aged 31, with three young children for a new life. Coming from a prosperous Southern family, primitive frontier life must have shocked her. In 1884, the school district was established, and she started teaching with an initial class of 75 students of all ages, with no desks, books, or blackboard. Due to a misunderstanding, she later was asked to resign. She opened a private academy but was then rehired in 1887 as a schoolteacher. Before returning to her home state of Kentucky, she later taught briefly in Marfa. She came back again to Fort Davis in 1919. Always busy, she tutored her grandchildren and played the piano into old age. She died in 1938. In 1940, Fort Davis's new elementary school was named after her.

Bodie Hunter

Bodie Hunter came to Marfa from Sanderson with his wife, Josephine, and daughter, Zoe, in 1942. He was coach of football and basketball and, later, became the high school principal. Since he lost most of his football games, the first few years were, in his own words, "lean and rough." In basketball, however, Coach Hunter achieved remarkable success, taking Marfa to the State West Tournament for six consecutive years. His football team was in Class B, so they could not participate past the regional level. However, for 10 years, they beat Alpine, more than two times the size of Marfa, in football conference games. Even today, his former students' eyes light up at the mention of Coach Hunter (seated, right). The board of trustees named Marfa High School Gymnasium is his honor. He died in 1955. (Courtesy Marfa and Presidio County Museum.)

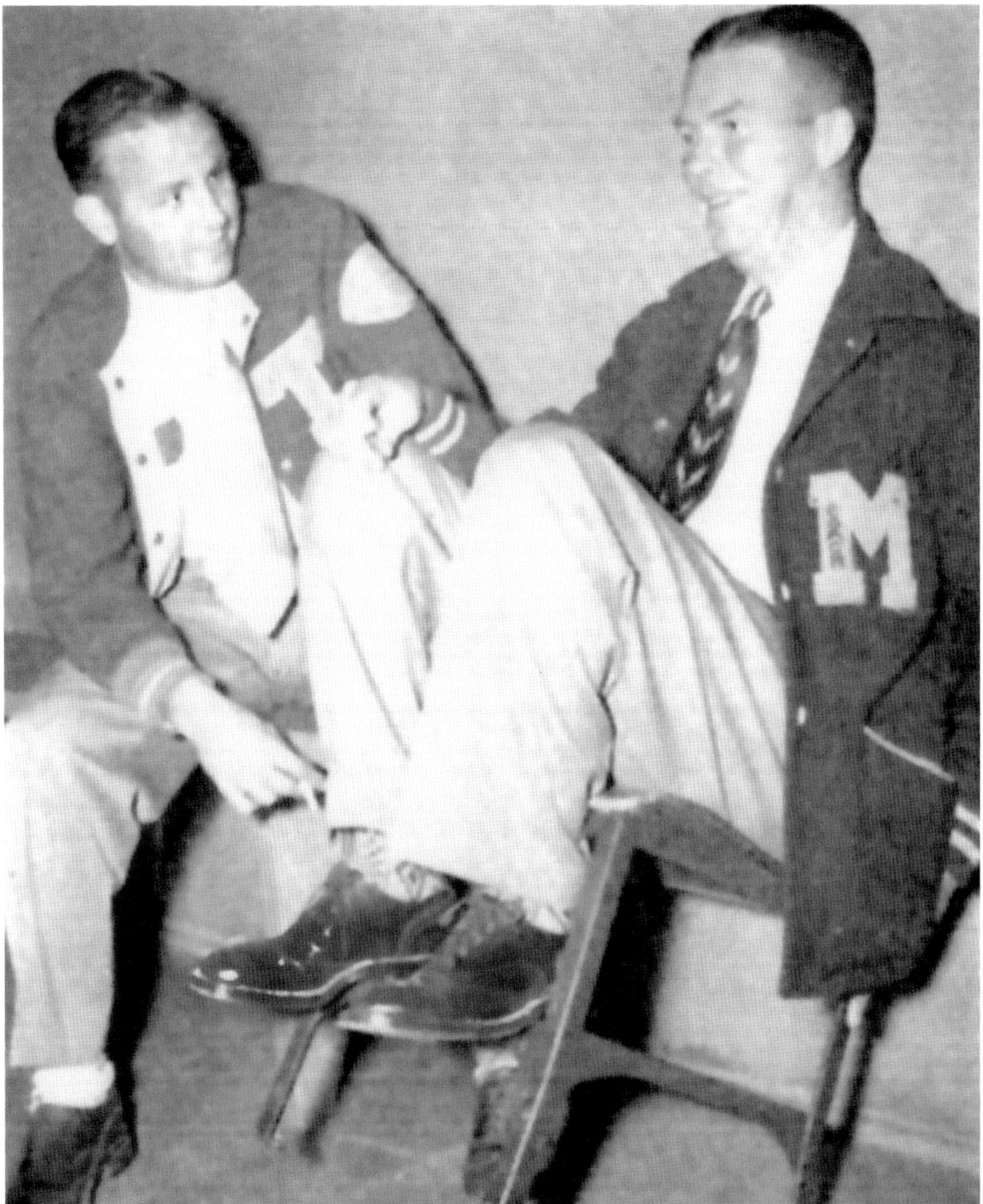

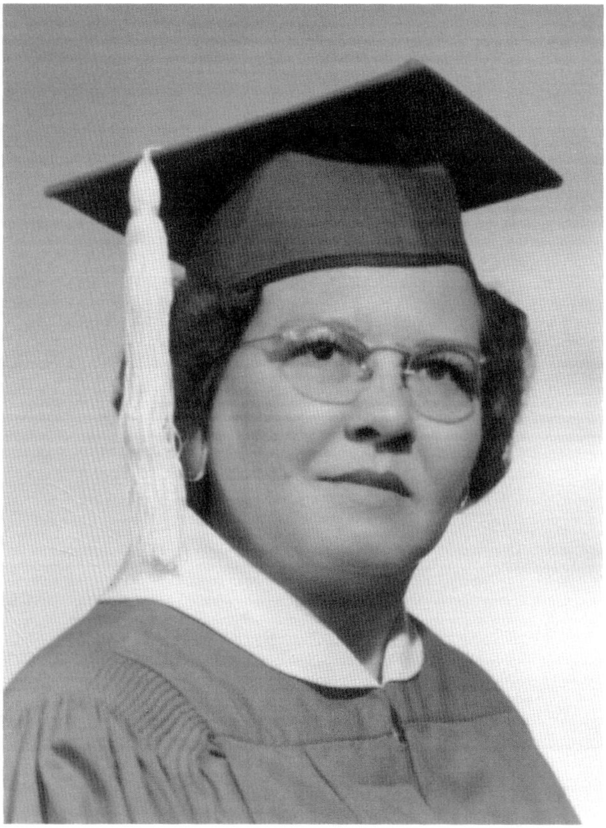

Amparo Montoya

Amparo Montoya was born in 1912, in Ojinaga, Mexico. A few years later, her family fled the Mexican Revolution and came north to the small mining town of Shafter, Texas. Her grandfather ran the mining company store.

Amparo's lifetime dream was to become a teacher. In Shafter, she balanced her time between working at her grandfather's store, caring for her extended family, and attending Sul Ross in the summer. Eventually, she became one of the first female Hispanics to graduate. In 1961, she married Porfirio Fuentes, a cowboy who was later inducted into the Big Bend Cowboy Hall of Fame.

Amparo's teaching career spanned 25 years. Her first teaching assignment was in El Indio, and her last was in Presidio. Amparo, beloved teacher to many, passed away at 98 and is buried in Shafter. (Both, courtesy of Julia West.)

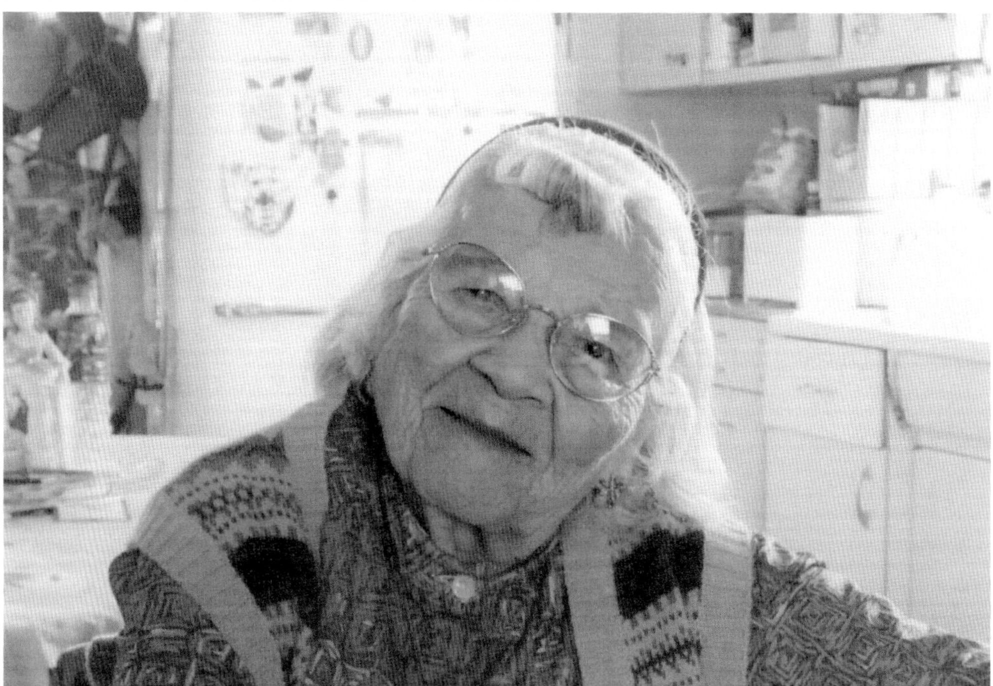

Dr. Horace W. Morelock

In 1923, the Texas legislature changed the name "Sul Ross Normal College" to "Sul Ross State Teachers College" and appointed Dr. Horace W. Morelock as president. His background experience in various fields in education made him well-qualified to guide the new college, which was only in its third year, through a period of growth and development. He served as president from 1923 to 1945.

Much of his time was taken up with the haphazard and inadequate physical plant. Over a period of 20 years, campus improvements instigated by Morelock through judicious grants and loans included the construction of a women's dormitory, the establishment of athletic grounds, Jackson Field, an outdoor theater, 41 modern cottages for student accommodations, and a library-classroom building.

Over the same period, Sul Ross moved from being a two-year college to a four-year state teachers college (1923) and was later admitted into the Association of Texas College (1929). The number of students increased dramatically also. In 1923, there were only 100 students registered. As Morelock summarized at the time of his retirement, during his tenure, 8,000 students had enrolled at Sul Ross, over 3,000 teaching certificates and 1,500 degrees had been awarded. When Morelock retired, student enrollment numbers were plunging as World War II started, but would soar after the war's end due to the GI Bill.

Every inch the dignified college president in appearance, Morelock instigated many practical changes but also pushed for qualitative improvements. He was a keen speaker at outside events, never failing to advertise the college's achievements. He started a campus newspaper, the *Skyline*, which continues today. He strove to encourage cultural activities on campus through literary organizations and scholarship clubs.

Morelock married Willa Battaile of Houston in 1907, and they had three children. He was awarded his master's from Harvard in 1917 and was a fine writer. He worked in the Alpine community on the campaign to establish the Big Bend National Park. Today, one of the handsome university buildings is named after him.

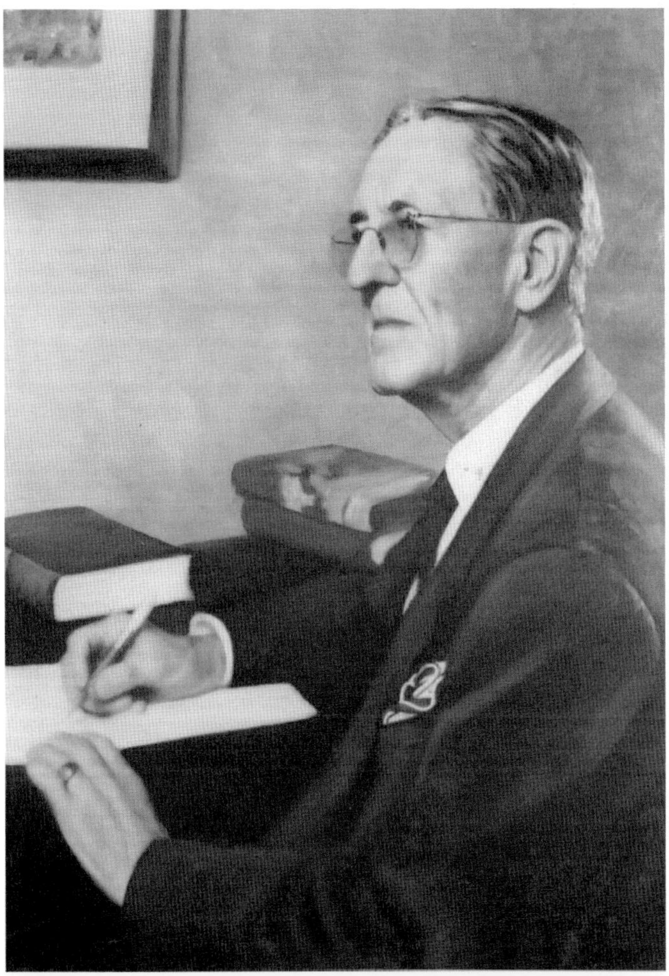

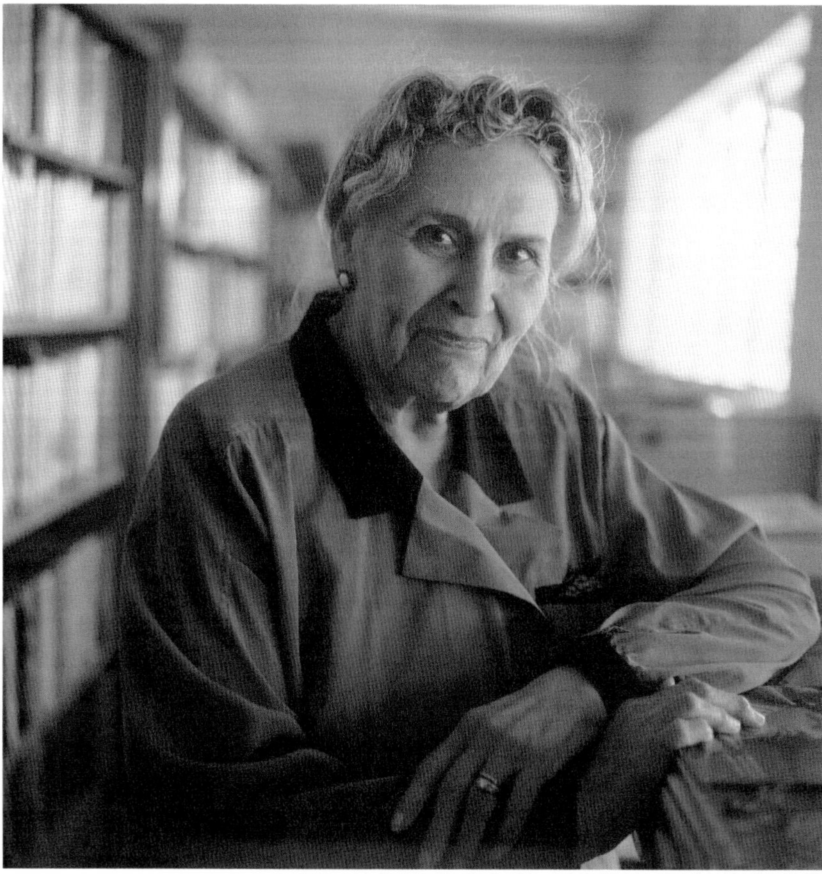

Lucia Madrid

Born in 1913 in the hamlet of Redford on the Rio Grande, eight miles southeast of Presidio, into a family long known in the area, Lucia was the sixth of eight children. Her father, Lujan, farmed and ran supply wagons to troops along the border.

The family prospered and was able to move to Marfa, 75 miles north, where the children could go to school. "Seven of us were able to go to college," Lucia recalled later; she was to become a teacher herself. Fifty-five members of her family graduated with college degrees at Sul Ross.

After graduation, Lucia taught in towns and ranches around Big Bend. She married Enrique Madrid of Redford in 1941, came back to where she was born, and had three children. While teaching in Redford, there was a severe lack of books; Lucia, also known as "Chita," had to regularly travel 75 miles to Marfa to pick up 25 books for the 80 children in her class—after teaching a full day.

On retirement in 1976, Chita was determined to start a lending library in Redford and used space in the corner of her husband's general store for this purpose. She found some old magazines, Sears catalogs, and about 25 books, and the word got around. Visitors saw what she was doing and started sending books and contributions. Soon, Chita had a collection of 20,000 books. Children and grown-ups flocked to the library, which had now outgrown the store, to study or just to read for pleasure.

Over the years, the library, La Biblioteca de El Polvo, gained regional, then national attention before closing in the early 1990s. In 1989, Lucia was inducted into the Texas Women's Hall of Fame. That following year, she visited the White House to receive from President Bush two volunteer awards. She died, aged 90, in 2003. Her son, Enrique (born in 1947), a scholar and historian of the border, received two awards from the governor of Texas for archeological work in the area. He lives with his wife, Ruby, among the books of the old library and keeps the memory alive. (Photograph by James H. Evans.)

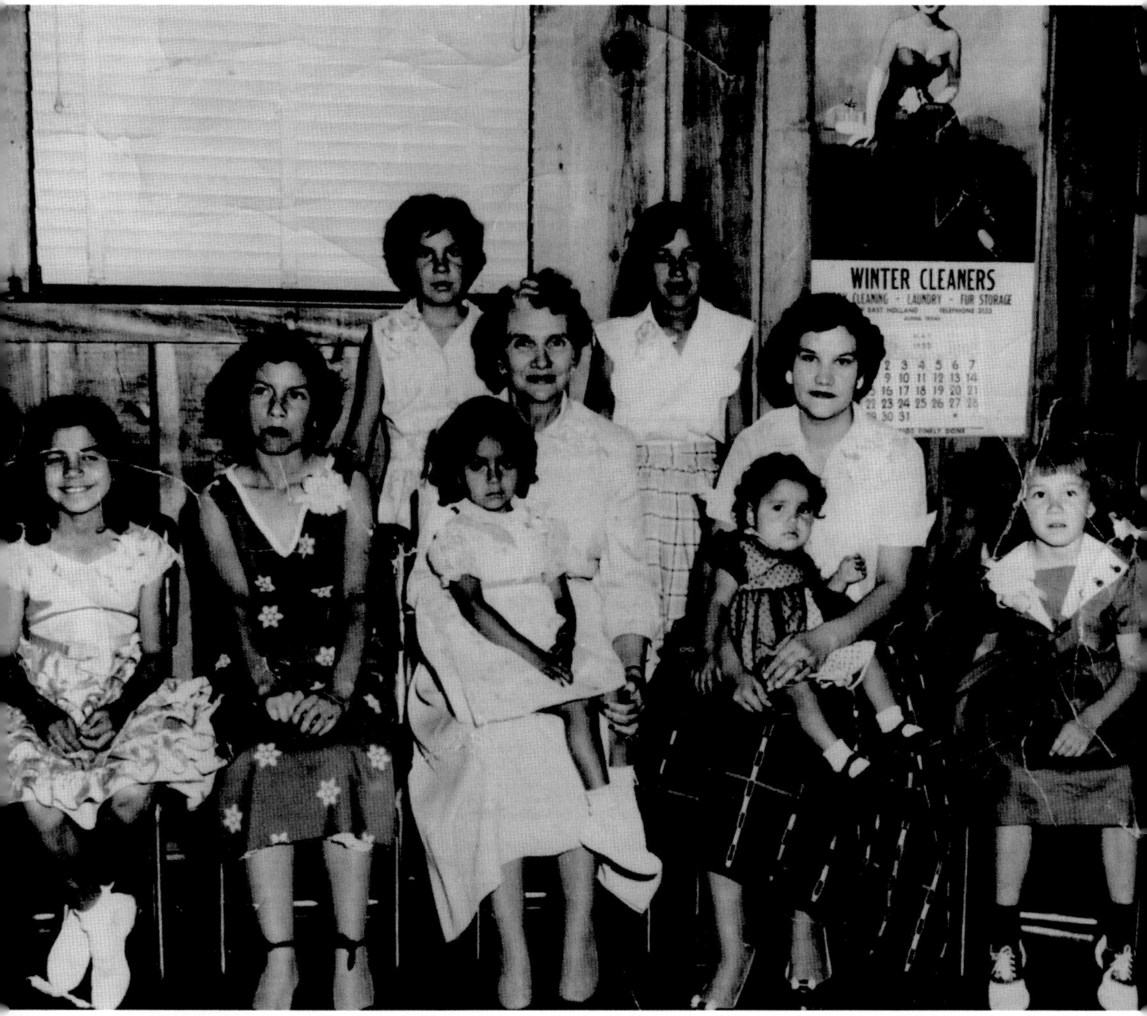

Berta Clark Lassiter

Berta Clark Lassiter was a most popular teacher at the Madero school in Alpine for Hispanic children, grades one through five. She taught in the 1920s and, in 1925, was named principal. A local account related the following: "Who can forget the PTA programs, staged each year by the legendary Berta Clark Lassiter, with the first graders in full costume and makeup performing before huge crowds in the gymnasium?" What gradually got the attention of the town was how many members of the community named their children after Berta. A photograph in 1952 shows Lassiter surrounded by eight other Bertas. They had all been name Berta by their parents out of respect for a remarkable teacher. A total of 15 Bertas in the community were named after this caring and loving teacher.

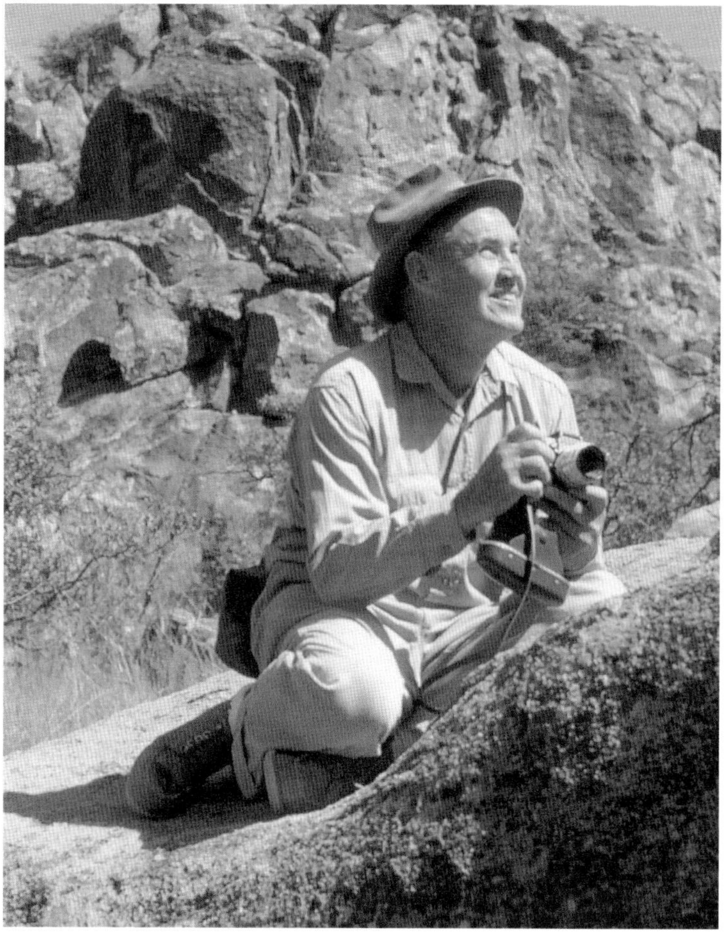

Barton H. Warnock

Barton H. Warnock, the legendary botanist of Sul Ross State University, where he taught for 33 years, was a prodigious plant collector. He discovered many new species, of which more than a dozen are named after him. His prolific collection forms the basis of the herbarium at Sul Ross State University, which contains around 100,000 plant species, mainly from the Trans-Pecos region.

He was a charismatic teacher whose popular botany inspired a new generation of botanists. His local plant-collecting exercises were planned and executed like military campaigns. He would pick out a target mountain, gather up his energetic graduate students, and send them up to high altitudes that are rarely visited by botanists. He would exhort his students with phrases like "Git after it!" and challenge them to beat him to the top.

The best-known part of his legacy is the trilogy of books on the common plants of the Big Bend region. The first, *Wildflowers of the Big Bend Country, Texas*, was published in 1970 and was illustrated photographically by the talented local photographer Peter Koch. After retiring from his professorship at Sul Ross, he kept active by assembling small collections of plants at ranches in the area, so the ranchers' families could understand what was growing on their land.

Growing up locally, the son of an alfalfa farmer, he graduated with his doctorate from the University of Texas, Austin, before joining Sul Ross. He lost his wife of 60 years, Ruel, shortly before his own death, at age 87, in 1998. He died with his boots on, having suffered a heart attack and driven off the highway to Fort Stockton. He is the only person in the region to have two buildings named after him: the science building at Sul Ross and the Barton Warnock Environmental Center in Lajitas.

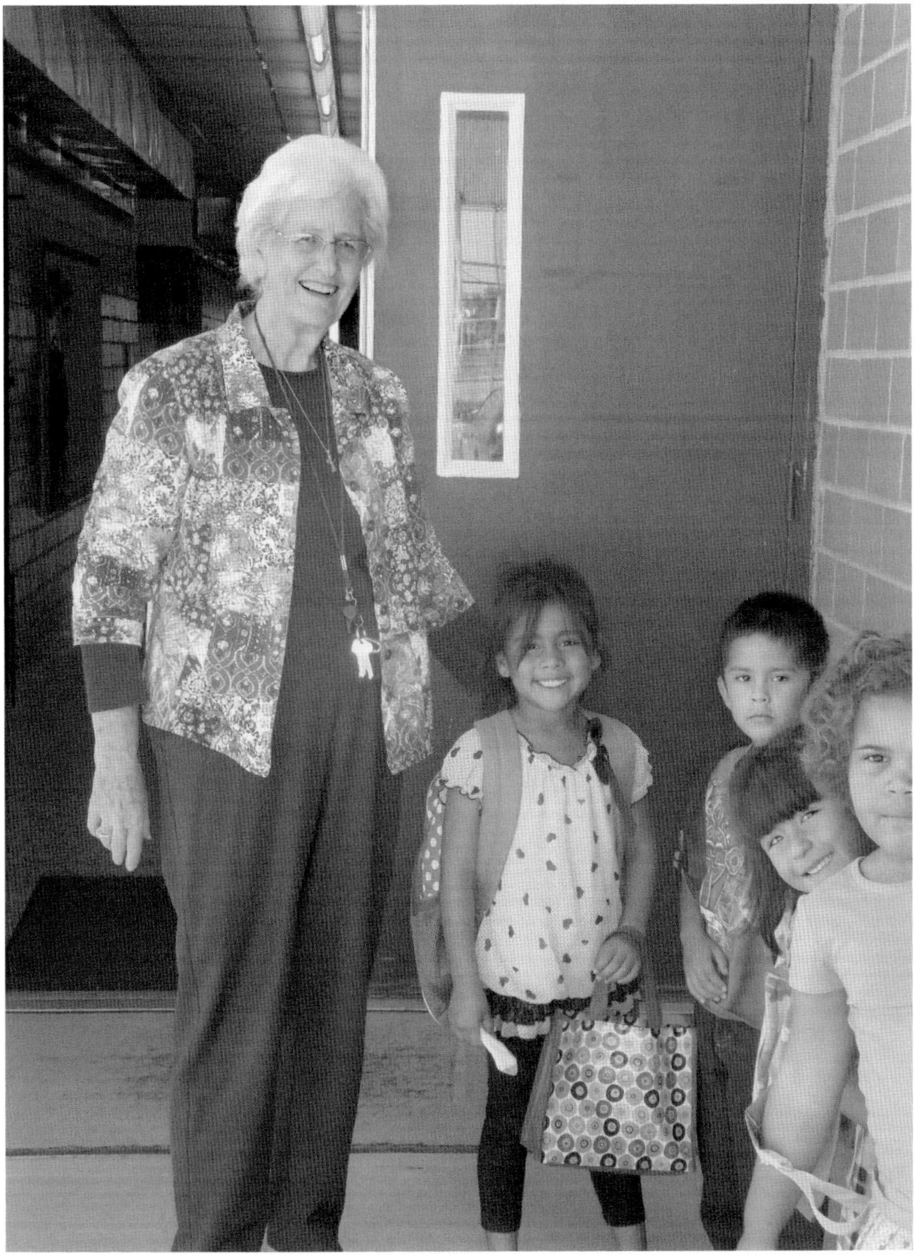

Laverne Gullihur

Born in Marathon in 1934, the eldest of six children of Fred Gullihur, Laverne seemed destined to be a teacher. First, however, she got married in her senior year at Marathon High School. She bore five children and spent 10 years raising them. Then, she thought about a career. Laverne graduated with a bachelor's in education (1965) from Sul Ross. Next, she bore her sixth child, Lonnie, and embarked on a teaching career. She transferred to a school in Odessa for higher wages. Before "retiring" in 1994, she opened a beauty salon in her carport and then taught for five years in Presidio. Still teaching the first grade, she smiles when talking about her young charges, one of whom remarked, "I didn't know you could do it," when the teacher, at age 78, sat down on the floor with them. (Author's collection.)

Dennis McEntire

Something has changed in the past 10 years in the Presidio Independent School District. Previously, the turnover of teachers in this small, dusty border town, with high unemployment, was 30 percent; today, it is one percent. In 2011, the high school graduation rate was 100 percent.

Dennis McEntire, the superintendent of the school district, has been on the job for 11 years and has been instrumental in helping to make this change. He came to the area because he already knew it, having run the Outward Bound operation in Redford (16 miles distant) in the 1970s, and loved it.

When asked what achievements he is proudest of, he replies that there is now a unified vision, from board members to those working in the cafeteria, based on the welfare of the students. The reason the teachers are staying is that they are driven by their heart, he says, which communicates itself to the kids.

Recent successes include the visit in 2012 to the White House by science teacher Shella Condino and her robotics class to receive an award from the president. Equally noteworthy was the visit, also in 2012, to the Smithsonian Institute in Washington, DC, by two teams of Presidio students, out of 1,125 across the nation. The presentation by the second team (seventh graders) was described as "stunning."

Now, the education authorities in Austin have designated Presidio as an Early College High School, one of six in the state. The challenge in the future for administration, teachers, and the students will be to justify this advancement. McEntire believes that his school can instill in the students a belief that they can compete in the world outside of Presidio. Achievements at Presidio High School recently suggest that he is moving in the right direction. (Photograph by Carmen Rubner, technology department, Presidio ISD.)

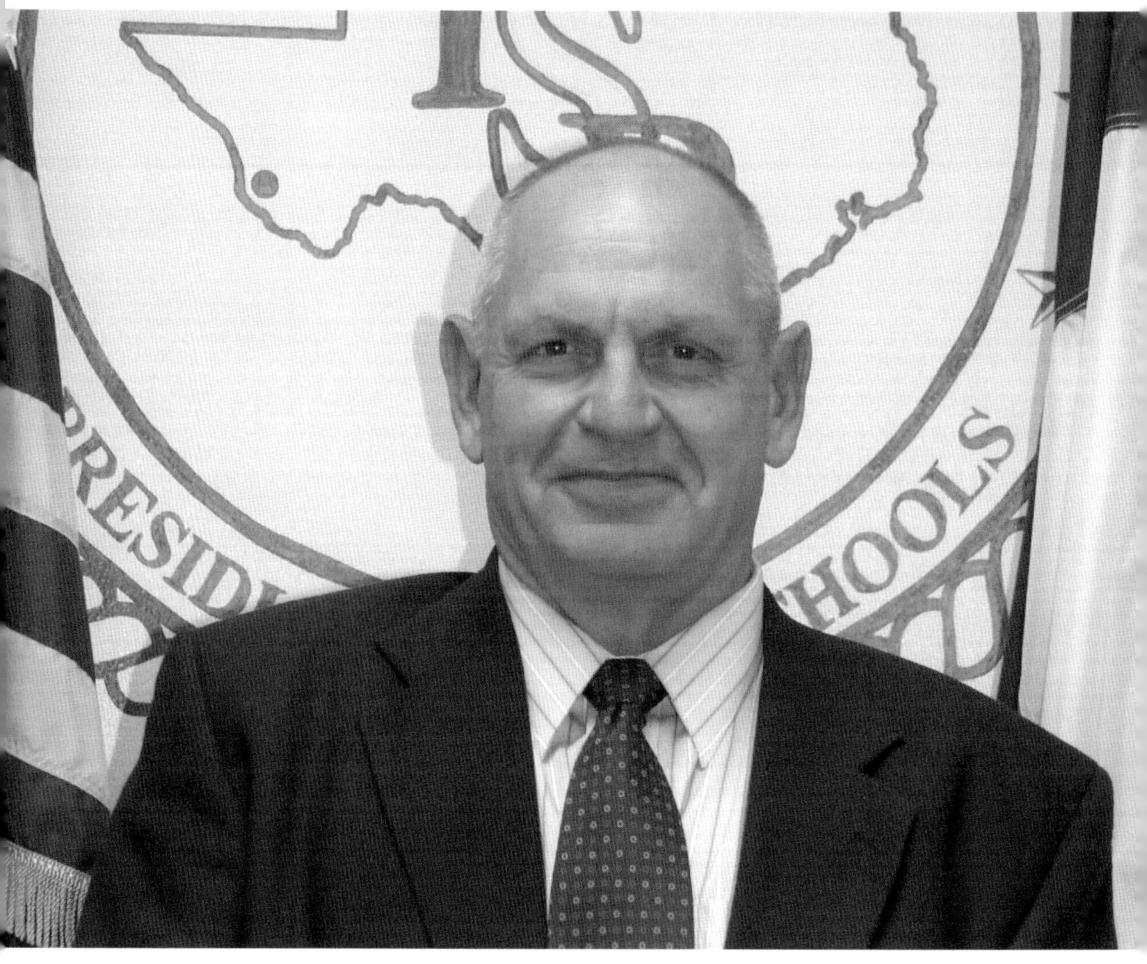

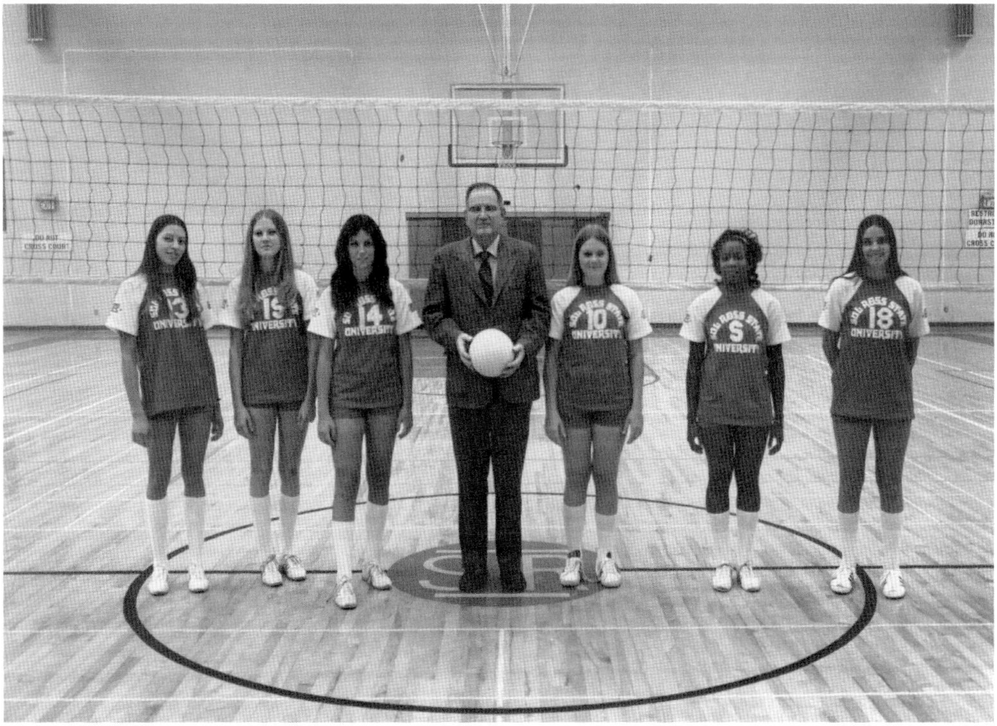

Paul E. Pierce

Paul E. Pierce was born in Hill, New Mexico, in 1914. He grew up in Fort Stockton, Texas, and graduated from Fort Stockton High School in 1932. An all-round athlete, he then attended Schreiner Institute Junior College in Kerrville, Texas, earning an associate of arts degree. He enrolled at Sul Ross Teachers College, graduating in 1936 with his bachelor's of arts in chemistry.

His first teaching/coaching job was at Fabens High School near El Paso, where his natural aptitude as a coach soon was apparent. After two years, he moved on to Wink, Texas, near Pecos, coaching all sports. From 1942 until 1946, Pierce served as a gunnery officer in the US Navy, while also coaching a Navy football team. At war's end, he returned to Sul Ross and was hired as instructor and coach of all athletics.

Then followed Coach Pierce's first highly successful term at Sul Ross. From 1946 to 1952, he became the most successful coach ever at the university, both in the number of wins and in winning percentage. The 1948 team was undefeated and played to a 7-7 tie in the Tangerine Bowl.

After the 1952 season, he moved to Sam Houston State College in Huntsville, Texas, and became the head coach for football and track and athletics director. The Sam Houston Bearcats shared the National Association of Intercollegiate Athletics Football National Championship in 1964, and the following year, Pierce was named Knute Rockne Little All-American Coach of the Year.

After earning his doctorate in education at the University of Houston, he retired from teaching and coaching to spend more time with his terminally ill wife, Lunelle, to whom he had been married for 42 years. In 1978, Pierce was inducted into the Sam Houston Hall of Honor, and nine years later, Sul Ross awarded him the same honor.

"Red" Pierce returned to Sul Ross in 1968 as head of the health and physical education department. Results began to show immediately. The Lady Lobos, coached by US Olympian Marilyn McCreary, led the Lady Lobos to two straight national championships; it was the dawn of a new era. Pierce was named head football coach and athletic director in 1976 and served in that capacity until his retirement in 1978.

Pierce then turned his attention to civic affairs, serving as mayor for 12 years, and various other civic groups. He died in 2004, aged 89. The Texas State legislature passed a resolution honoring him, and the gymnasium at Sul Ross bears his name.

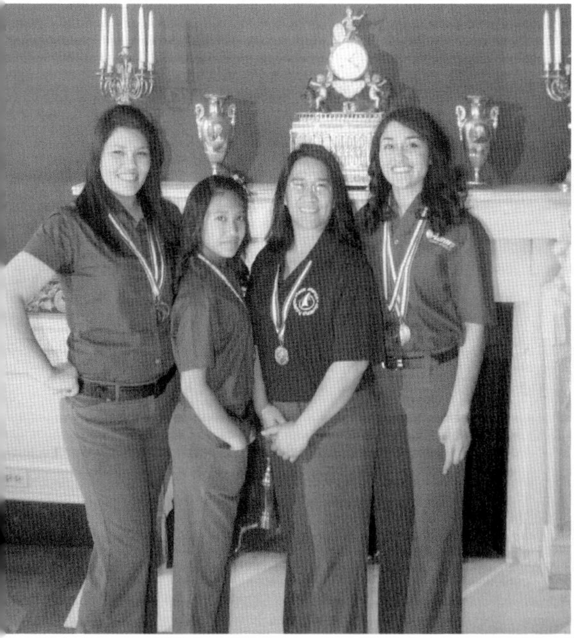

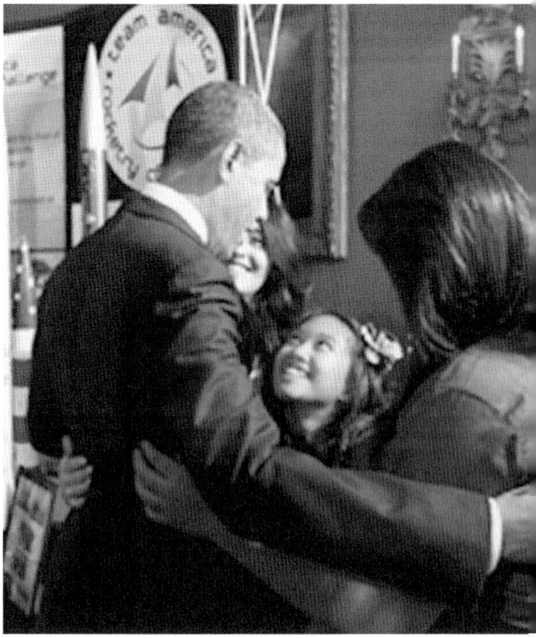

Shella Condino

Growing up in the Philippines, the oldest of eight children, Shella Condino struggled with poverty and the responsibility of helping bring up her sisters. Yet, she obtained degrees in science from the University of Manila (1993). She then taught chemistry and physics for eight years before immigrating to the United States. She flew to El Paso in 2003. From El Paso, she relocated to Presidio, Texas. Here, she made an immediate impact, bonding with the students and impressing the administration by initiating a rocketry and robotics class. In national competitions, her class excelled, and Shella was honored with various awards, including a National Aerospace Teacher of the Year Award (2011). This rapid recognition culminated in a visit to the White House Science Fair in 2012, where her students met with President Obama, who gave them a hug. (All, courtesy of Shella Condino.)

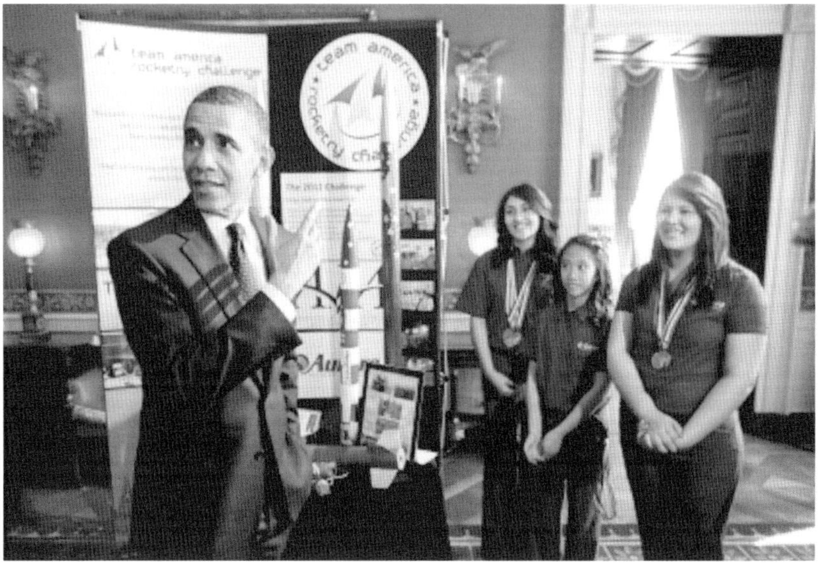

CHAPTER FOUR

Art, Music, and Letters

It may be the beauty of this landscape of mountain and desert, the small population, or the region's history, but there is no doubting that a substantial number of artists, musicians, and writers have chosen, and are still choosing, the Big Bend and Davis Mountains as their home. Their destination is not just Marfa—a moribund cow town transformed into an active center for modern art—but the region as a whole.

Terlingua has long been a magnet for creative, talented people who relish the unstructured life in this ghost town. They live simply, sometimes hauling water to their rock houses or trailers, far from the pressures of city living. Terlingua has been host to an annual chili cook-off for many years, attracting thousands of visitors each November. Less well-known is the annual Word-Off, a reading by local writers of their work in the famous Starlight Theatre in the ghost town. No more than five minutes of reading time is the first rule of the evening. Hallie Stillwell is an artist that participated in this. Although, she was a teacher, rancher, cowboy's wife, and justice of the peace, her three books made her known across Texas.

The quality of desert light attracts photographers to the Big Bend National Park. James Evans, Bill Wright, Luc Novovitch, Jim Bones, Dan Klepper, Laurence Parent, and Todd Jagger are a few of a long list of photographers who capture the landscape, wildlife, and people. There is also lots of good weather for shooting pictures.

Painters have been drawn to the Big Bend and Davis Mountains landscapes for many years. Among contemporary local artists, Wayne Baize, Bonnie Wunderlich, and Mary Baxter stand out, but there are many more as the walls of Alpine's three galleries, Kiowa, Catchlight, and Gallery on the Square, attest. Priscilla Wiggins occupies a special position among artists. For 26 years, she has painted outdoors in the Big Bend National Park; see the entry later in the book.

Local musicians have for years played at popular venues like the Starlight Theatre and La Kiva in Terlingua, and the Railroad Blues in Alpine. Some, like Butch Hancock and Craig Carter (65 tours in Europe), have toured extensively overseas. Texas-Mexico border music (*cumbias* and *conjunto* music) is particularly popular. The names of the bands speak volumes; Pinché Gringos and Doodlin' Hogwallops are two examples of typical band names. There is even a recording studio in Terlingua, which has produced 50 CDs.

Marfa stages many music events, from periodic performances by visiting bands (like the Tuareg band Tinawiren), hosted by Ballroom Marfa, to the ever-changing schedule at Padre's Marfa (a former funeral home). El Cosmico, an alternative accommodation place with teepees, vintage trailers, and safari tents, also hosts concerts with big name bands from Austin. There is music all around, and the price of admission is low.

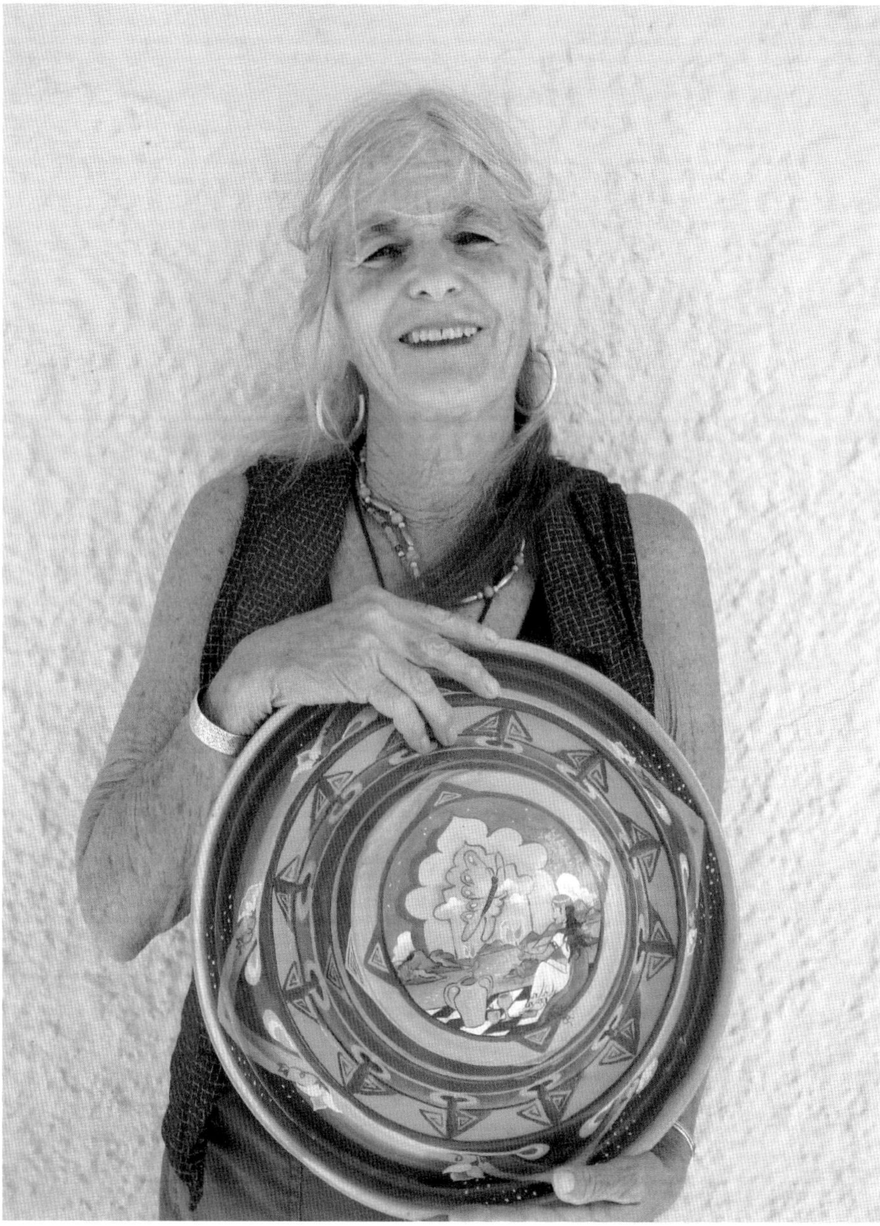

Collie Ryan
Collie Ryan (born in 1946) arrived in Terlingua in 1980 from California, where she took art classes, wrote poetry, and recorded songs. She loved the silence of the desert around Terlingua, and felt safe. For 23 years, she lived in a bus on the banks of the Rio Grande and started painting mandalas. Mandalas are ancient circular designs used in Eastern cultures. The circle represents the universe and provides a geometric plan into which the painter can present his or her private dreams. Collie has painted 2,000 hubcap mandalas over 25 years, each one taking two to three days, with many of them being special orders. Hubcaps are lightweight and recyclable, an important point for someone who lives close to nature. They are an industrial 21st-century medium, on which an artist paints timeless spiritual concepts. (Author's collection.)

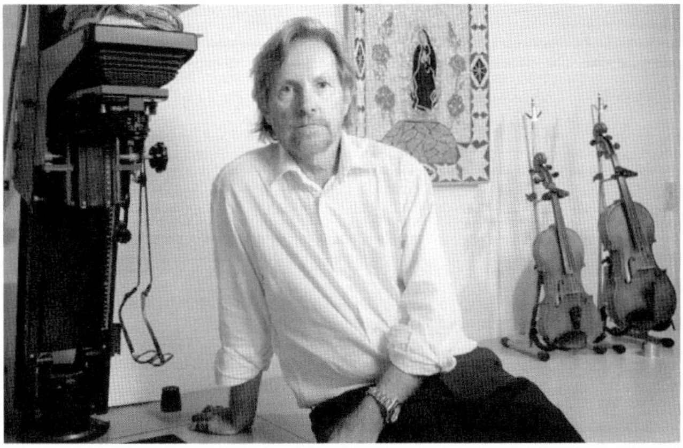

James Evans

James Evans arrived in Marathon from Austin in 1990 and took a job in the Holland Hotel kitchens. His aim was to live in the Big Bend region and photograph it. In over 20 years, he has established the oldest gallery, produced two sizeable coffee table books (both selling well), and has captured the spirit of the place through his landscape and people photographs. His first book, *Big Bend Pictures*, showed black-and-white photographs, including legendary character Hallie Stillwell, numerous landscapes, and some quirky shots too. His recent book *Crazy from the Heat* is part black-and-white photography with some color and some nighttime shots. What is noteworthy is how he portrays the independent, sometimes eccentric, nature of the area's residents through unusual pictures, such as the back of a man's neck, some dancing feet, and a shot called "David's grave." (Photographs by James H. Evans.)

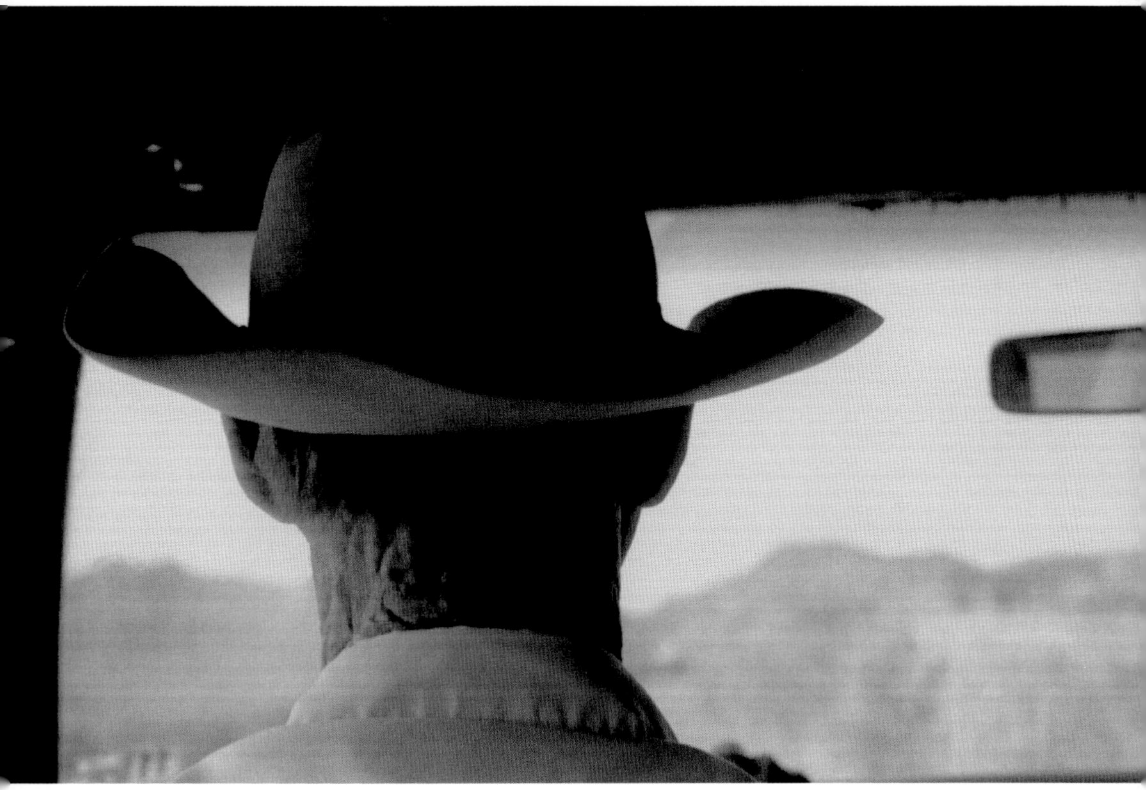

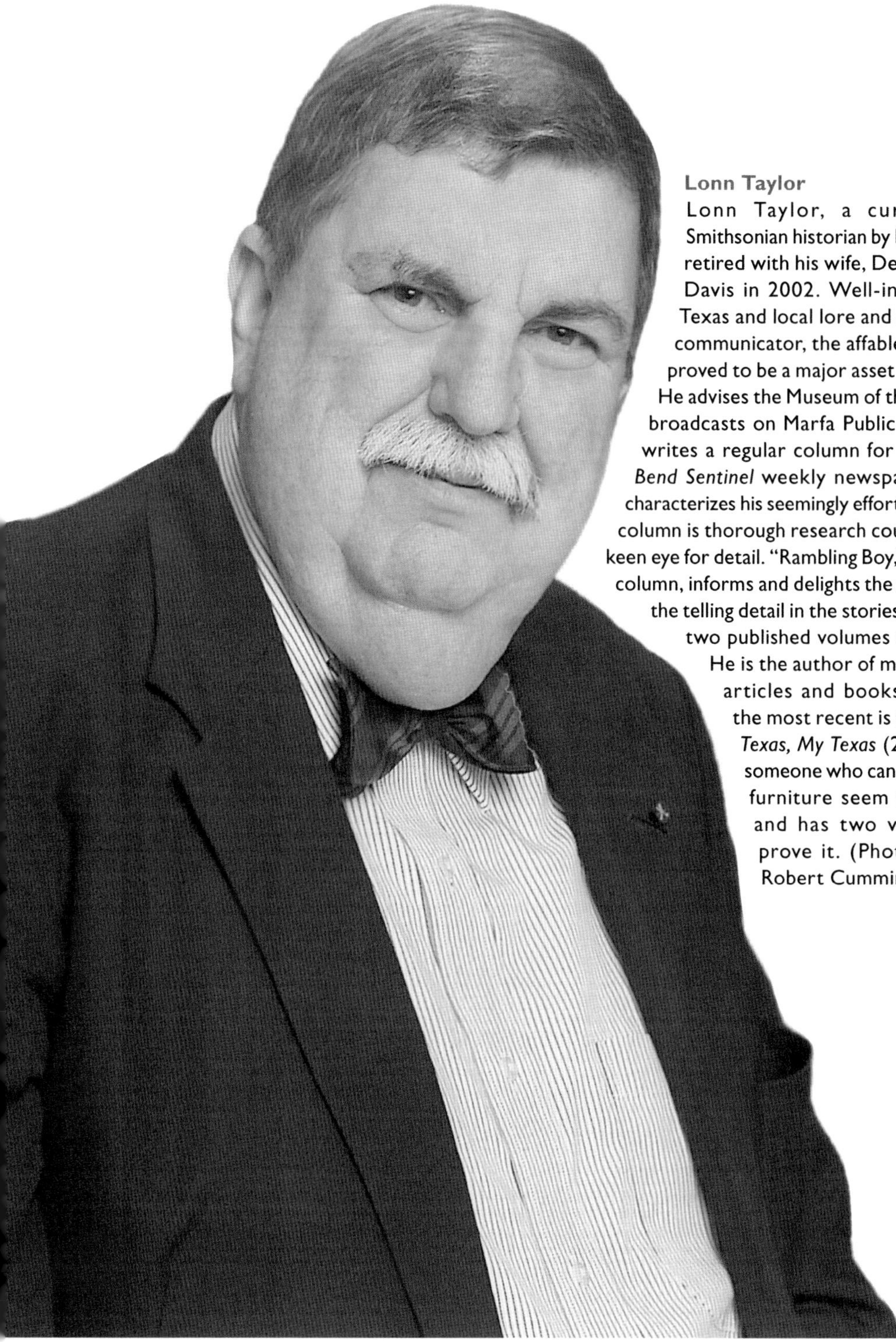

Lonn Taylor

Lonn Taylor, a curator and Smithsonian historian by background, retired with his wife, Dedie, to Fort Davis in 2002. Well-informed on Texas and local lore and an effective communicator, the affable Taylor has proved to be a major asset to the area. He advises the Museum of the Big Bend, broadcasts on Marfa Public Radio, and writes a regular column for Marfa's *Big Bend Sentinel* weekly newspaper. What characterizes his seemingly effortless written column is thorough research coupled with a keen eye for detail. "Rambling Boy," his weekly column, informs and delights the reader with the telling detail in the stories, and he has two published volumes to prove it. He is the author of many learned articles and books, of which the most recent is the popular *Texas, My Texas* (2012). He is someone who can make Texas furniture seem interesting and has two volumes to prove it. (Photograph by Robert Cummings.)

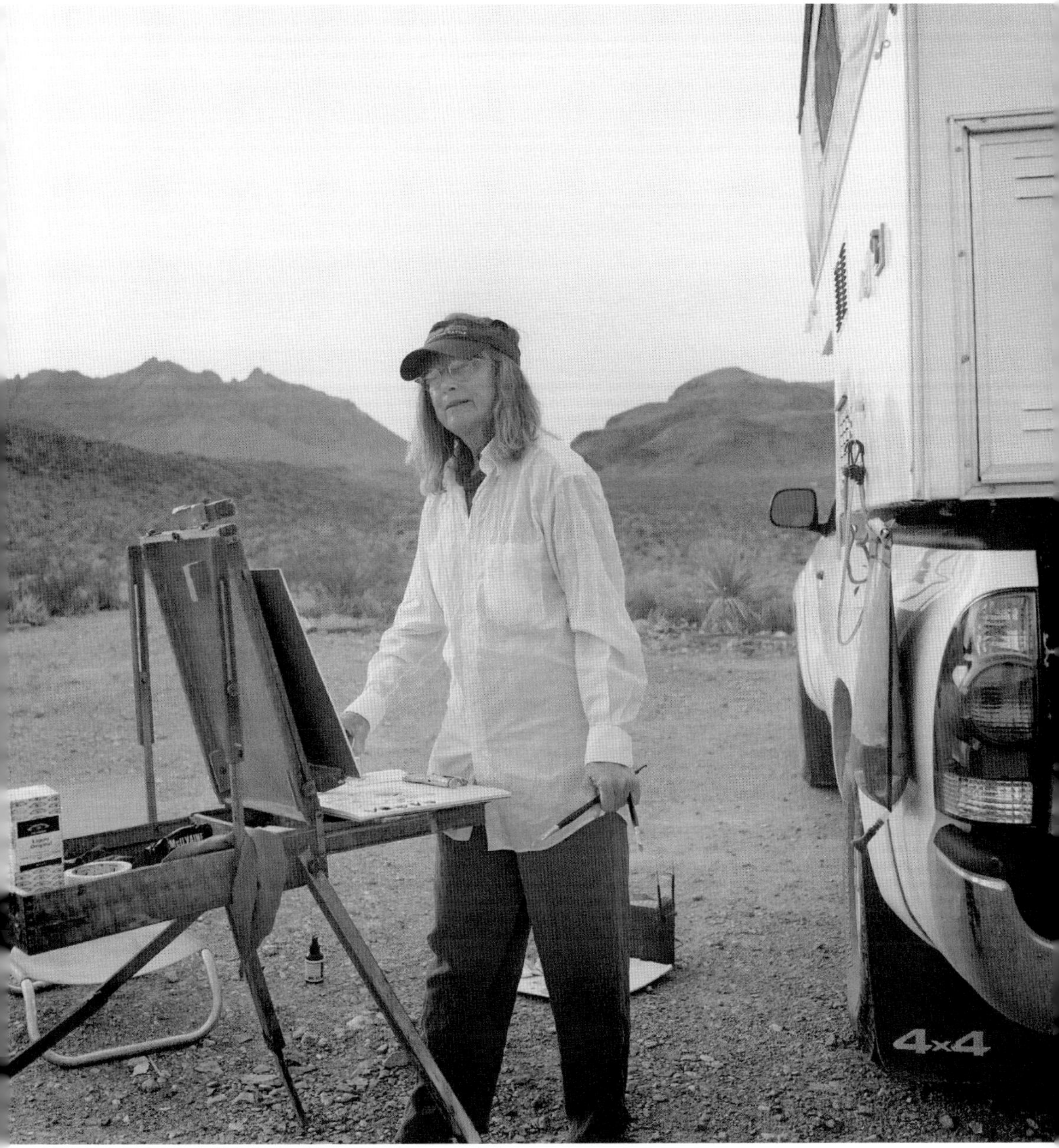

Priscilla Wiggins
Priscilla Wiggins remembers painting at an easel at the age of three. She grew up on the East Coast and attended schools and colleges, mainly for art classes, until she was 27. Interested in the Hopi Indians, she moved to Albuquerque and obtained a bachelor's degree in art in 1972. She says, "In 1977, I decided to dedicate the rest of my life to camping and painting." In 1981, she found Big Bend National Park, and from then, she divided her year between Colorado in the summer and Big Bend in winter—for 26 years. She continues, "I was struck by the immense silence and the layers of landscape stretching for miles in every direction." Her exquisite landscape oil paintings are displayed at Eve's Garden Bed-and-Breakfast in Marathon, and she has periodic solo shows in Santa Fe. (Photograph by James H. Evans.)

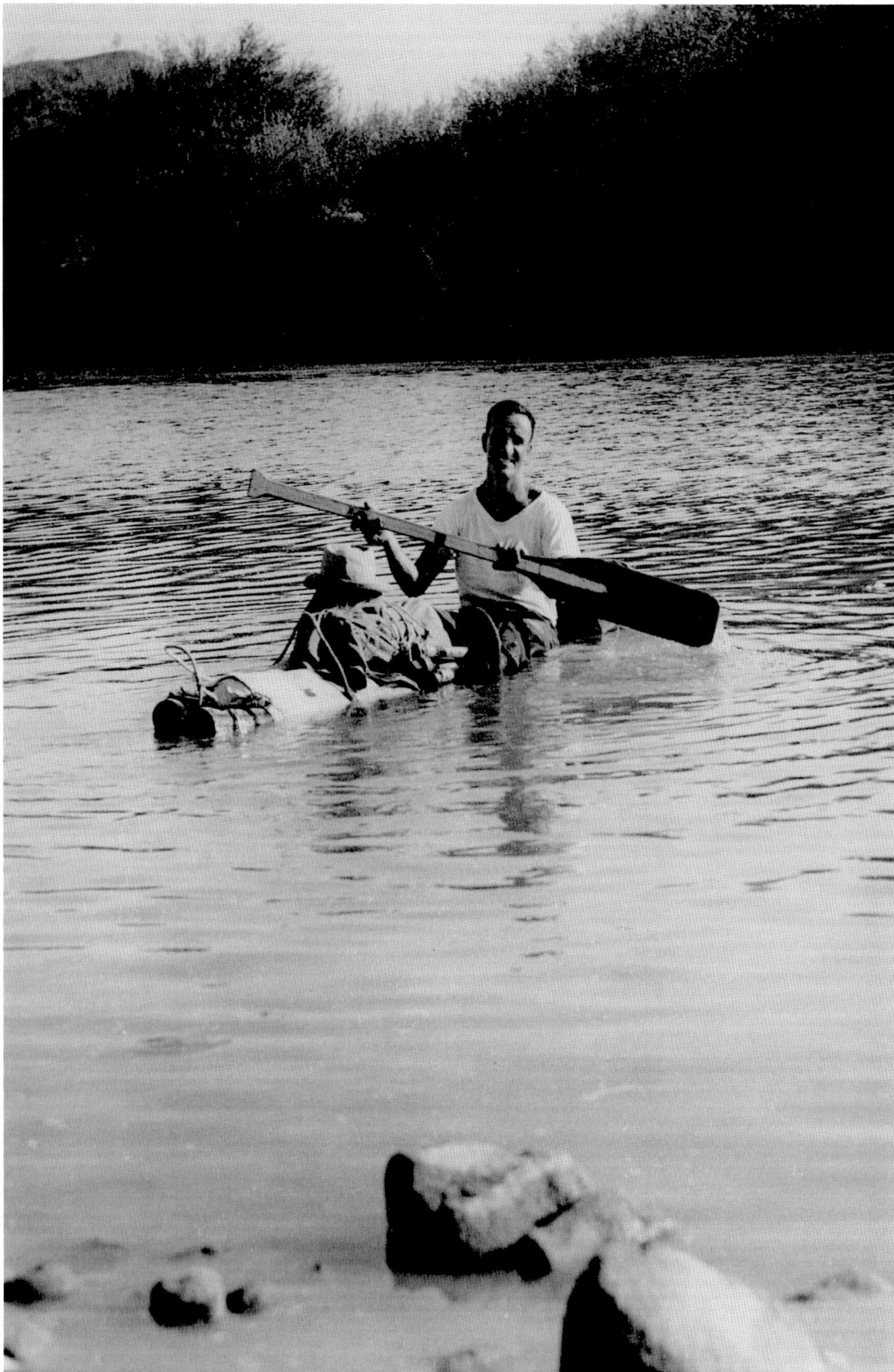

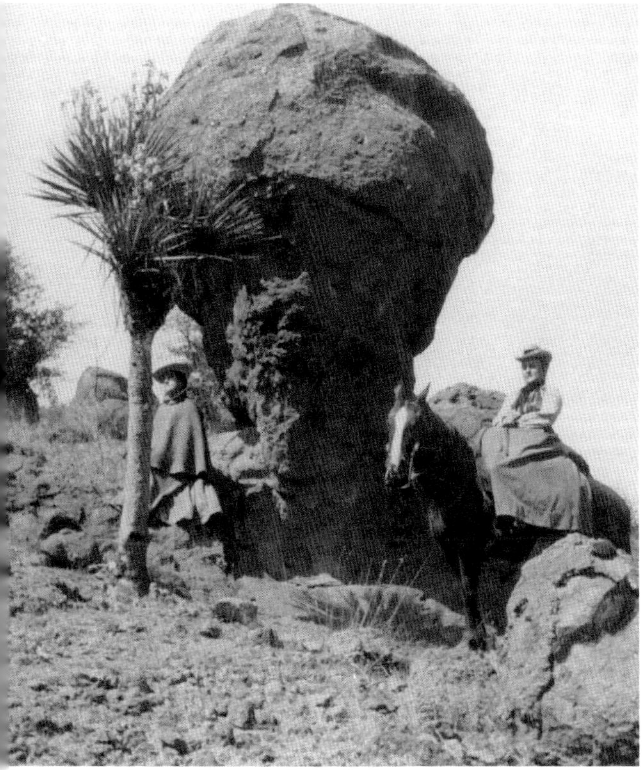

Susan Janes
John L. Janes was hired by Colonel Grierson to operate the military telegraph line between Fort Davis and Marfa. He and his wife, Susan, arrived in Fort Davis from New Hampshire in 1893 with their two children. She was an energetic woman and roamed the countryside photographing Indian relics. She made seven trips to the top of Mount Livermore, where a particularly important find of arrowheads had been made. When she heard that local people started to remove the arrowheads, she remonstrated with them and got the artifacts, which she believed had religious significance, into a museum. This important find is known as the Livermore Cache. She opened a photography studio in Fort Davis. After her husband died in 1906, she moved with her daughter to El Paso, where she died in 1910.

Peter Koch (OPPOSITE PAGE)
The man sitting on a half-submerged, homemade boat in the Rio Grande is Peter Koch.

He was employed by the National Park Service in 1945 to take pictures of the brand new Big Bend National Park, which opened to the public the previous year. Koch planned to stay two weeks in the park but ended up spending the rest of his life there.

He was born in Romania and came to the United States at the age of nine. An early introduction to photography as a Boy Scout became a lifelong passion. Later in life, married and with three daughters, he worked as chief photographer for the *Cincinnati Times-Star.*

Pining for wilderness and anxious that his wife, Etta, reach a dry climate better suited to her health, in 1944, he took leave of absence from the paper and headed for Texas. The family loaded up a trailer, which they called "Porky the Road Hog," and drove south.

Koch was a born naturalist and a self-taught photographer, and so, coming to the Big Bend National Park was a wonderful match. In 1945–1946, he produced two full-length film documentaries on the Big Bend. One, *Desert Gold,* proved popular, and Koch embarked on lecture tours through the Northeast and Midwest. Meanwhile, Etta's health improved, and she took a secretarial job with the National Park Service.

After six strenuous years of touring and lecturing, Koch returned to Big Bend. He started a camera shop concession in Big Bend National Park and collaborated in writing a tourist handbook, *Guide for the Big Bend.* In 1955, the family moved to Alpine, and Koch threw himself into tourism promotion, opening a travel agency and collaborating with famed botanist Dr. Barton Warnock, who produced three wildflower books in the 1970s. He wrote a weekly column for the *Alpine Avalanche* newspaper, always stressing the importance of conserving the environment, which nourished and stimulated his creative energy. Koch died in 1986.

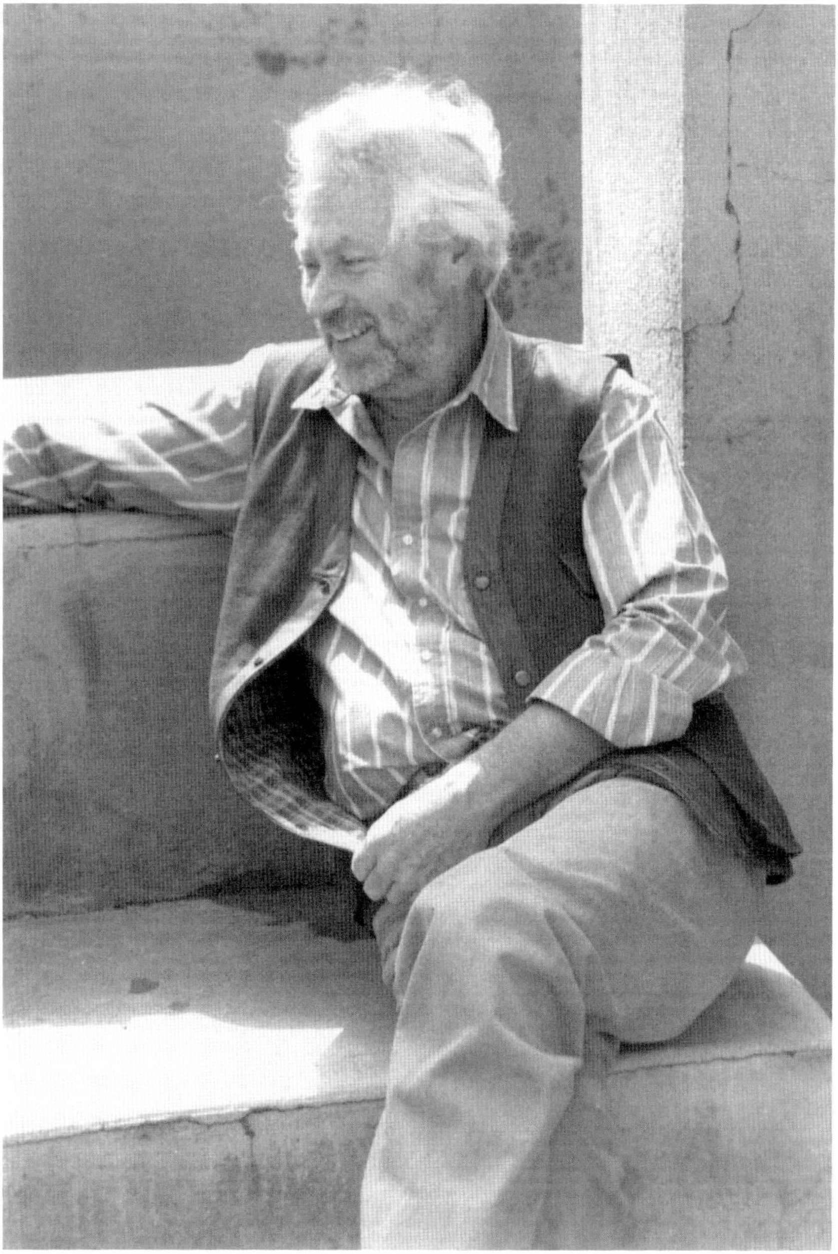

Donald Judd

In 1976, Donald Judd arrived in Marfa from New York, where he had been an art critic. He sought the austere landscape and desert light to display his own work, large sculpture pieces, which were designed to stay in one place. He purchased old Fort Russell, south of town, for this purpose. Judd died in 1993 but had already set in motion events that would make Marfa internationally recognized. He was a private man and was initially misunderstood by Marfa's residents. He brought economic life back to the ailing town. His best known work is a collection of 100 aluminum cubes or boxes, no two the same, set in a hangar building with huge windows opening onto the desert. The changing light constantly alters the appearance of the work. (Photograph by Chinati Foundation.)

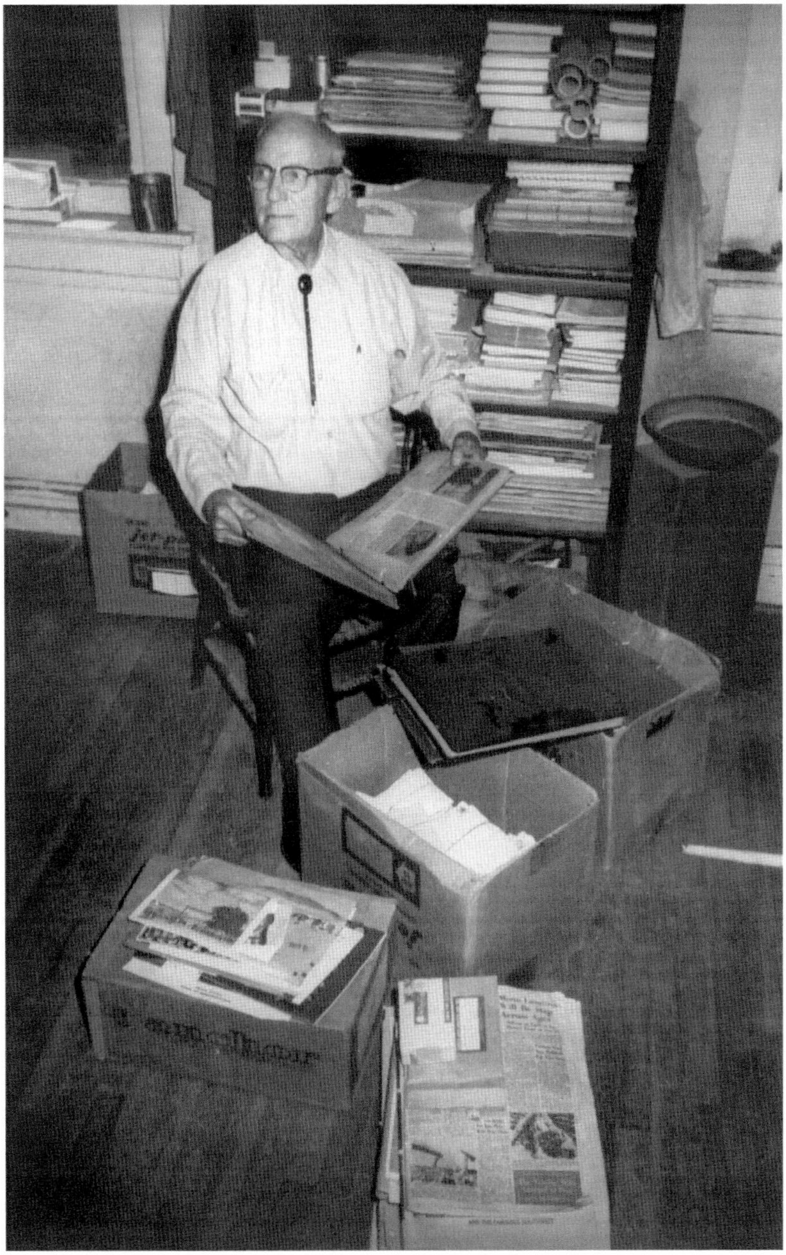

Barry Scobee

Someone once said that Barry Scobee was "never one to let truth stand in the way of a good story." He also is probably the only pulp fiction writer to have a mountain (near Fort Davis) named after him.

Born in Missouri in 1885, he arrived in Fort Davis in 1917, after serving in the US Army in the Philippines. He churned out countless short stories for magazines, mainly popularizing the lore of the West. Later, he turned to writing about local history; he helped to preserve the history of old Fort Davis.

At age 55, he served on a merchant ship in World War II and, once done, he returned to Fort Davis for a second career as justice of the peace and county coroner. He had long since become a Texan and died in Texas in 1977, aged 91.

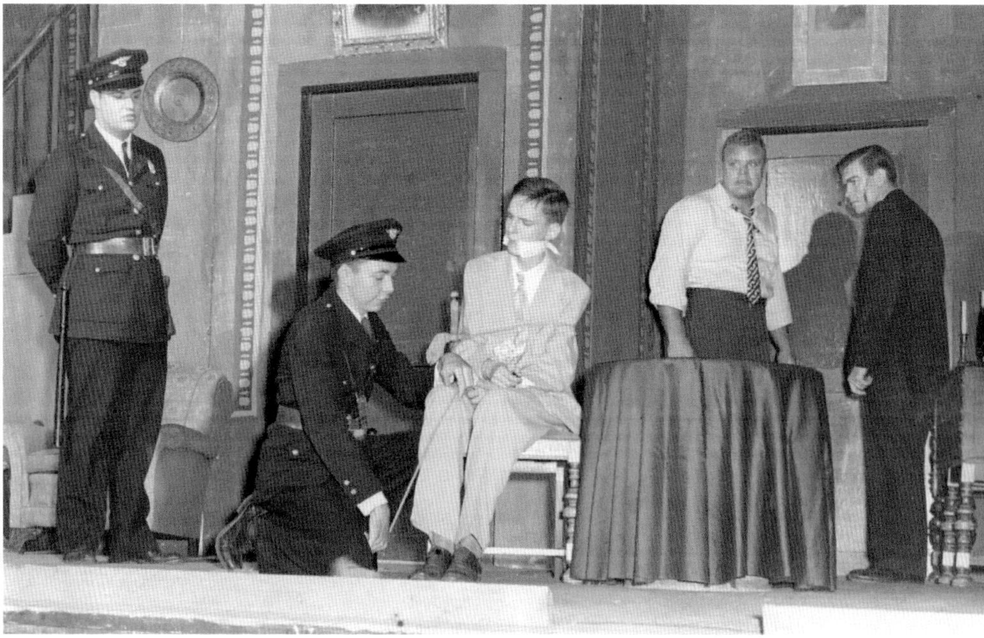

Dan Blocker

In 1946, a 350-pound teenager named Dan Blocker arrived on Sul Ross campus, accompanied by his mother. He played football but did not excel. However, he acted in one or two plays (pictured here, second from right) and graduated with a degree in speech in 1950. He served in Korea as a sergeant (1950–1952), came home to Alpine, married Dolphie Parker, and had four children. He completed his master's and anticipated doing a doctorate program in Los Angeles. Instead, he got a role in *Gunsmoke*, which led to a 13-year role in *Bonanza*, as Hoss Cartwright (see picture). He died from a failed gallbladder operation in 1974. His classmate Gene Hendryx summarized the following about Dan: "This jolly giant of a man was the most amazing buffoon, the cleverest storyteller, the most hilarious and pleasurable person to come up the pike." (Below, courtesy Museum of the Big Bend Collection.)

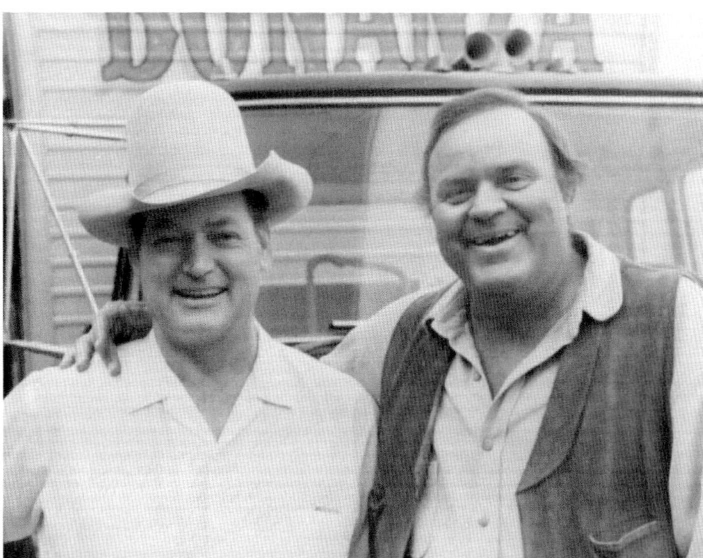

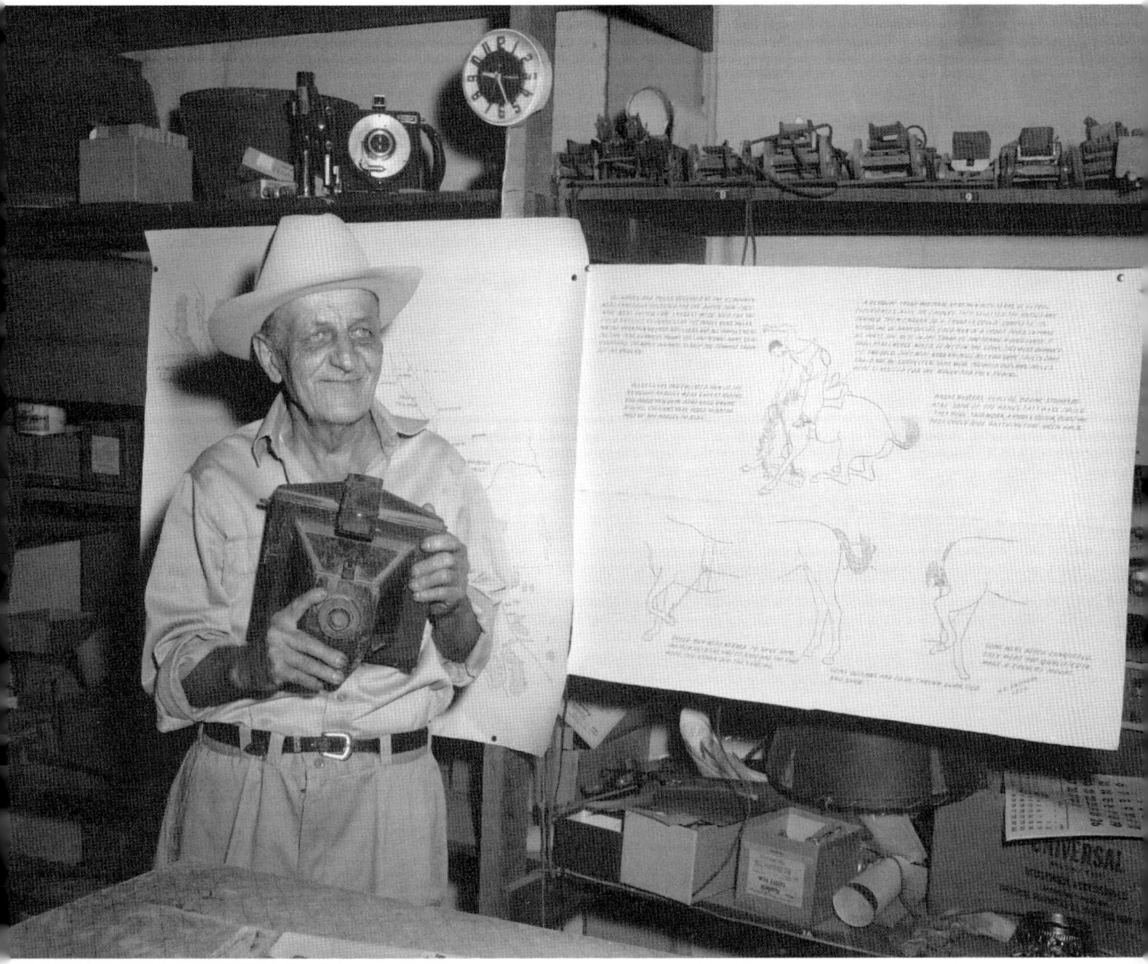

William Dudley Smithers

Having been born in San Luis Potosi, Mexico, where his father kept books for a US mining company, and growing up as a teenager in San Antonio gave William Dudley Smithers a Mexican cultural outlook, which later showed up in his pictures of people along the border.

In San Antonio, he worked as a hauler for 12 hours a day and then learned the basics of photography at night in a studio. In 1915, he enlisted with the US Army Quartermaster Corps, handling horse-drawn wagons. He arrived in Alpine as a teamster with an Army Pack Train, delivering supplies to cavalry posts, which had been established along the Big Bend border as a result of surging violence. Many of his pictures from those days are of horse pack trains, cavalry, motorized columns, and military aircraft, which operated as spotters to the mounted units.

The 9,000 photographs in Smithers's collection, which he bequeathed to the University of Texas, Austin, are the result of his presence as an eyewitness in the Big Bend region during this time of military activity. He recorded through his lens the working cowboys, the Mexican families, drug smugglers crossing the Rio Grande, and mule trains hauling goods. His pictures helped E.E. Townsend sell the idea of a Texas park along the Rio Grande to the legislature in Austin.

Later, living in Alpine, he got into the business of selling what he called "magic lantern slides" and also postcards of his photographs. This picture shows him in his Alpine studio. In 1976, he wrote *Chronicle of the Big Bend: A Photographic Memoir of Life on the Border*, an evocative account of conditions in the area at that time. He died in 1981, never having married.

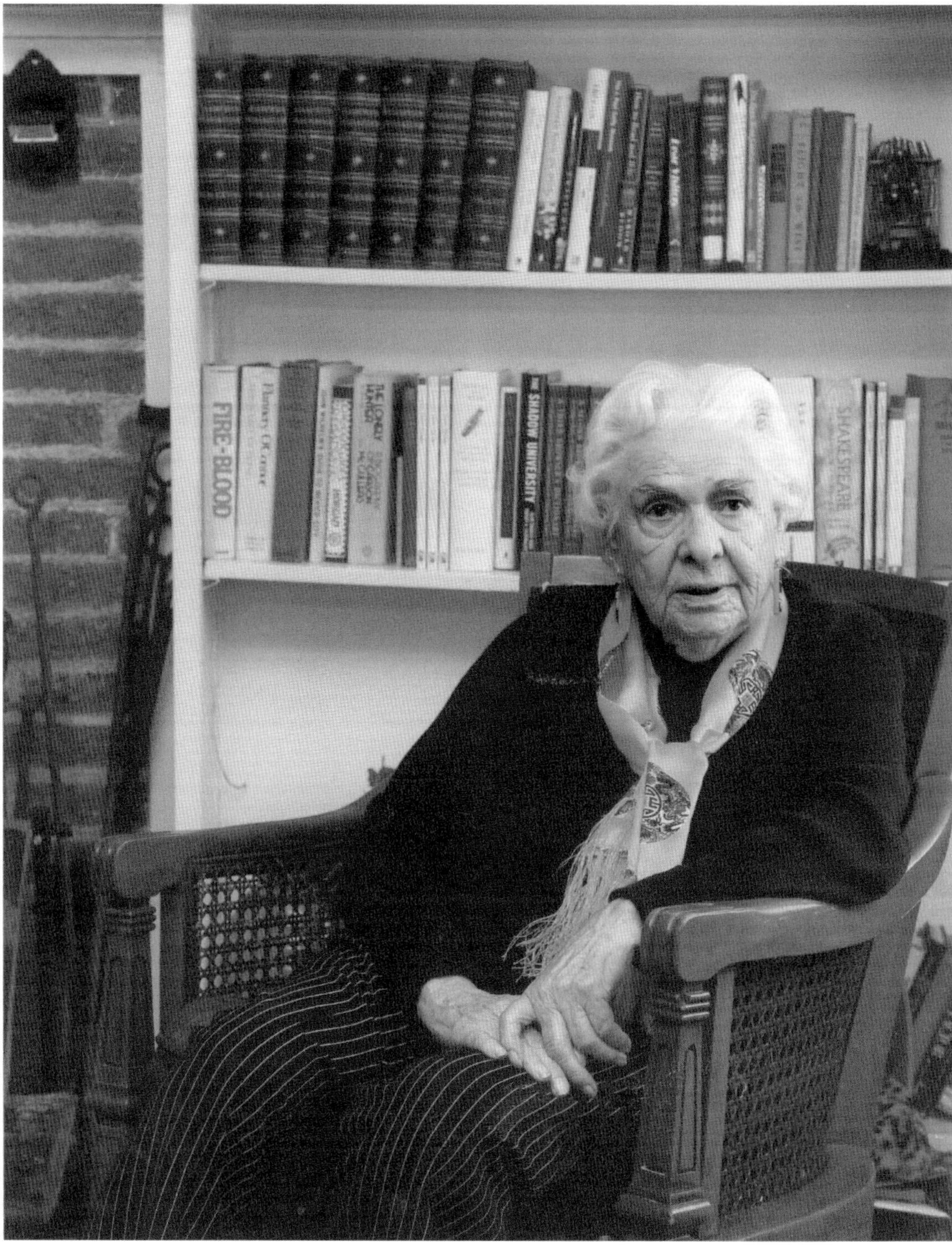

Cecilia Thompson

At age 92, blind and requiring a secretary to act as her eyes, Cecilia Thompson finished compiling the third volume of the *History of Presidio County*. She had already completed the first two volumes, which won the Fehrenbach Book Award for best county history.

She graduated in 1954 with a doctorate in theater arts from Iowa University and, 65 years later, still had the artistic energy to direct a play in Marfa, *Our Town*. In the last two years of her life she also wrote, coauthoring with Louise O'Connor, Images of America: *Marfa* for Arcadia Publishing. She died in May 2012, aged 94.

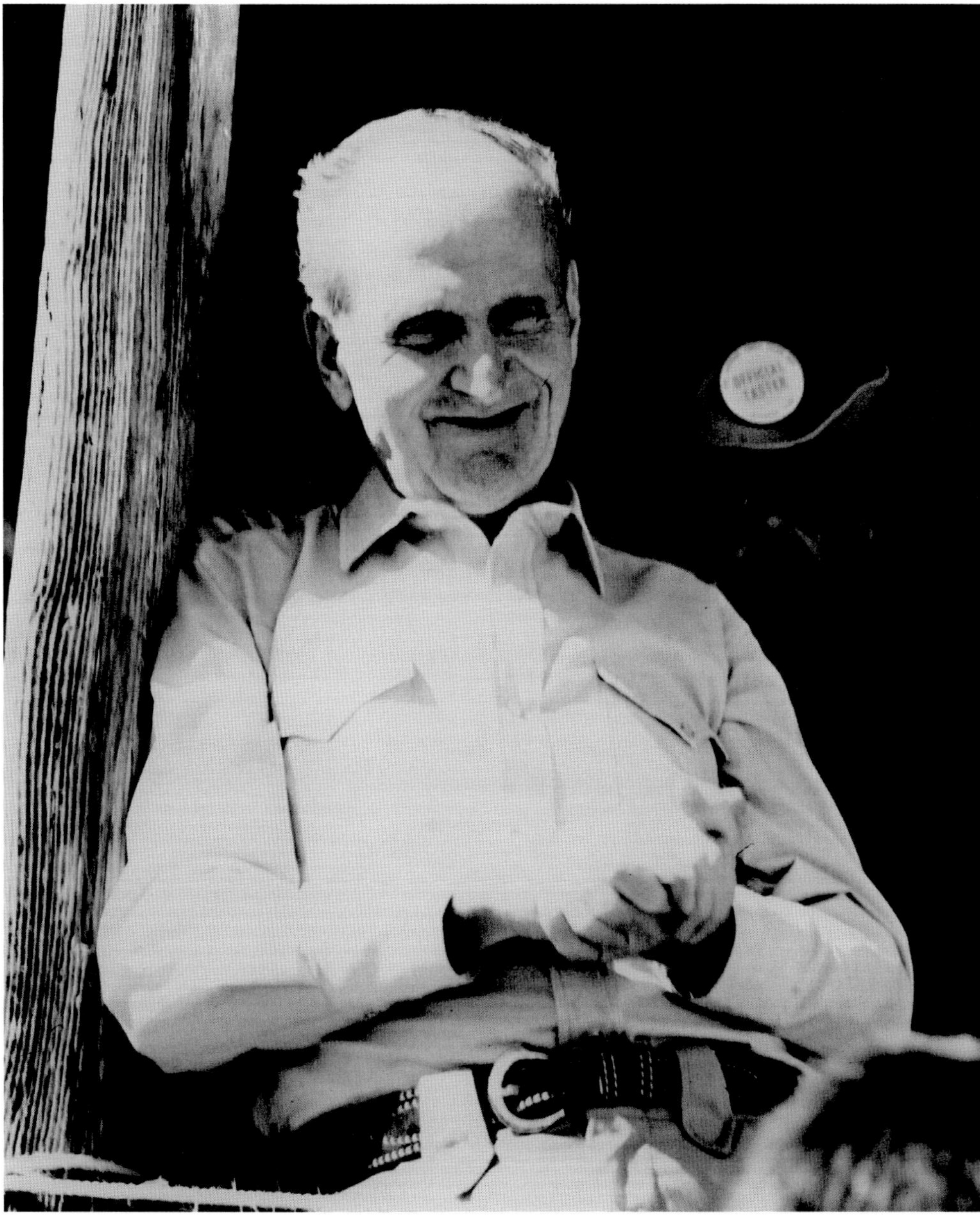

H. Allen Smith

H. Allen Smith, a famed East Coast humorist who wrote 36 books in the 1940s and 1950s, came to Alpine in 1967 looking for a quiet and peaceful retreat. But local residents found nothing humorous in his comments about them—"I have never seen such a goddamned bunch of bigoted, pious, lying, cheating bastards in all my life."

A naturally cantankerous man who felt cheated by his house builder in Alpine, Smith refused to apologize. Reciprocal feelings of disdain were shown by Alpine's residents. Smith later donated generously to local libraries and struck up a few friendships, and so a wary truce broke out. His one success was a relationship with Wick Fowler over how to cook chili, the reason he had come to Alpine in the first place. He died in his hilltop Alpine home in 1976, aged 69.

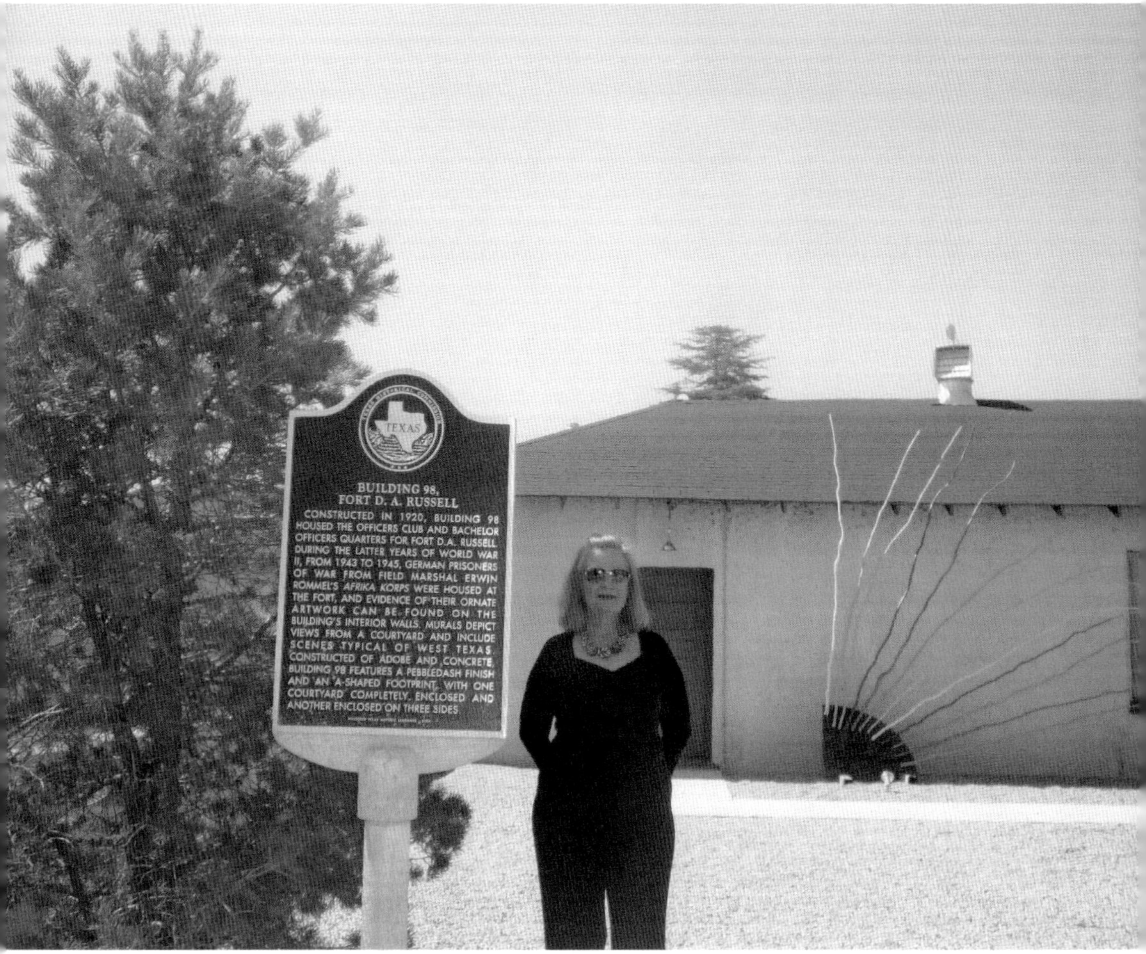

Mona Garcia

After her husband, Rudy, retired in 1995 from the oil business, in which he had worked around the world, Mona Garcia opened a bed-and-breakfast in Marfa. Little did she know that it would lead to a challenging task of unearthing, documenting, and recreating art treasures housed in Marfa's former military base. Mona decided to open an International Woman's Foundation in the old officers' quarters at Camp D.A. Russell, a center where mature women artists could live and develop their work. Ten years later, the center is open. Rooms are available to visiting artists. On the walls, murals painted by World War II German prisoners who were housed here in 1944–1945, have been restored. Periodic exhibitions are staged, such as the current Grand Retrospective of Wilhelmina Weber Furlong, described as "America's first woman modern artist." (Author's collection.)

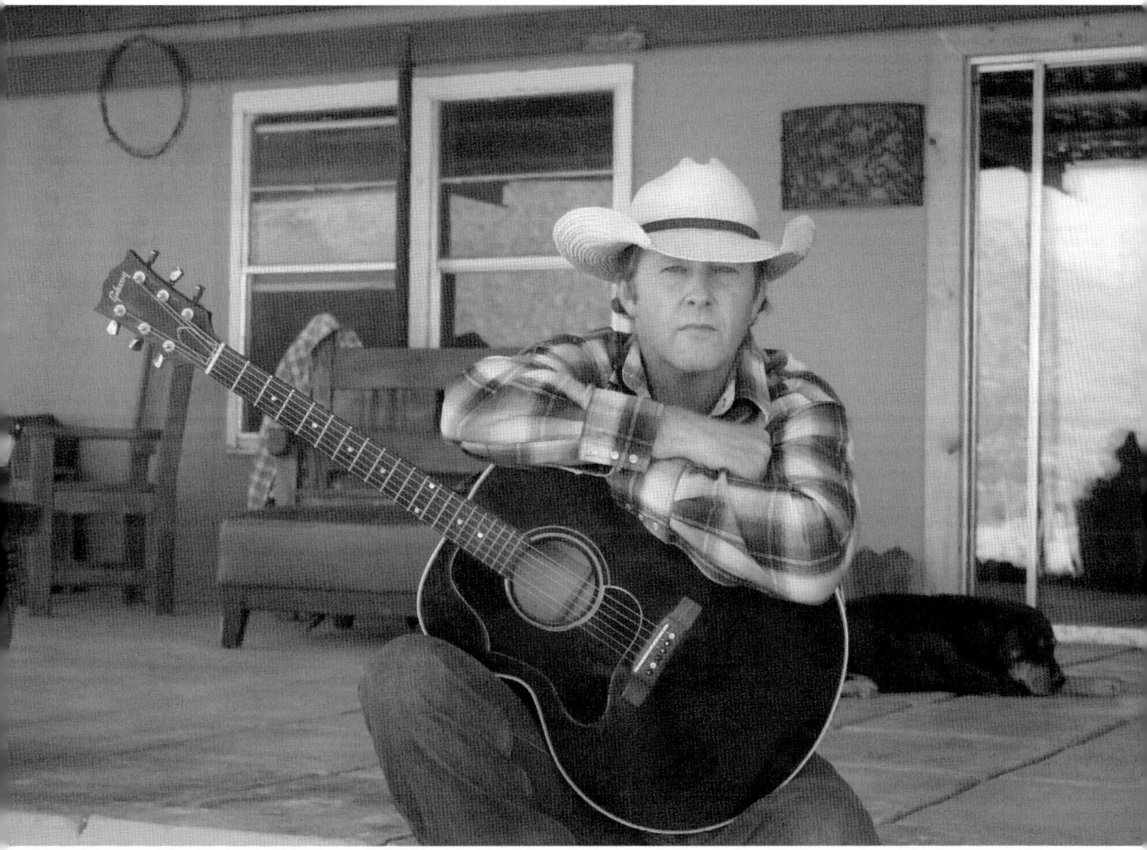

Craig Carter
"My career has been horses, music, movies," says Craig Carter. He also adds that his marriage at age 44 changed his life. Most local people know his Spur of the Moment Band because it plays each Fourth of July.

Craig (born in 1963) grew up working in the Big Bend National Park horse concession with his father, Lynn. He also played music from age 17 with his dad. Soon he formed a band and started playing the club scene in New Mexico, then nationally, and later toured Europe 65 times,

Today, Craig, still writing and playing music, also works in the movie business as an animal trainer. He met his wife, Shannon, on a television show, and they married in 2007. Baby girl Sadie Phlynn was born in 2008. They live south of Marathon on Spring Creek Ranch. (Photograph by Shannon Carter.)

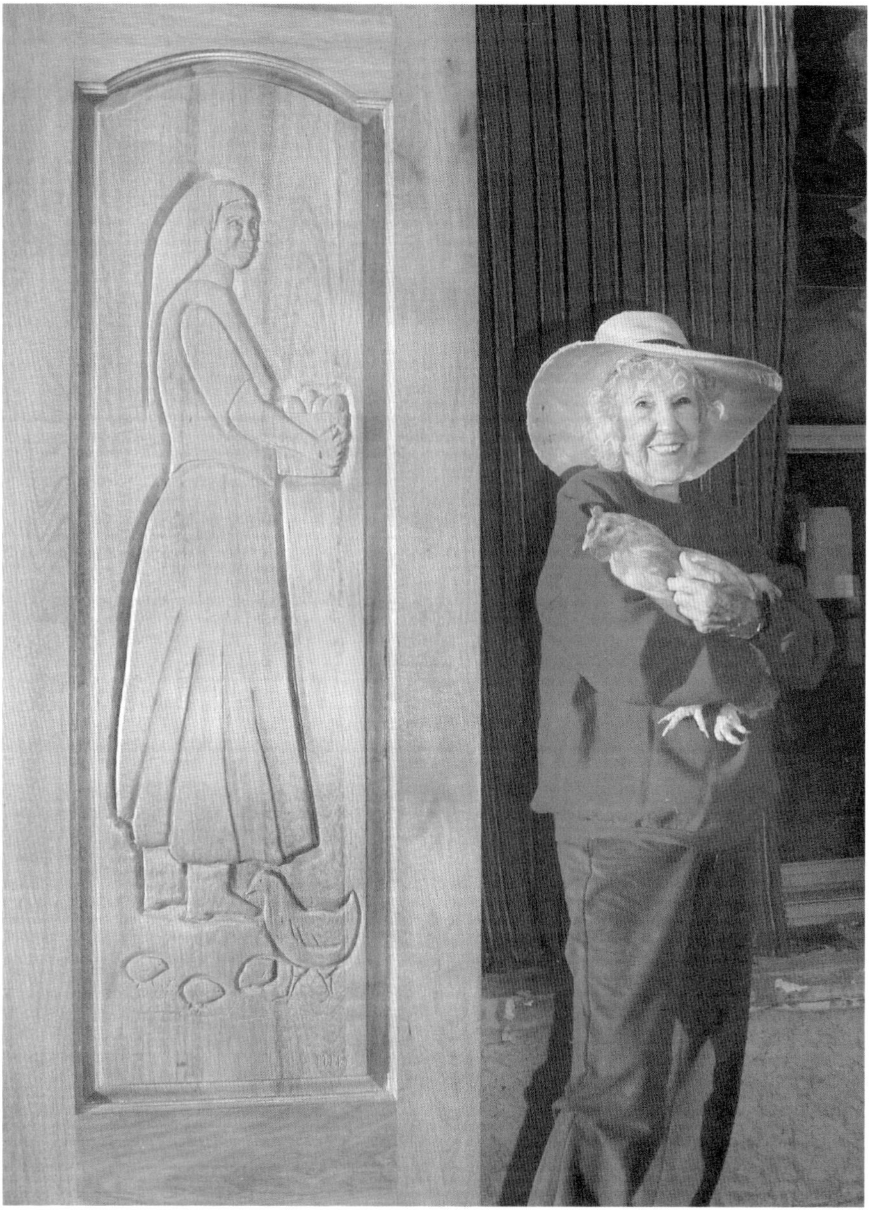

Maisie Kane Lee

From Australia, where she was born, by way of Florida, where she attended elementary school, Maisie Kane Lee and her family were in West Texas when the 1929 stock market crash occurred; her father, Frederick, was left penniless. Stranded in Marathon, she met a tall, muscular cowboy named Guy Lee, whom she married in 1939, a marriage which lasted 55 years.

Maisie's mother, Mary, had been a sculptor, and Maisie had drawn pictures from her earliest years. Her brother Victor gave her a piece of wood, and she carved a face on it using her husband's pocketknife. Over the years, she has sold and traded many, many sculptures. Some were traded for medical treatment. The San Antonio HemisFair in 1968 displayed three. A local rancher has five. She works on her art most days. She has just published a memoir called *A Stick in a Whirlwind*. (Photograph by E. Dan Klepper.)

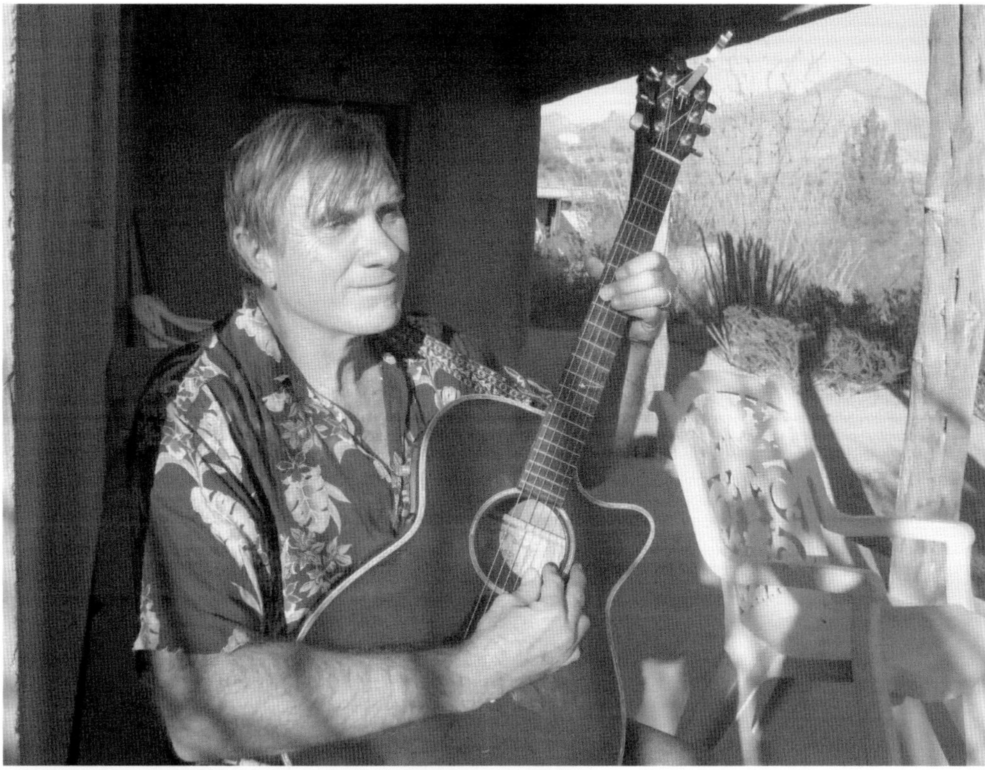

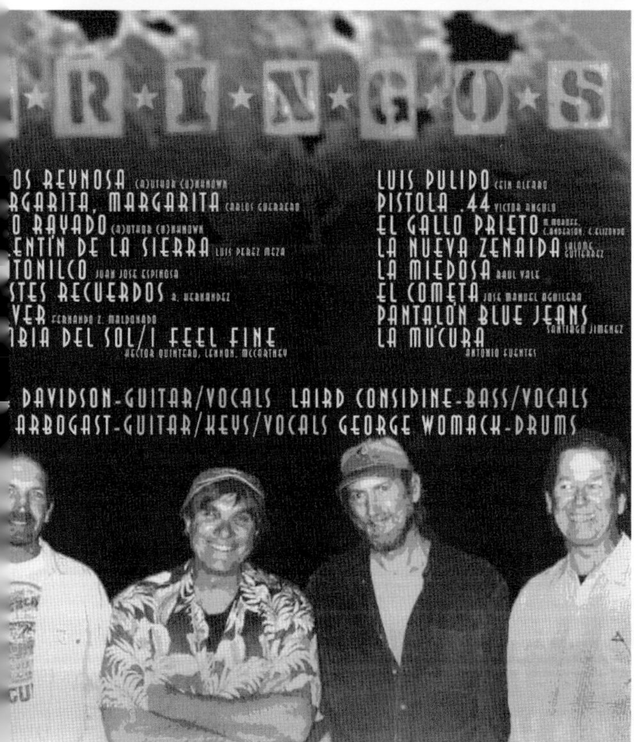

Ted Arbogast

In an area that is rich in musical talent, Ted Arbogast stands out because of the many hats he wears. He arrived in Terlingua from Arizona 20 years ago and immediately took to the freedom of the place. He played with Craig Carter's well-known band and went on to form the Pinché Gringos band with Mike Davidson. He opened a recording studio in 1995 and has produced 50 CDs. He lives with his wife, Joanne, and they share the parenting of their three boys, Gus, Gage, and Kevin. He fixes the computers at Terlingua School, where he is also band director. The opening of these young minds to music is important to him. He plays solo gigs locally and also directs the Terlingua Community Choir, combining musical creativity in this desert community with a steady job. (Above, photograph by Joanne Brooke Arbogast; left, photograph by Lauren Stedman.)

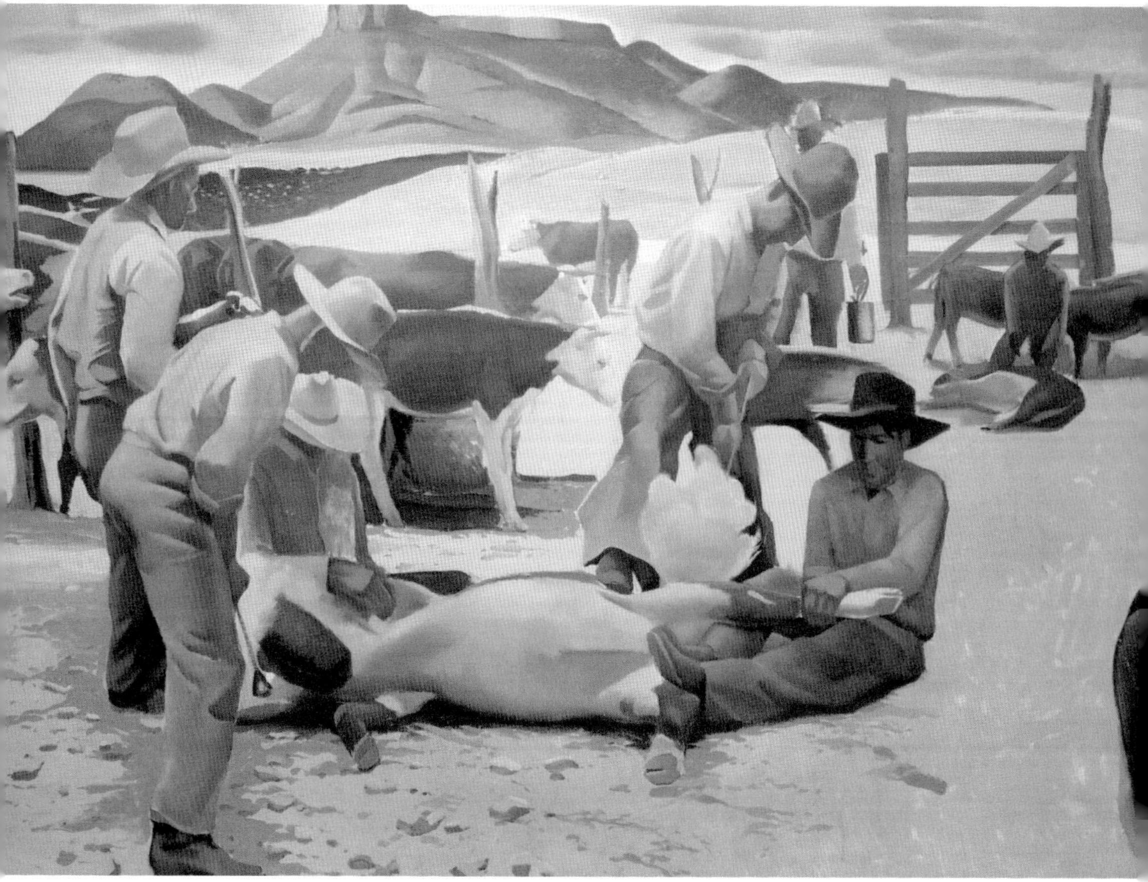

Julius Woeltz

The Department of Drawing at Sul Ross State University played a surprising but important role in the Texas Regionalists Art Movement of the 1930s—surprising because the college was new, remote, and unknown. The desert and mountain landscape played a large part, but the artists involved were the key. The result was a number of impressive paintings that have lasted well, and the Department of Drawing at Sul Ross became the Department of Art.

Julius Woeltz (1911–1956), a muralist, art teacher, and landscape painter, was born in San Antonio and studied in Chicago, Paris, and Texas. He was appointed director of the art department at Sul Ross (1932–1936). For more than 15 years, artists and students were invited to Alpine on this popular and successful summer course. Woeltz left Sul Ross in 1936 to teach in New Orleans. (Courtesy Museum of the Big Bend Collection; photograph by Jim Bones.)

CHAPTER FIVE

Groups

Polo is an exotic sport for the desert terrain, but the cavalry regiment stationed at Fort D.A. Russell in Marfa in the early 1930s had a polo team, and matches were arranged with their Mexican counterparts. More recently, Alpine had a different experience of polo when Al Micallef, a local rancher, offered residents the chance to watch polo at his ranch north of Alpine. For a $1 parking fee, visitors could watch polo and were even offered a glass of champagne if they helped replace the divots between chukkers.

A local outfitter of note is Big Bend Stables in Study Butte, the only horse stables open to the public near Big Bend National Park. In business for 27 years, this is a thoroughly professional and child-friendly operation. A different sort of outfitter is Desert Sports, located close to Terlingua ghost town. It specializes in mountain bike trips and also offers rafting and hiking options. Wonderful people work at this small outfit. The largest outfitter, Far Flung Outdoor Center, even provides casitas for clients.

Also falling under the category of groups are ranchers, railroad employees, and miners. The stories of early ranchers are legend, and their achievements today are no less impressive despite fickle weather and an interfering government, as many ranchers see it.

The railroad is 140 years old, and few know or care that the eastbound track laying was done mainly by Chinese labor. In Marfa, they left an unusual souvenir—some deodar trees, which originate in Asia. Today, 20 freight trains daily pass through the area, and Amtrak offers passenger service three times weekly.

For more than 70 years, the region has been well served by KVLF in Alpine, "The Voice of the Last Frontier." Gene Hendryx provided, and his son Ray still provides, sterling service laced with good humor, keeping residents informed about weather, football games, deaths in the community, stuff to sell, local emergencies, city council meetings, and more.

Five years ago, Marfa Public Radio sprang up to provide a new type of radio. A "Talk at Ten" daily interview show with visiting and local persons, history and science programs, many music programs hosted by residents, and National Public Radio news broadcasts provide a new listening service to the community.

On the print side of communications, the *Big Bend Sentinel* of Marfa is streets ahead of any other local paper and winning awards to prove it. Relay for Life is in its own category, a self-help volunteer group, with outstanding participations in an area where volunteerism is strong.

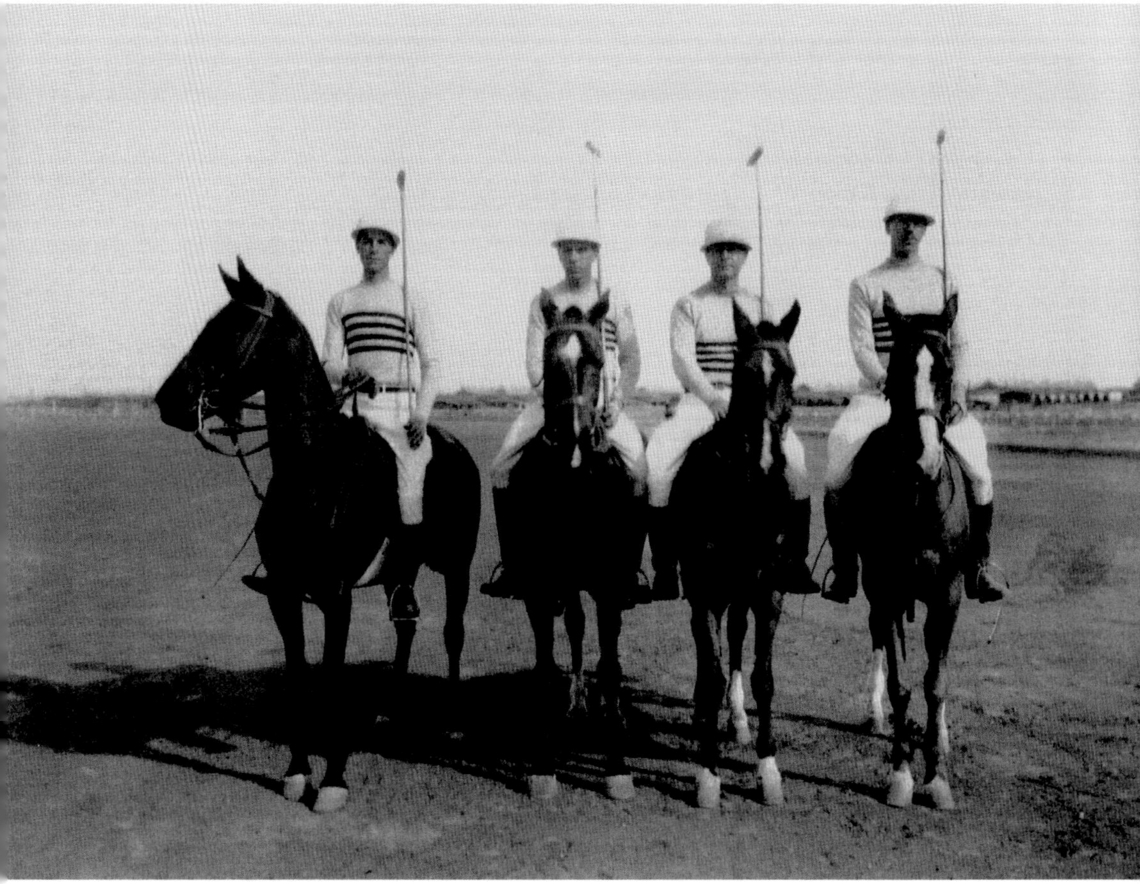

Fort D.A. Russell

Opened as Camp Marfa in 1911, during the early years of the Mexican Revolution, and renamed Fort D.A. Russell in 1929, the major military establishment in the region engaged in recreational activity as well as military maneuvers. In July 1930, a Mexican Army team visited Marfa and defeated the 1st Cavalry poloists 5-2.

Reciprocating the visit, a large contingent left Marfa in November 1930 by special charter train for Mexico City. The party included 38 officers, 33 ladies, 36 enlisted men, 18 Marfa residents, and 46 polo ponies. In Mexico City, "a royal welcome was arranged for the Americans' arrival. Lavish entertainment attended by the pomp and circumstance which wealth and position could bestow, was provided for the guests," according to *History of Presidio County*, Vol. II, by Cecilia Thompson. The score was not recorded. (Courtesy Marfa and Presidio County Museum.)

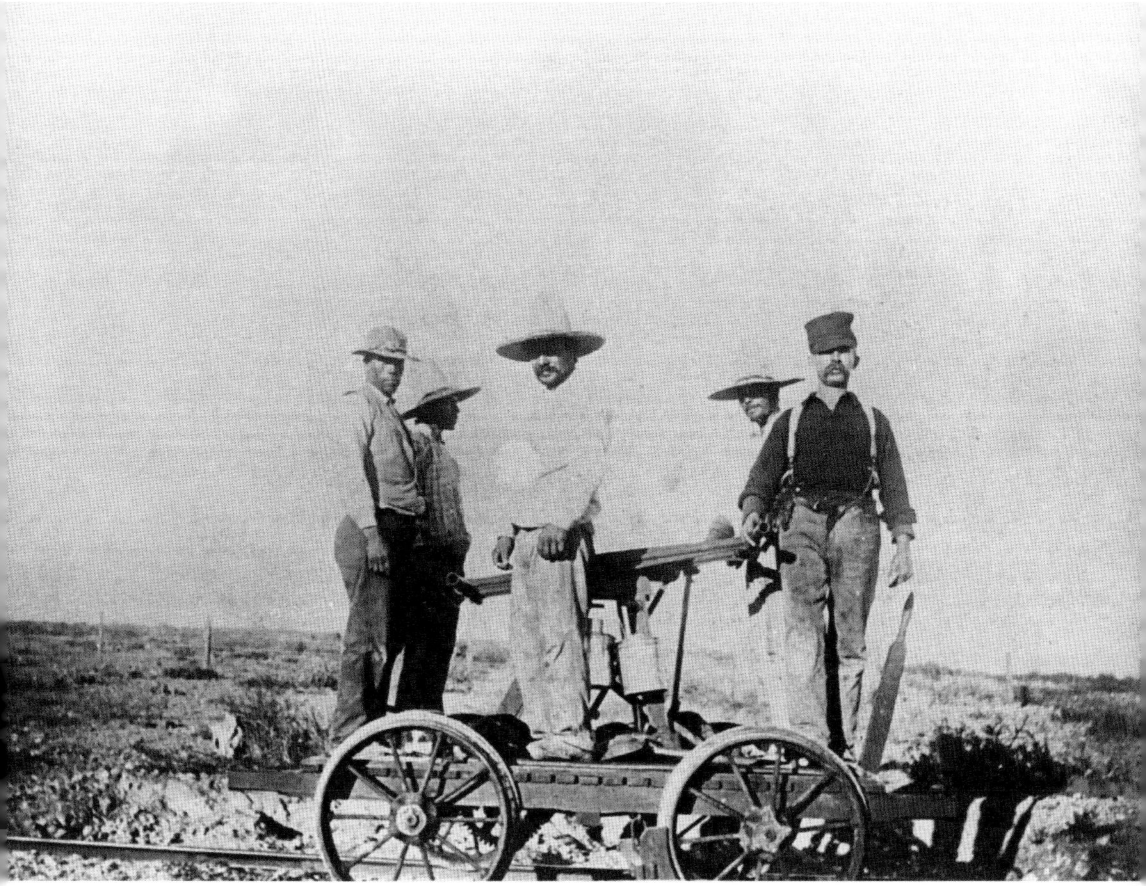

The Southern Pacific Line
Building from the West Coast, predominantly Chinese workers laid the tracks along a southern route across the United States. They met their mainly Irish counterparts, building from the East, near Pecos High Bridge, and the Southern Pacific line was complete. Few, if any, graves mark the spots where many Chinese workers died. Only the deodar tree, found in Marfa, acts as a testimonial to their labor. The Chinese workers used the seeds of the deodar as a relaxant, their marijuana. Each section of railroad measured 10 miles and included a section house and sometimes a water stop. Small crews, an Anglo foreman, and usually four Hispanic section workers were on permanent duty to maintain the line. In the early days, residents of Marathon could catch a train to Alpine, for shopping or a movie, and return home at night.

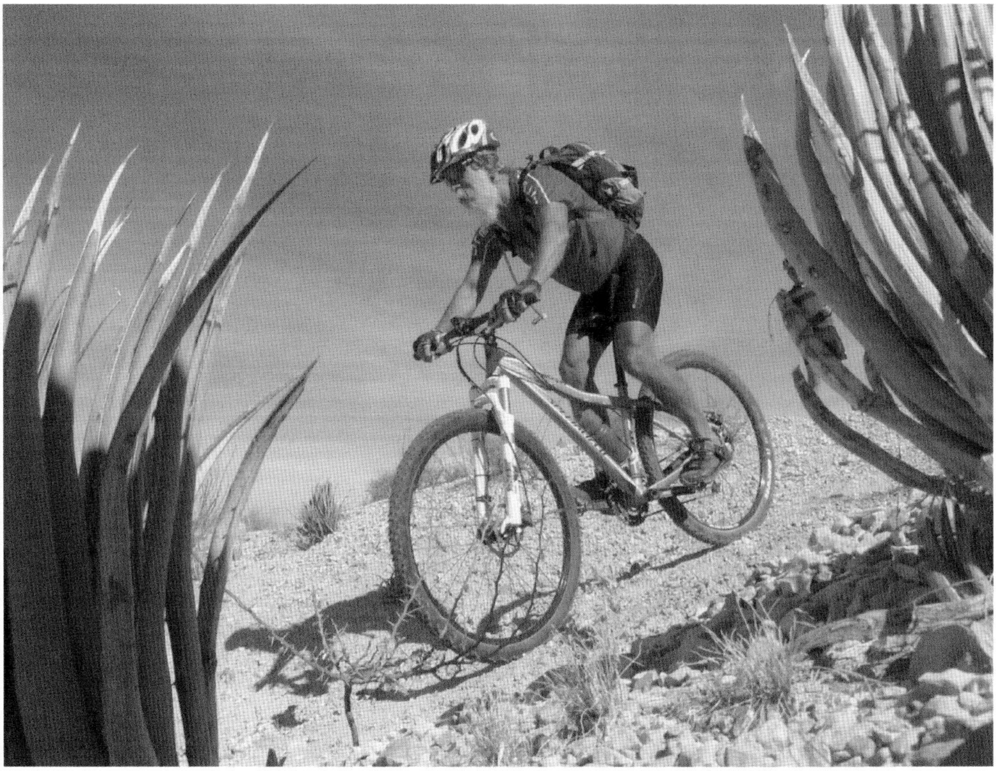

Mike Long and Crystal Allbright, Desert Sports

Located outside of Terlingua ghost town, Desert Sports offers a choice of hiking, rafting, and biking or all three. But biking is its specialty, and the business organizes the annual Chihuahuan Desert Bike Fest, which takes place during February. Mike Long (pictured above) is second-to-none in biking experience, while Crystal Allbright adds an extra touch in photography talent. They are professionals with tons of experience and they are also fun to be with. Guided, overnight trips may include steaks in the evening and pancakes the next morning. Or, if one has been on the river before, he or she may want to go on his or her own; in which case, Desert Sports can rent the equipment and arrange a shuttle. These folks are the smallest outfitters here, and they say they have worked hard to keep it that way. (Photographs by Crystal Allbright.)

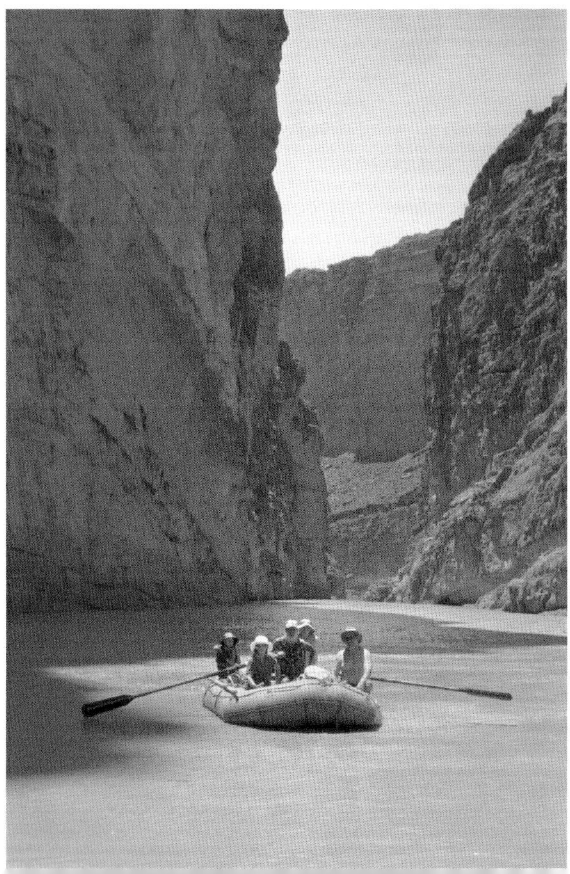

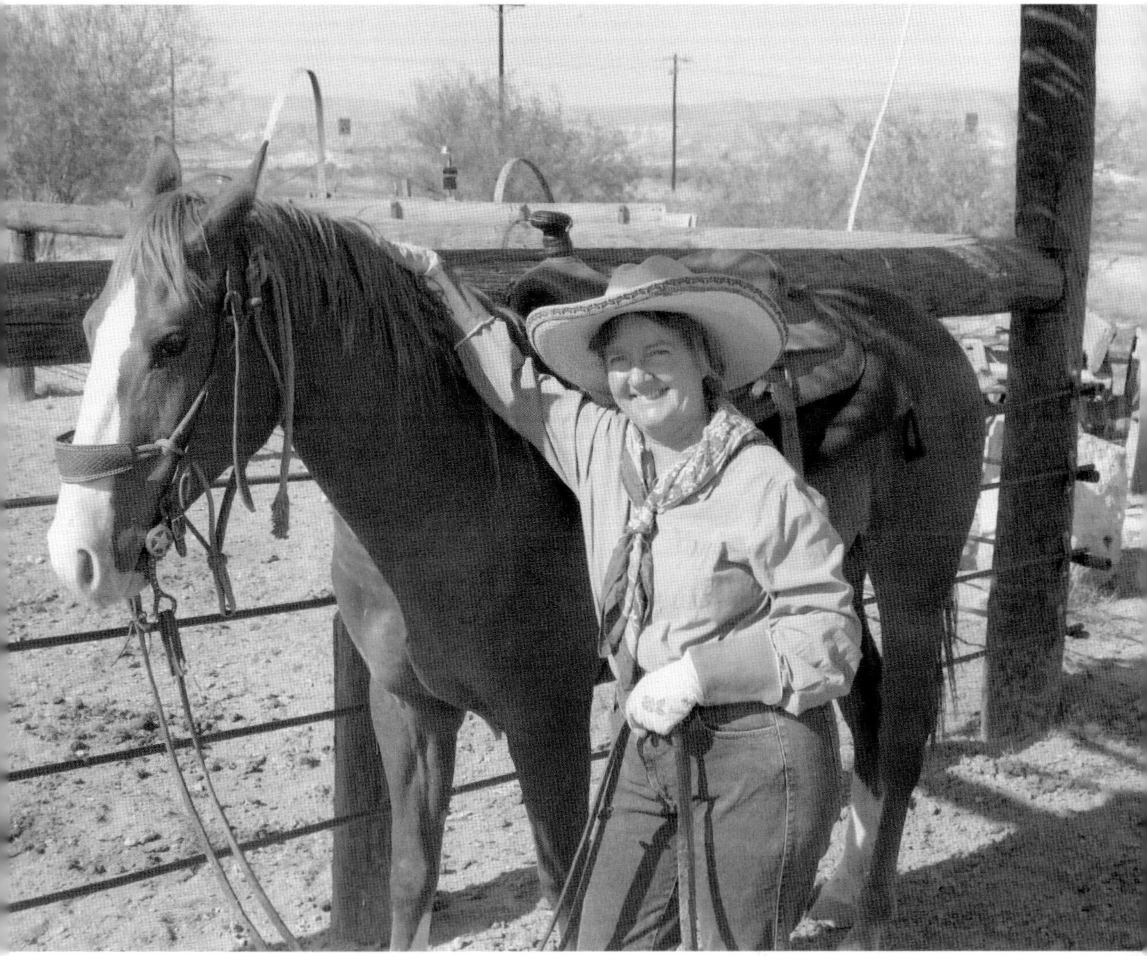

Linda Walker and Big Bend Stables
Visitors driving through Study Butte to the Big Bend National Park sometimes notice a corral filled with horses on the left side of the road. This is Big Bend Stables, the one and only horse stables open to the public near to the park, now in its 26th year of operation under the spirited ownership of Linda Walker. Originally, the stables were in Lajitas, 18 miles west, and there is still an operation there, which takes riders into the Big Bend State Park. Previously, the stables ran horseback trips into Mexico, until visits across the Rio Grande became risky. The bulk of the tourist clients want something safe that they can handle. A horseback ride on a gentle horse with an attentive wrangler is what gives visitors, adults, and children, a feel for the desert and for the history of this region. (Courtesy of Big Bend Stables.)

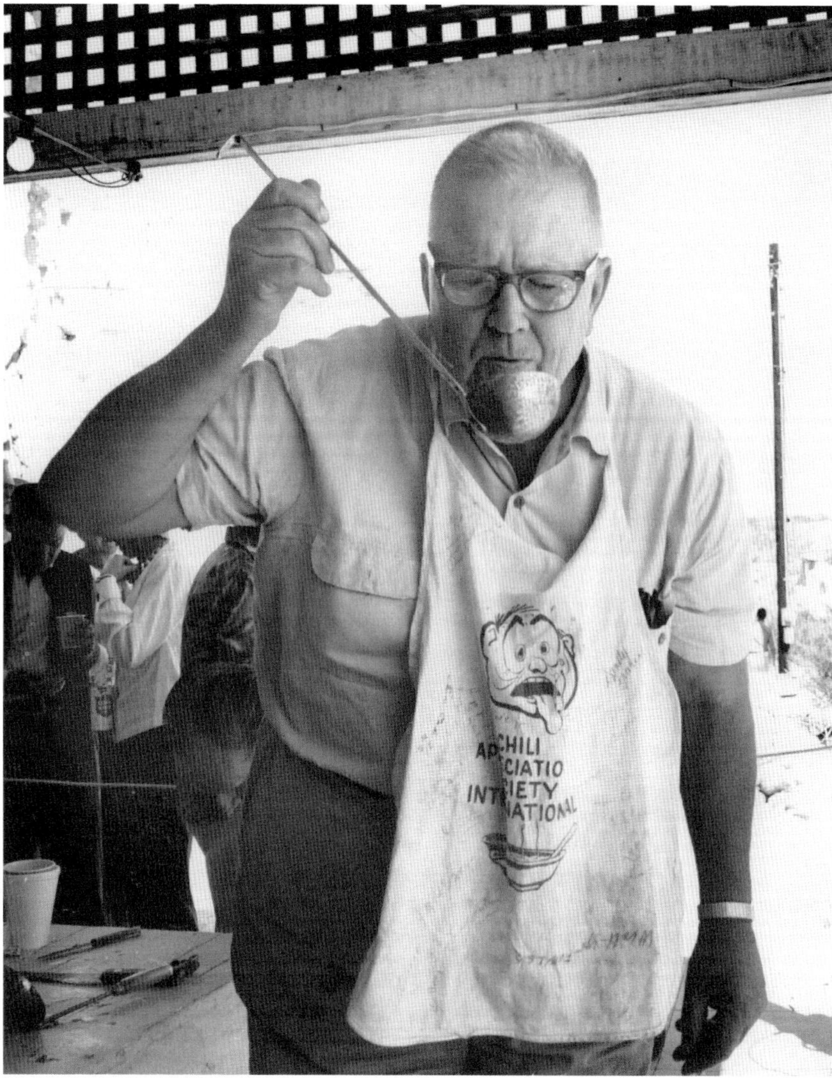

Chili Cook-Off

The coming together in 1967 of three quite different men in a remote patch of desert near the Mexican border was the start of an annual event, which today draws thousands of chili lovers and partygoers.

H. Allen Smith, a nationally known writer from the East Coast, who retired in Alpine, wrote, "No one knows more about chili than I do," in an article, which caused widespread offense in Texas among chili enthusiasts. Meanwhile, Carroll Shelby, who later would become known internationally for his racing cars, had bought with partners 300,000 acres in South Brewster County. In the hope of selling some real estate, and to make a good story, a plan was hatched for a chili-cooking competition.

The Texas competitor to face off against H. Allen Smith was Wick Fowler. After a long and varied career as a reporter, starting in Europe in World War II, and a political activist, in 1964, he started a chili company called Wick Fowler's Two-Alarm Chili.

The competition was set for October 21, 1967, in Terlingua, Texas. The three judges included Hallie Stillwell, the locally known writer, ranch woman, and justice of the peace. The vote was inconclusive, and the referee, Frank X. Tolbert, the recognized Texas chili expert, declared the contest a draw. There was no winner, but the chili cook-off idea had arrived, and it continues to this day.

70

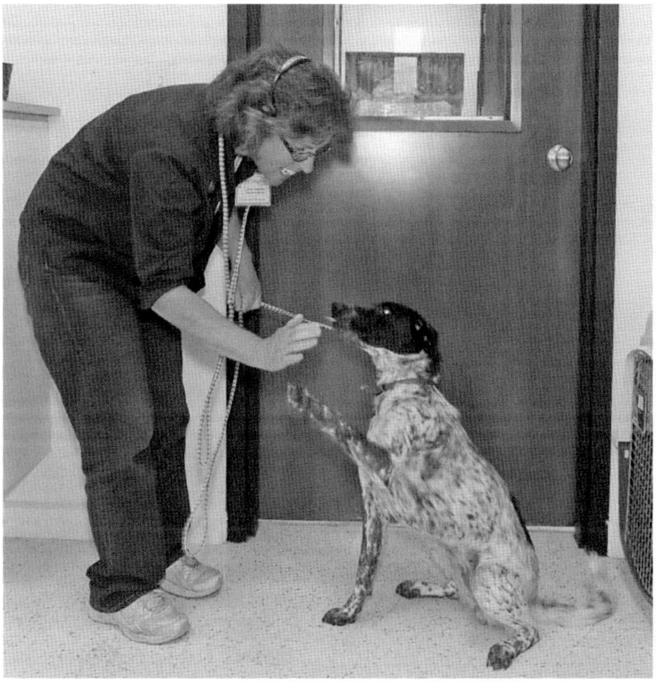

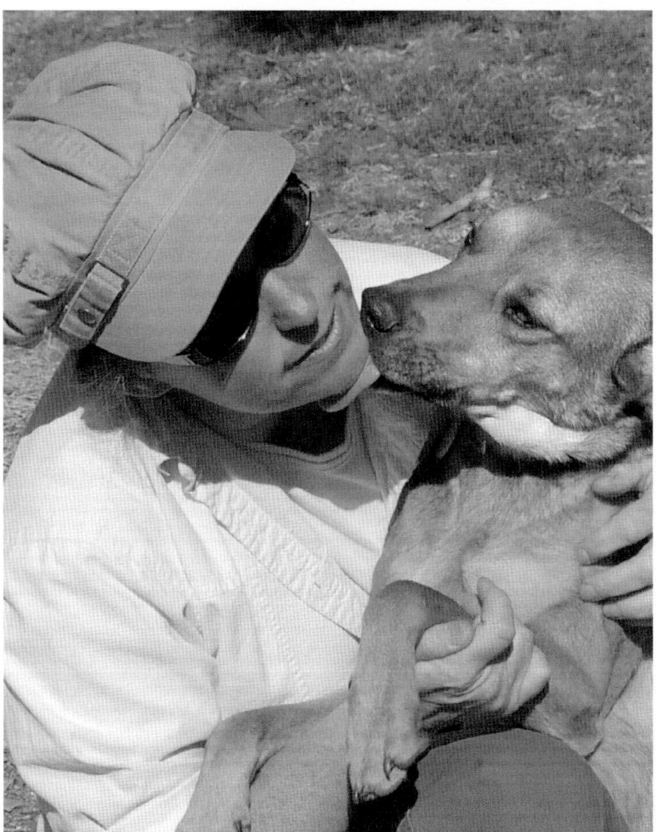

Grand Companions Humane Society
Established in Fort Davis in 1989, Grand Companions Humane Society has grown by leaps and bounds, in size and in quality, and has just put into operation a radical new concept. The new Miriam McCoy Pet Adoption Center takes pet adoption to a new level, offering a home environment rather than a warehouse and facilitating more easily the later move to the pet's new home. This change from the traditional shelter image of pet caring is the brainchild of Laura Langham, the longtime director. "A socialized, well-adjusted animal is an adoptable animal," she says. Thus, the animals and staff intermingle, each staff member being responsible for 9–12 dogs in his or her work area. This is the Sweet Suites concept. No cages, kennels, or dog runs. The pets are being socialized. The system is working, and there are plans to expand. (Both, courtesy of Grand Companions.)

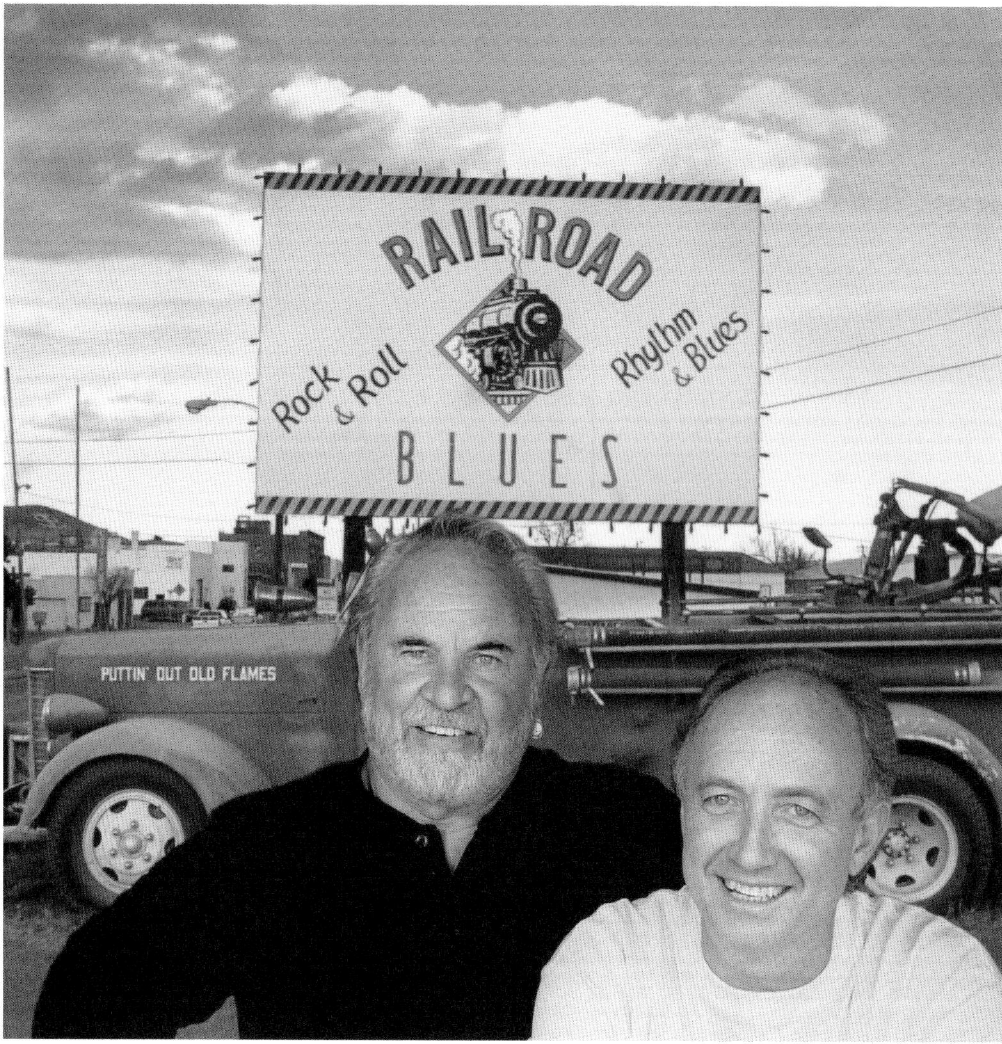

Richard Fallon and R.J. Toler, The Railroad Blues

Richard Fallon (right) and his business partner took over the Railroad Blues in 1993. Over the years, the Railroad Blues became the first choice of contemporary and country music lovers in Alpine. It is a well-run bar with a selection of 133 beers and an old-world dance floor in front of the stage. Outside during the winter months, a wood fire is often burning to warm the patrons seeking escape from the crowded interior. Located halfway between Austin and Los Angeles, the Railroad Blues is well-placed to attract bands traveling between those two centers of music. Over the years, musicians of note, such as Arlo Guthrie, have played at the Blues, as well as a rich variety of local bands, like the Doodlin' Hogwallops. This place is serious regarding its music and is fun to visit. Fallon's background experience of bar management, previously in Austin, and his talent for treating visiting bands just right bring those bands back to Alpine. (Photograph by Mike Howard.)

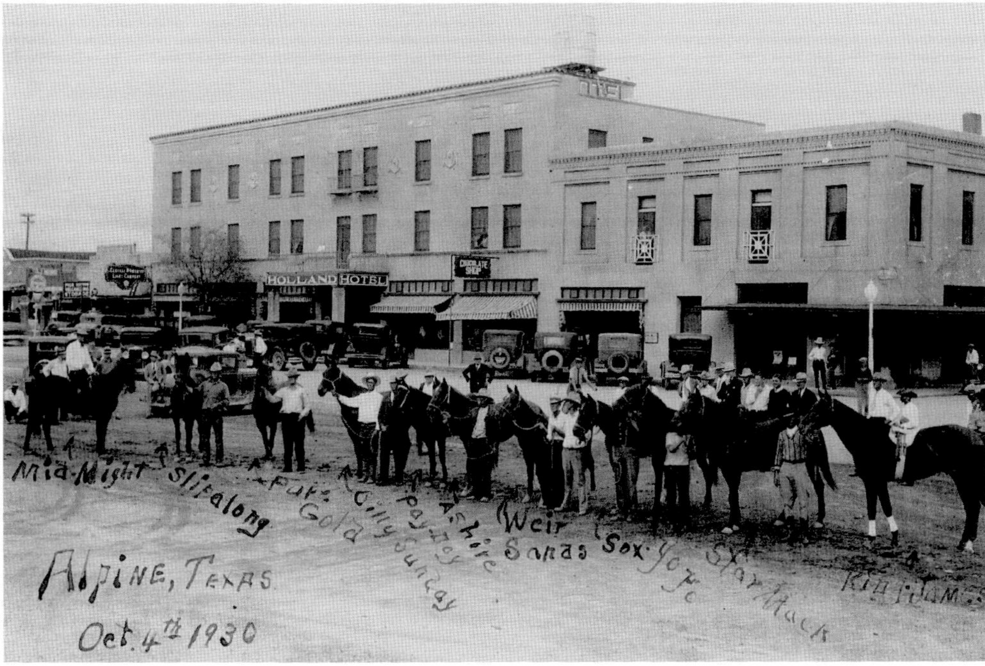

The Holland Hotel

Built in 1912 by wealthy rancher John Holland, the Holland Hotel was expanded in 1928 by his son Clay Holland. The 40-room annex, designed by architects Trost & Trost, brought the room total to 70. The hotel soon became the meeting point for civic, social, and business groups. More telling is the reputation the hotel gained as having the longest-running poker game in Texas, also a murder or two and some hauntings. Horses, shown here in 1930, were still hitched outside until the early 1990s.

Myra Jo McFarland and her daughter Carla, pictured here outside the hotel, bought it in the mid-1980s. Carla put in a new restaurant and ran the hotel for 21 years, restoring its old reputation. From 2011, the Holland Hotel underwent a major upgrade under new owners Charles Mallory and Konrad Wos. (Below, photograph by Griff Smith, Texas Department of Transportation.)

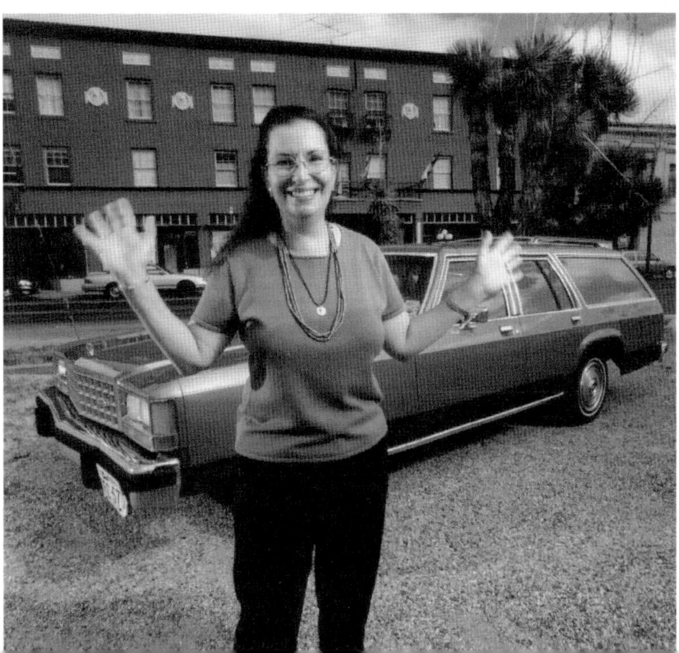

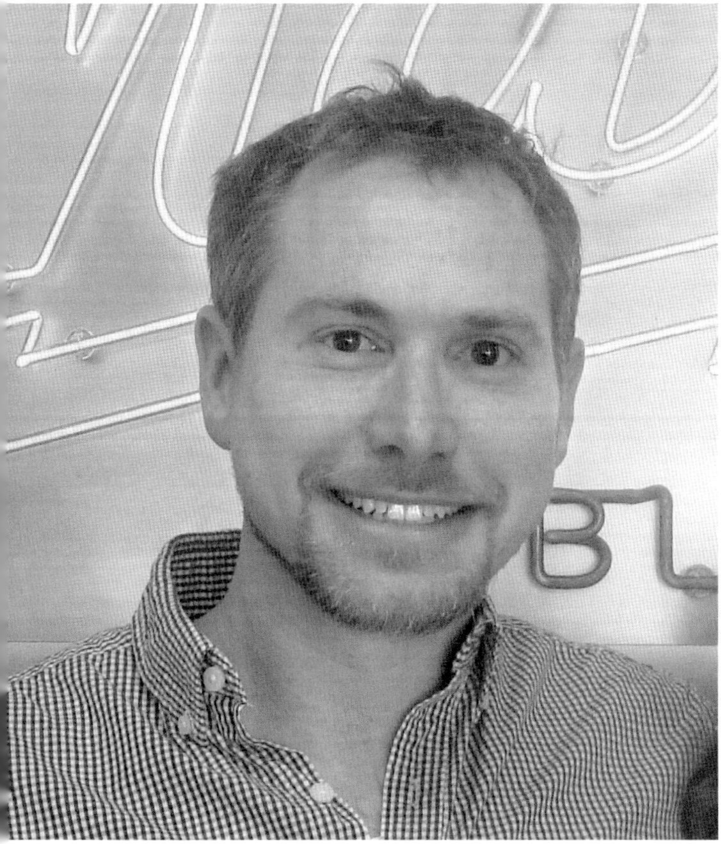

Tom Michael and KRTS

In March 2007, following a concert by Willie Nelson the year before and with newsman Dan Rather as guest, West Texas gained its first public radio service, thanks to the generosity of sponsors, principally Kay Burnett of Alpine. Since then, under the energetic guidance of Tom Michael, KRTS Marfa has gone from strength to strength. Tom and his two paid staff, Anne Adkins (left) and Rachel Osier Lindley (center), host "Talk at Ten" each morning, offering lively interviews with residents and visitors. Weekly science and history shows complement a wide variety of volunteer-hosted music programs. Most listened to is the NPR *News Program*. A turning point came in April 2001, when the station moved swiftly to cover the disastrous local wildfires. The community found that its station was of vital use in a time of crisis. (Photographs by Marfa Public Radio.)

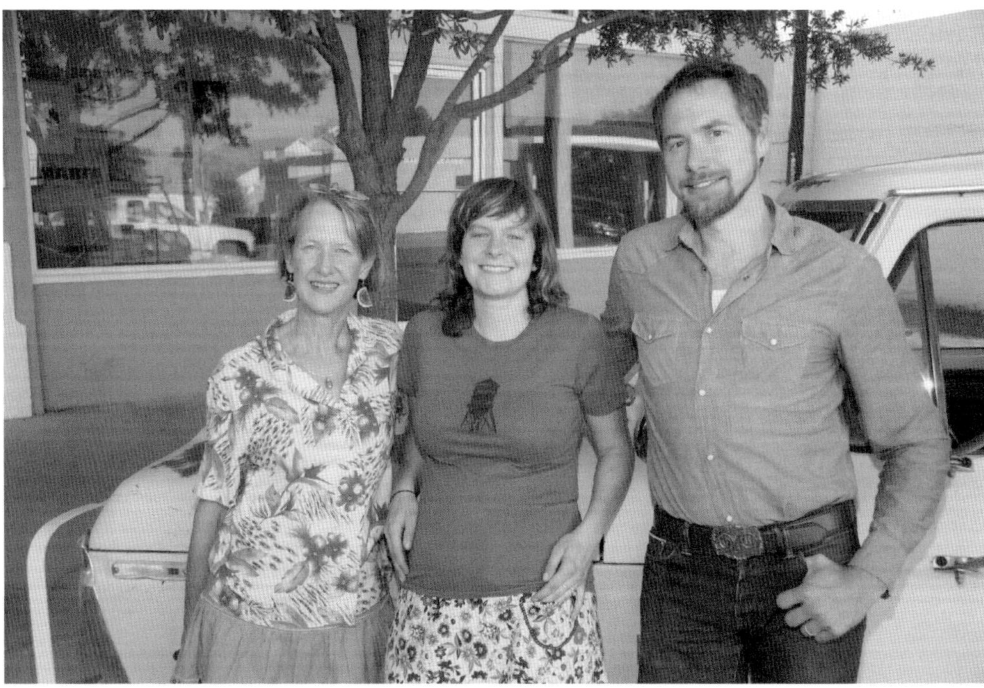

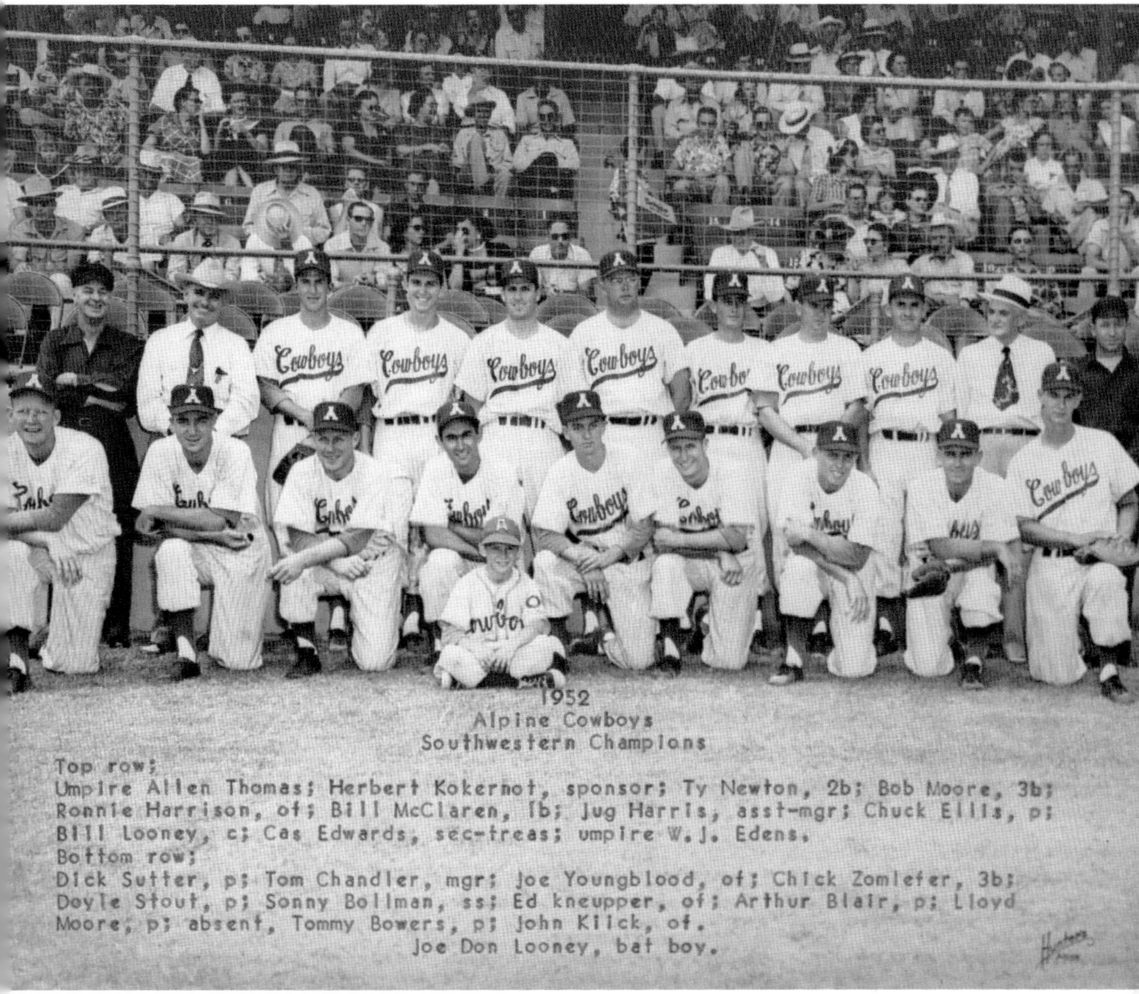

Alpine Cowboys

In 1947, H.L. Kokernot Jr., a local rancher and philanthropist, bought a local semiprofessional baseball team and renamed it the Alpine Cowboys. He also built on the edge of town, at a cost of $1.5 million, a handsome baseball field with red stone and wrought iron, modeled after Chicago's Wrigley Field. *Sports Illustrated* magazine called it "A gem of a place . . . the best little ballpark in Texas (or anywhere else)." In addition, Mr. Herbert, as he was known, employed as team manager Tom Chandler, a natural and popular leader who was also a savvy recruiter.

The first Alpine Cowboys got off to a good start, winning a dozen regional semiprofessional championships and, on one occasion, they were national runners-up. In 1959, the Boston Red Sox moved their minor league affiliate to Alpine, took the name "Cowboys" for the team, and were immediately successful. But in 1962, the Sophomore League, in which they competed, folded, and the team moved to Idaho under a new name in a different league. The early days of baseball in Alpine were over.

Professional baseball returned to Alpine in 2009 with the Big Bend Cowboys of the Continental Baseball League (CBL). Successful on the field, becoming CBL champions the following year, their success was interrupted when the CBL folded after the second season. The team was reorganized in 2011 as the Alpine Cowboys in a new league (Pecos League), which they won in 2012. Encouraged by new sponsorship, they now look forward to the 2013 season. Alpine residents and visitors will again have the chance of watching baseball in the "loveliest ballpark in America," (*Sports Illustrated*, July 31, 1989).

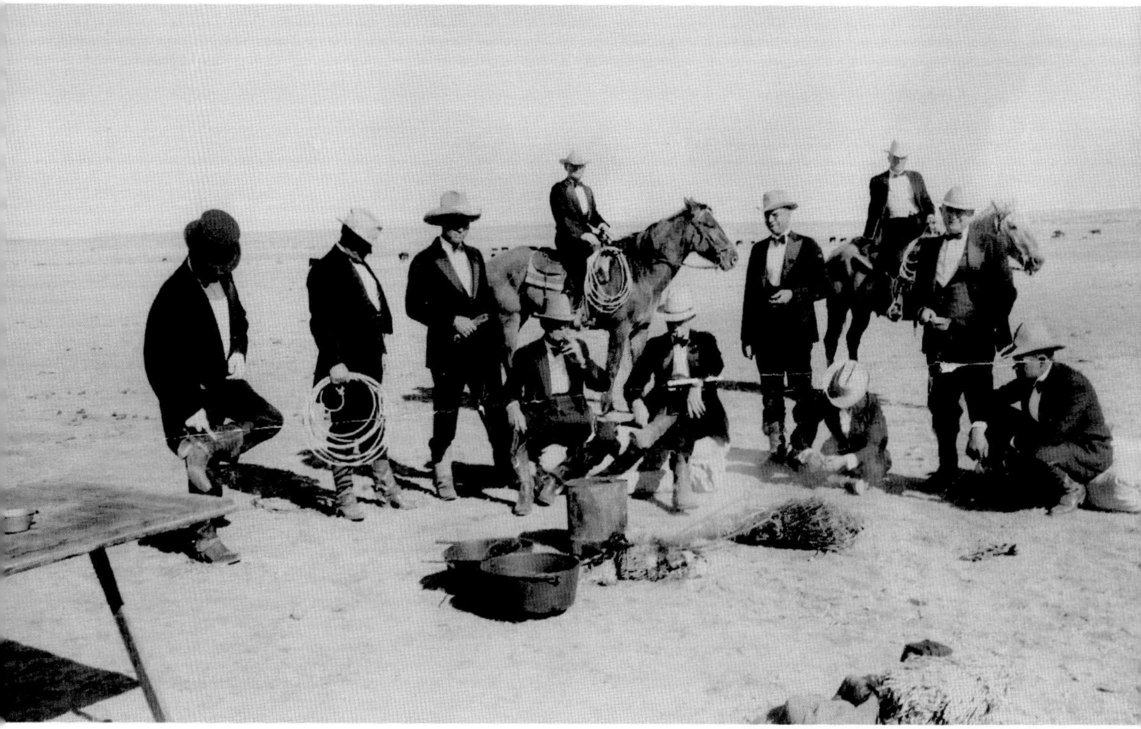

West Texas Ranchers

West Texas ranchers are a hardy breed, as they need to be to survive the fickle weather, which too often brings drought (pronounced here as "drouth"). Even 60 years on, old-timers remember the 1950s drought, aptly described in Elmer Kelton's book *The Time it Never Rained.*

They have a sense of their historical role and their own standing. In 1929, the *Big Bend Sentinel* wrote the following: "The Cowman today is a businessman. His wife is a prominent club woman. His daughter has been to Europe. His office is in the most convenient building in town. His son is at the 'U.'" That year, 7,000 persons attended the Fair of the Highland Hereford Breeders Association in Marfa.

They also have a sense of humor. As the Depression got worse, one rancher was heard saying he could not afford to buy any new work clothes and would have to wear his tuxedo when his present clothes wore out. This remark prompted a Depression roundup in tuxedos. The ranching families in this picture include names like Mitchell, Rawls, Jones, and Highsmith. Shortly after the Depression roundup, the rains came. And things improved until the next drought came around. (Courtesy Marfa and Presidio County Museum.)

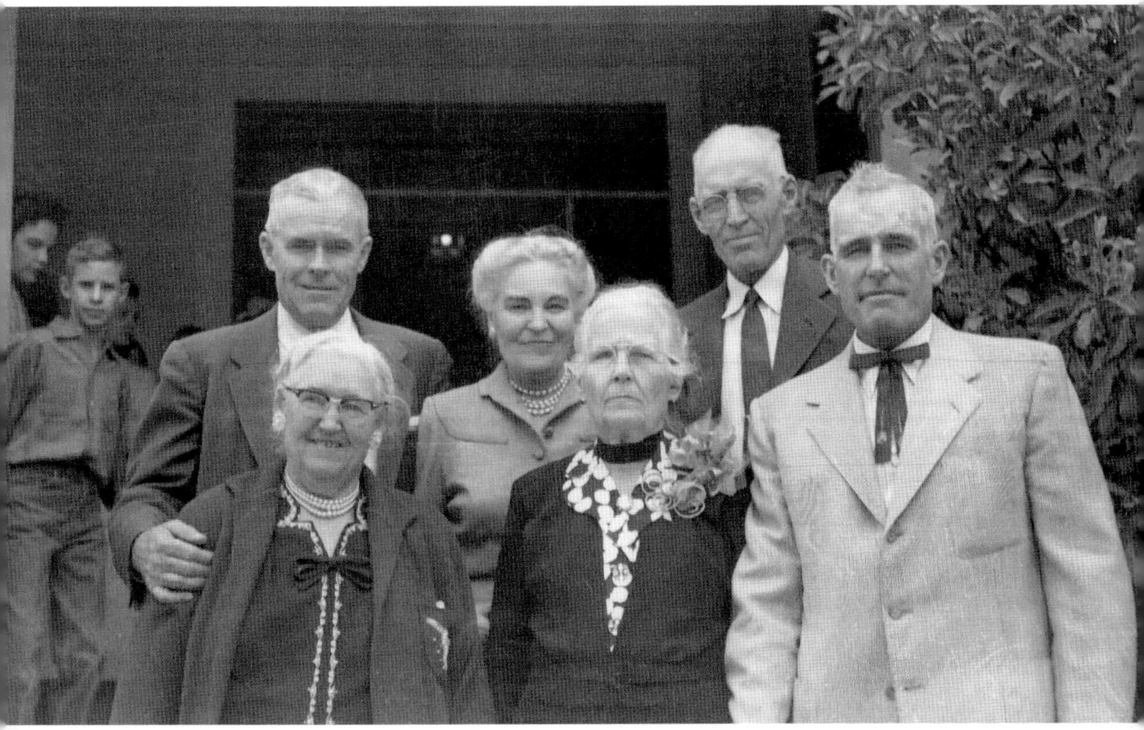

The Prude Family

The Prude family is one of many in notable ranching families in Jeff Davis County, some of whom (like the Espy, Means, and Pruett families) warrant a book just on themselves. The Prudes, however, stand out because of how they transitioned from ranching into other activities.

Andrew Prude arrived in Fort Davis in 1900 and acquired land six miles north of town. In the 1920s, much of the land was sold, due to the drought. The Prudes then announced that they were going into the "people business" and taking in visitors for a ranch experience. The timing was good, and the idea took off.

In 1951, the family introduced the first summer camp for kids, a long-lasting and successful operation. In 1985, following a drastic drop in oil prices affecting visitation from Midland/Odessa, the Prudes moved forcefully into general tourism promotion. They produced videos, even in Japanese, and won awards from the State of Texas. To hear family patriarch John Robert (at age 75) singing "Old Strawberry Roan" in front of a group of visitors eating hamburgers was to watch a piece of history. In more recent years, Prude Ranch has developed star-watching programs and gone after groups such as cyclists, churches, and tour operators.

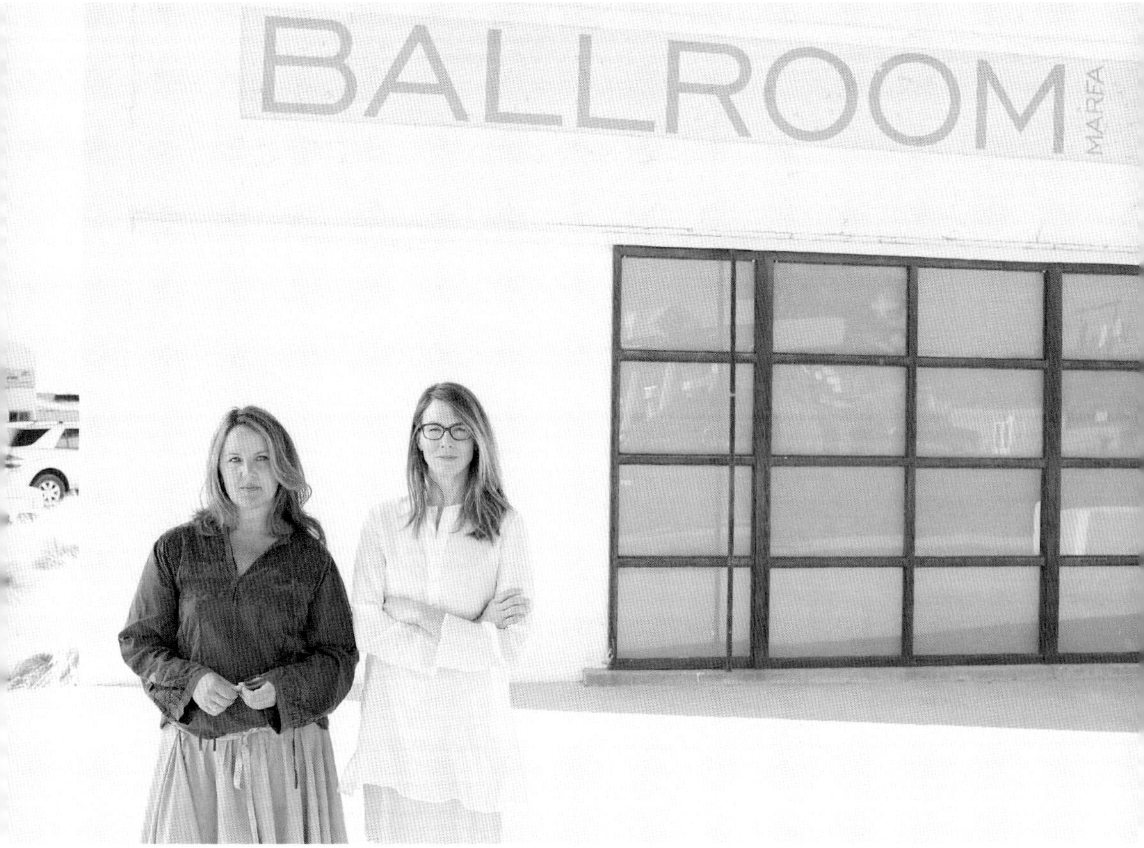

Ballroom Marfa

Ballroom Marfa was founded in 2003 by Virginia Lebermann and Fairfax Dorn. Native Texans, they had moved from New York City to Terlingua, where they recognized the contrast that locale brought to visual and performing arts. They chose Marfa as their site and bought a former ballroom property.

Ballroom Marfa has already proved itself a creative force on the edge of the extraordinary. Over 10 years, they have exhibited significant works and hosted memorable performances impossible to realize elsewhere. To date, they have presented more than 60 visual arts and film programs, including group shows, solo exhibitions, and site installations, as well as 90 musical performances from Tinariwen to Lyle Lovett. Next, they plan to open Ballroom Marfa Drive-in, an outdoor amphitheater and screen under the big West Texas skies. There is no stopping their inventive drive. (Photograph by John Hubba.)

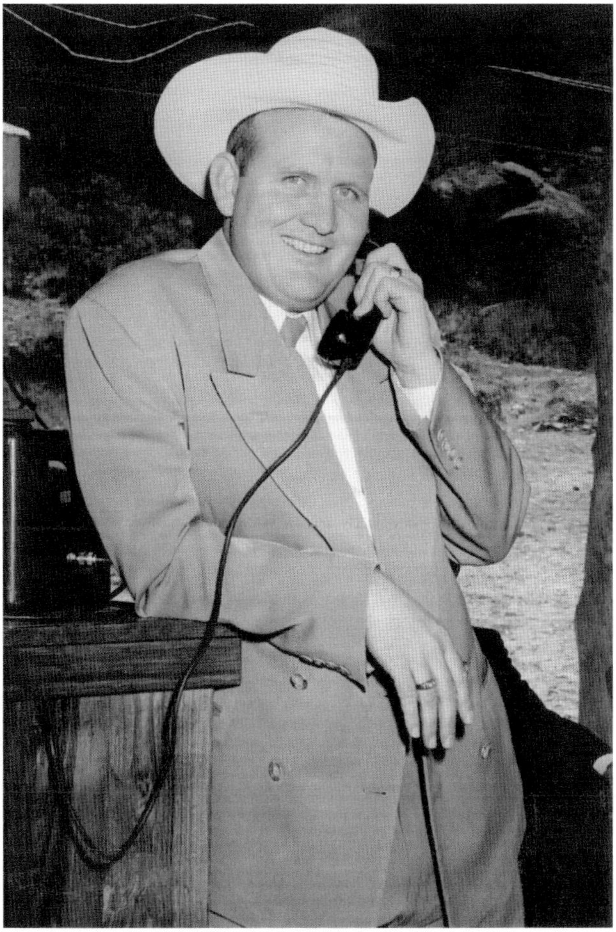

Gene Hendryx and KVLF

Born in 1927 in Ochiltree County, Texas, Gene Hendryx enlisted in the US Marine Corps at age 15, serving in the Pacific, including the Iwo Jima campaign. Moving to Alpine after the war, he obtained a bachelor's and master's degrees at Sul Ross and worked part-time as an announcer at the fledgling radio station KVLF.

In the mid-1950s, he acquired a controlling interest in the radio station and, in 25 years, turned it into a piece of radio history. Many varied and often-hilarious accounts of those early radio programs are in his book *Voices of the Last Frontier*, published in 1996. Typical is the piece titled "Elvis:" "Each year, on the anniversary of Elvis's death . . . newspapers write stories about Elvis being in their town on his first West Texas trip. That's a lot of bull. Elvis's first West Texas trip was to Alpine in 1953 when he was seventeen years old. I paid him $250 to come out here and put on a show, and I lost $30 on the deal."

Later in life, Gene Hendryx was elected as representative to the 58th, 59th, and 60th Texas Legislatures. He served two terms as a county commissioner and was appointed to the Texas Historical Commission. He also wrote *Semper Fi: The Story of the Ninth Marines* about his career in the Marines.

After the passing of his first wife, Lucille, he established at Sul Ross the largest privately endowed scholarship at the university. He had three sons by Lucille, Ray, Forrest, and Houston. He later married Nancy Roberts. By the mid-1970s, his health was beginning to fail, and his eldest son, Ray, stepped in to run the "Morning Show" by 1978. He died on September 21, 1998, at the age of 71. The Texas Department of Public Safety Building north of Alpine on Highway 118 is named for him. KVLF continued, under the expert guidance of Ray Hendryx, to broadcast for 24 years, justifying its accolade "Voice of the Last Frontier."

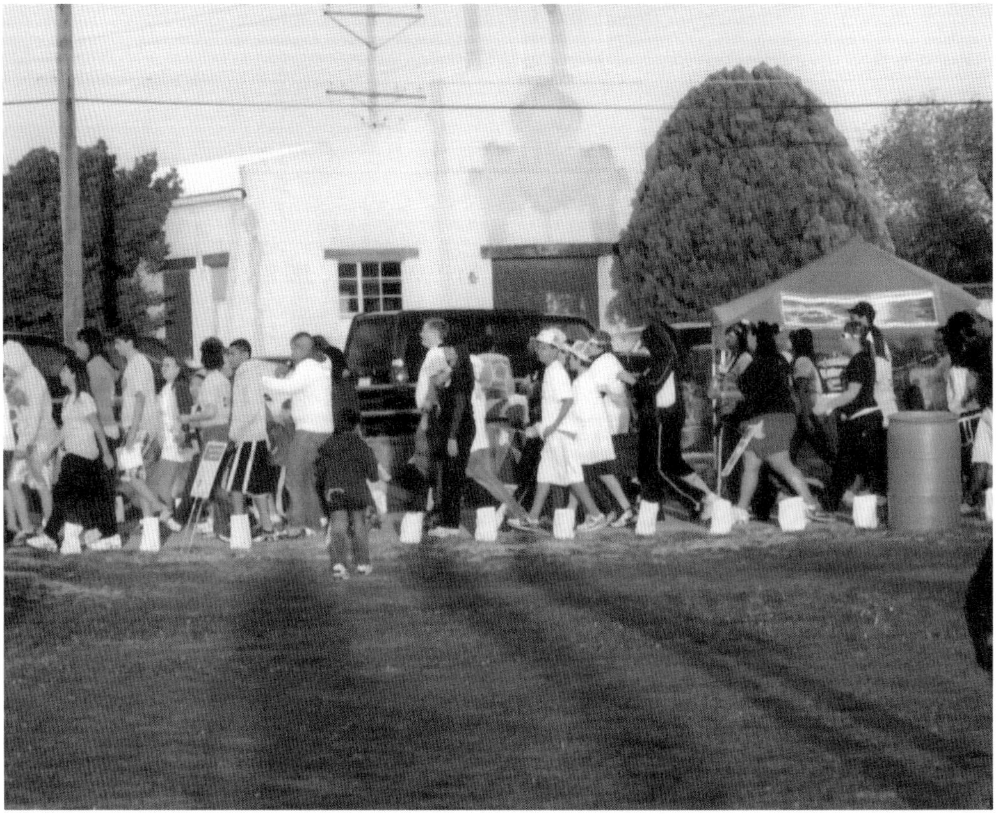

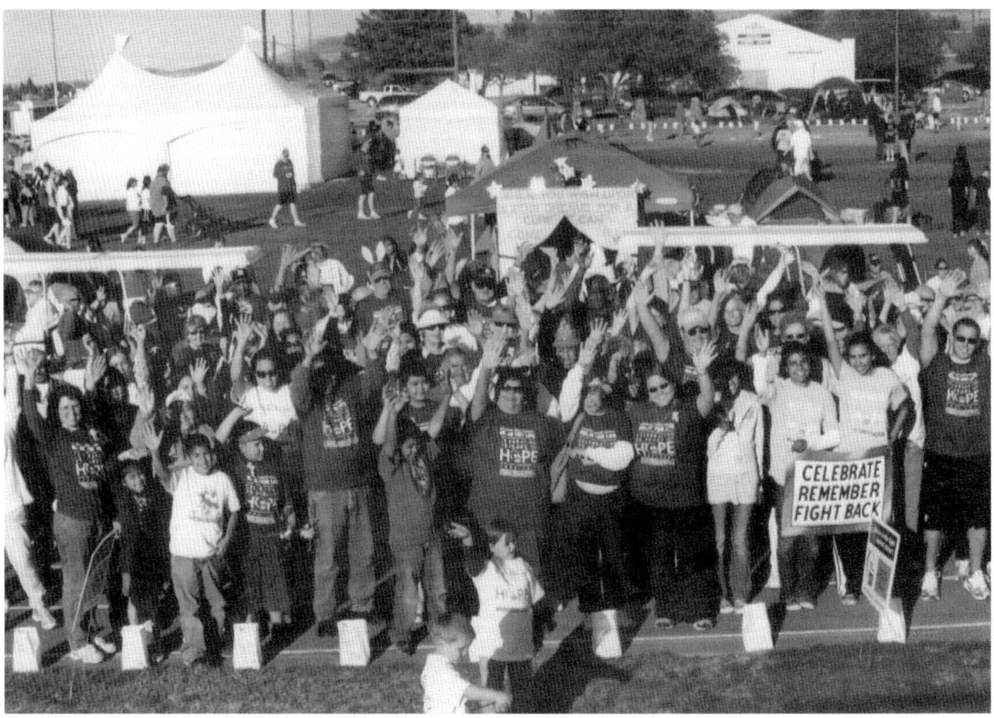
CELEBRATE
REMEMBER
FIGHT BACK

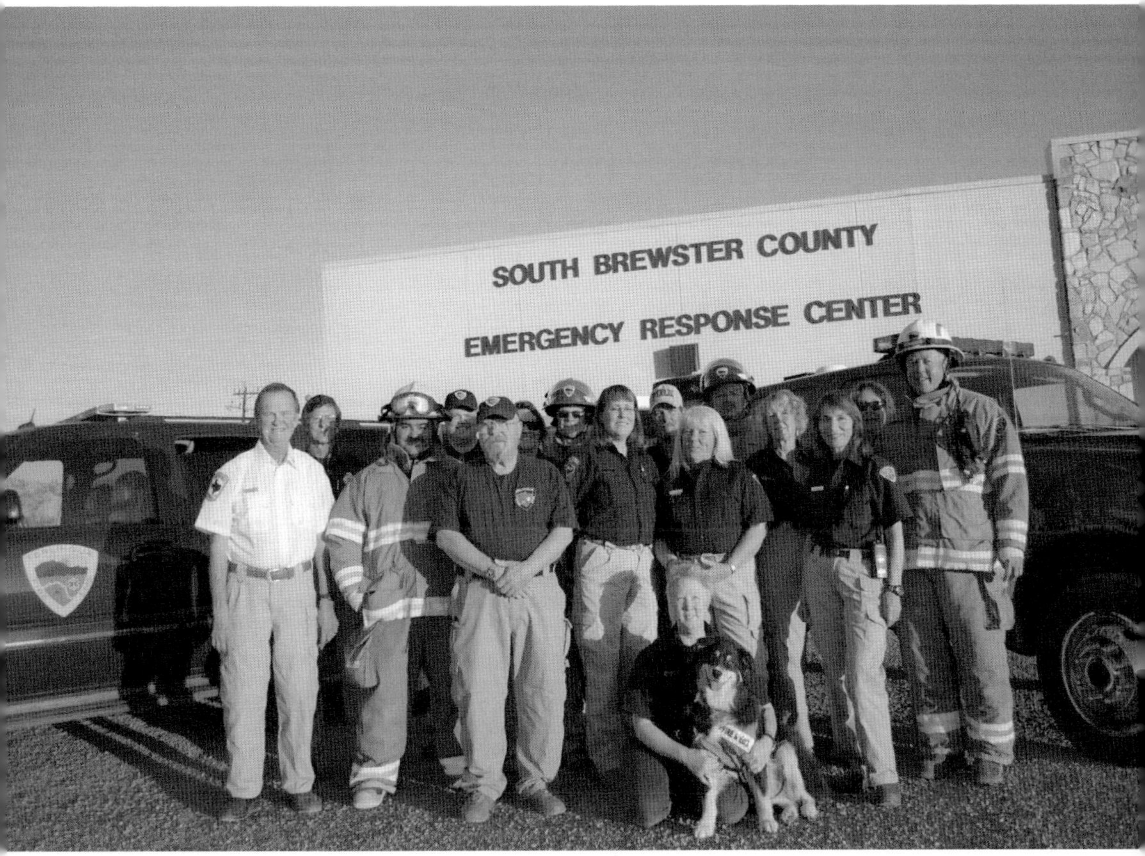

Greg Henington and the South Brewster County Medical Services
Founded nearly 25 years ago as a medical services provider in South Brewster County, today's department now provides both fire and medical services. It covers an area of 3,000 square miles and deals with approximately 200 medical emergencies and 25 fire calls a year, with a crew of 16 volunteers. They may travel five hours round-trip to the nearest hospital or drive an hour just to get to a house fire.

Wilderness medicine is their forte, under Chief Greg Henington, who is in demand around the nation teaching the subject. This is in addition to his regular job, running the outfitter Far Flung Outdoor Center. One day, the team had a call for a boy with a broken arm. They arrived on the scene to find a 54-year-old man with a fractured pelvis. He had to be carried out by team members for over a mile. (Photograph by Greg Henington.)

Relay for Life (OPPOSITE PAGE)
In 1985, Dr. Gordon Klatt walked 24 hours on a Seattle track as a cancer fundraiser. The American Cancer Society embraced the idea and made it their signature event, naming it Relay for Life. In 1996, the Big Bend area brought together 22 teams on the Sul Ross track in Alpine and raised about $26,000. Since then, a group of 20 volunteers, spearheaded in the past by local residents Shirley Eoff, Carole Causey, and Marvie Burton, have each year repeated the event. In April, the weather can be cold or wet, but nothing stops the participating teams and general members of the public from circling the track for many hours. A total of close to three-quarters of a million dollars has been raised over 17 years from a tricounty area with a population of 18,000. (Photographs by Relay for Life.)

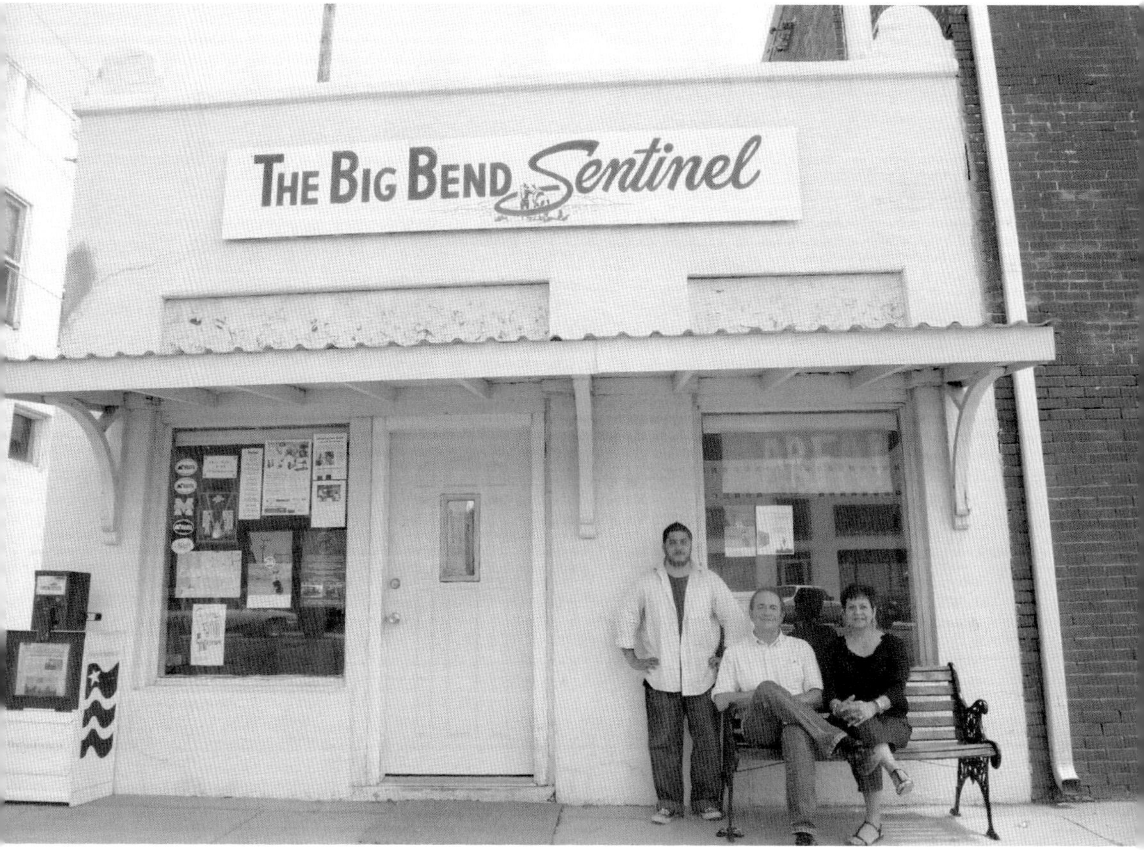

Big Bend Sentinel

Founded in 1926 and acquired in 1993 by the present owners, the *Big Bend Sentinel* is the newspaper of choice for tricounty residents. It covers local events and people and also offers articles in more depth and breadth than otherwise available. Editor-publisher Robert Halpern gained a journalism degree and worked at two larger papers as well as the *Big Bend Sentinel* before purchasing it with his accountant-qualified wife, Rosario. All three Halpern children have worked in the newsroom, and the youngest, Tomas, is presently the main reporter-photographer.

The *Big Bend Sentinel* routinely wins Texas Press Association awards for the subject matter and quality of its reportage. Being in Presidio County, with a large Hispanic population, the *Sentinel* covers border issues and events in nearby Mexico like no other local newspaper. It also has a sister newspaper, the *International*, which appears weekly, partly in Spanish, and covers more extensively the news in Presidio on the border.

The paper has had its fair share of scoops and some able reporters who have gone on to better things, such as Jake Silverstein, the current editor of *Texas Monthly*, and 15-year veteran reporter Sterry Butcher, who obtained a writers' fellowship to Stanford as a result of her writings for the *Sentinel*. Scoops by the paper include revealing plans by Midland oilmen to mine water in Presidio County (the Rio Nuevo water scheme), which failed as a result of the exposure, and breaking the story how Redford teenager Ezekiel Hernandez, while tending his goats on the Rio Grande, was shot dead by a detachment of US Marines. The editor's favorite headline, from September 10, 2009, goes as follows: "Man assaults woman, rams police vehicle, flees, hits train, fights paramedics, and jumps from courthouse." (Photograph by *Big Bend Sentinel*.)

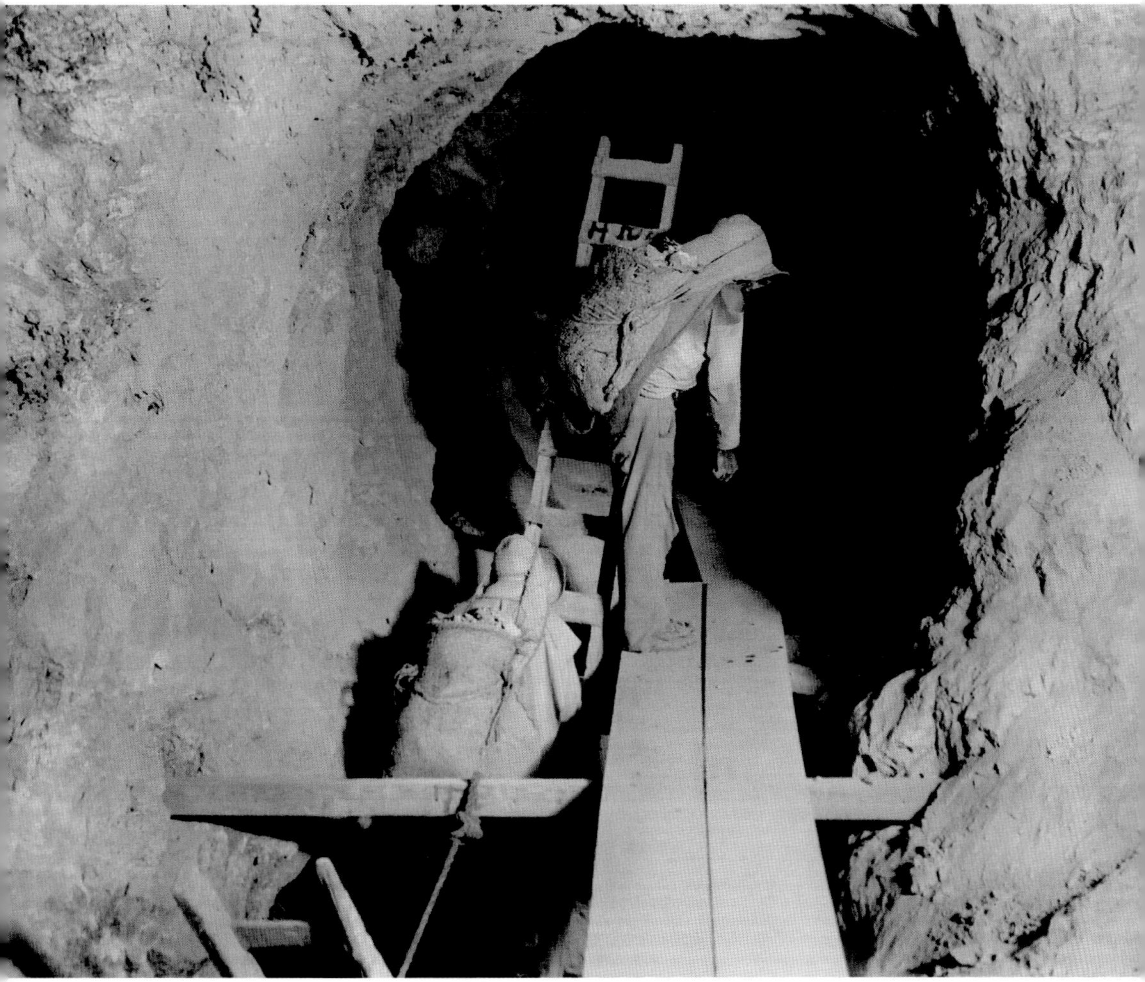

Chisos Mining Company

Mining in the region has a long history, on both sides of the border. Best known was the Chisos Mining Company in Terlingua, which, using Mexican labor and shrewd geological research, mined cinnabar (mercury). Due to World War I, cinnabar was in high demand for explosives. The story of mine owner Howard E. Perry is documented in Kenneth Ragsdale's "Cinnabar." Large amounts of zinc, lead, some silver, coal, and other ores were also mined. The "Old Ore Road" in Big Bend National Park is evidence of early-20th-century activity. Ore was transported by aerial containers across the Rio Grande from Mexico, then hauled by mule train to Marathon, where it was loaded onto trains. With the closing of the DuPont Corporation's fluorspar (used in making freon) mine at La Linda in 1990, mining operations seemed finished. However, the silver mine at Shafter has recently reopened, using new techniques.

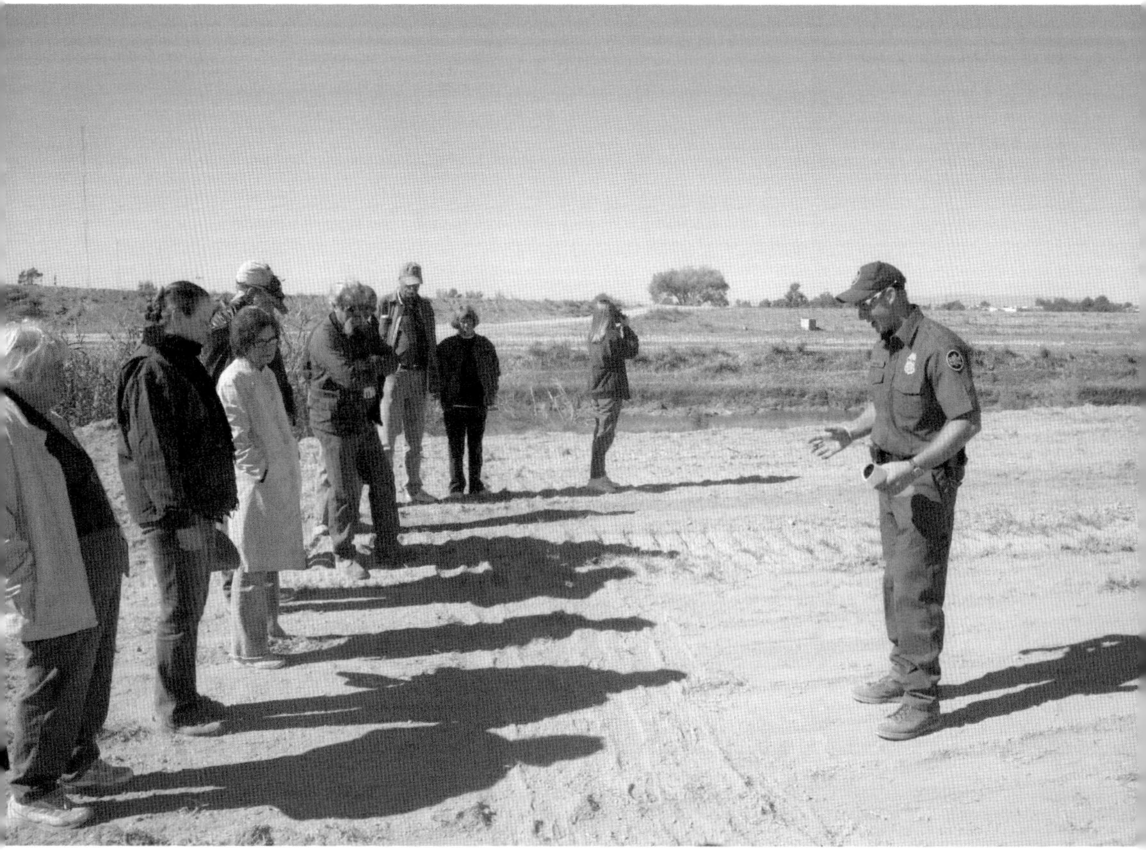

Bill Brooks and Customs and Border Patrol

Founded in 1924 and hugely expanded after 9/11, Customs and Border Patrol (CBP), Department Homeland Security, is a major presence in the area. Its work ranges from high-tech electronic surveillance to low-tech checking for footprints on dirt roads. Checkpoints on highways leading north from the border and a regional office in Marfa with a wide jurisdiction and responsibility are the visible signs of CBP presence, together with helicopters and many vehicles.

The public sees these young men and women, often from Northern states, when they perform the unglamorous and repetitive job of asking car drivers passing through checkpoints their citizenship. Sometime in the past, heavy-handed treatment of local residents has caused resentment. To correct this, CBP started a "Citizens' Academy," a four-evening, one-day, seminar explaining their work and offering some hands-on simulated training. This picture shows students examining footprints on the border. This workshop, under the guidance of CBP public affairs officer Bill Brooks, who previously was editor of a local newspaper, has been popular. (Photograph by Marfa Sector, Border Patrol.)

CHAPTER SIX

Business

There are no major manufacturing plants in the region; although, one mine (the silver mine at Shafter) has reopened. Previously, there was a mouse factory (to supply zoos) and also an ostrich factory (to provide feathers for Las Vegas show girls). Over the years, the Big Bend and Davis Mountains region has seen rubber production, a candelilla wax business, mining and ranching, and government at all levels.

Today, government jobs, including those at Sul Ross State University and a much-increased Department of Homeland Security, are numerous. The Big Bend Regional Medical Center and the Big Bend Telephone Company are two sizeable independent employers. Some of those in business in the area, such as J.P. Bryant, who owns the Gage Hotel in Marathon, are employed elsewhere, in his case as an oil company executive.

Joe and Lanna Duncan have always lived in Fort Davis and have a different story of how they expanded in the hotel business. They had built up the Hotel Limpia over some years, adding other accommodations around town and also a boutique. Then there was an auction in Marfa of the Paisano Hotel. Almost on a whim, the Duncans bid on the property and found to their surprise they were the new owners.

Their natural business acumen kicked in and, while the turnaround took time, eventually they were happy with the new Paisano Hotel on Highland Avenue in Marfa, a restored historic hotel, originally designed by the well-known firm of architects, Trost & Trost. Sometime later, a Trost & Trost property in Van Horn came on the market, and the Duncans added this to their workload. More recently, they have divested themselves of the Hotel Limpia to spend more time with their son in California.

"Don't call me before twelve," said Lewis Gordon. Having worked for years in the restaurant business, including nine years as owner-chef, Lewis Gordon now relishes sleeping late. Growing up black and poor in Alpine, Lewis gained experience in the Army and, upon discharge, worked in the Holland Hotel kitchen, where he learned about cooking. Years later, he bought the Ponderosa Restaurant in Alpine as his own business—he has not forgotten the long hours and early start to the day.

German immigrant Louis Forchheimer and, later, his son Paul ran a large and successful general store in Alpine. Natural shopkeepers, they observed the changing taste of the community and supervised the transition from serving mainly ranchers to selling to the public at large, as a department store.

Recent years have seen an increase in the variety of small businesses, catering to tourists and to the changing tastes of residents. Coffee shops serving up espressos, art galleries, and bike repair shops are now common.

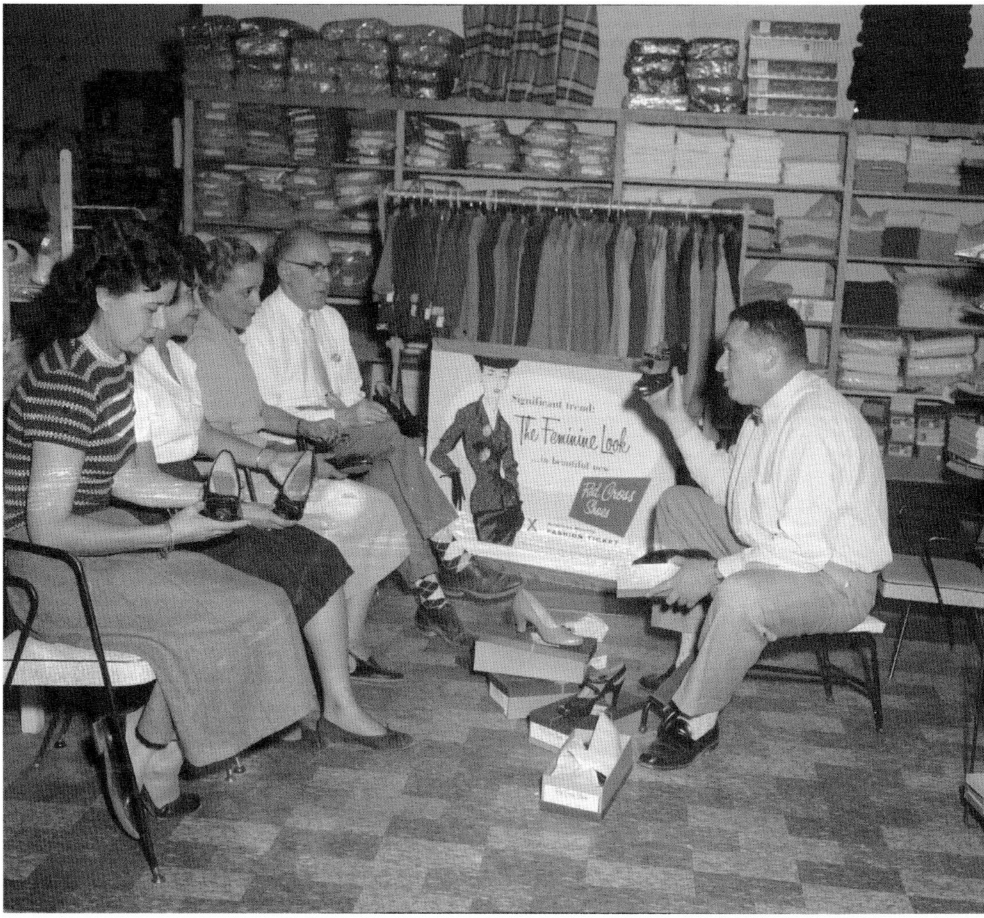
Significant trend:
The Feminine Look
...in beautiful new
Red Cross Shoes
FASHION TICKET

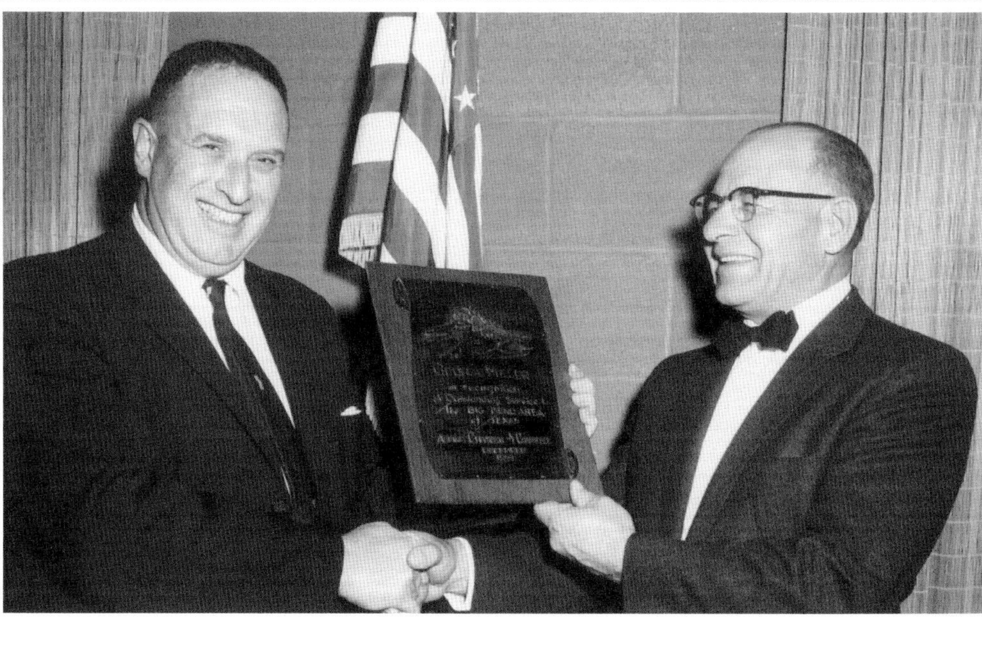

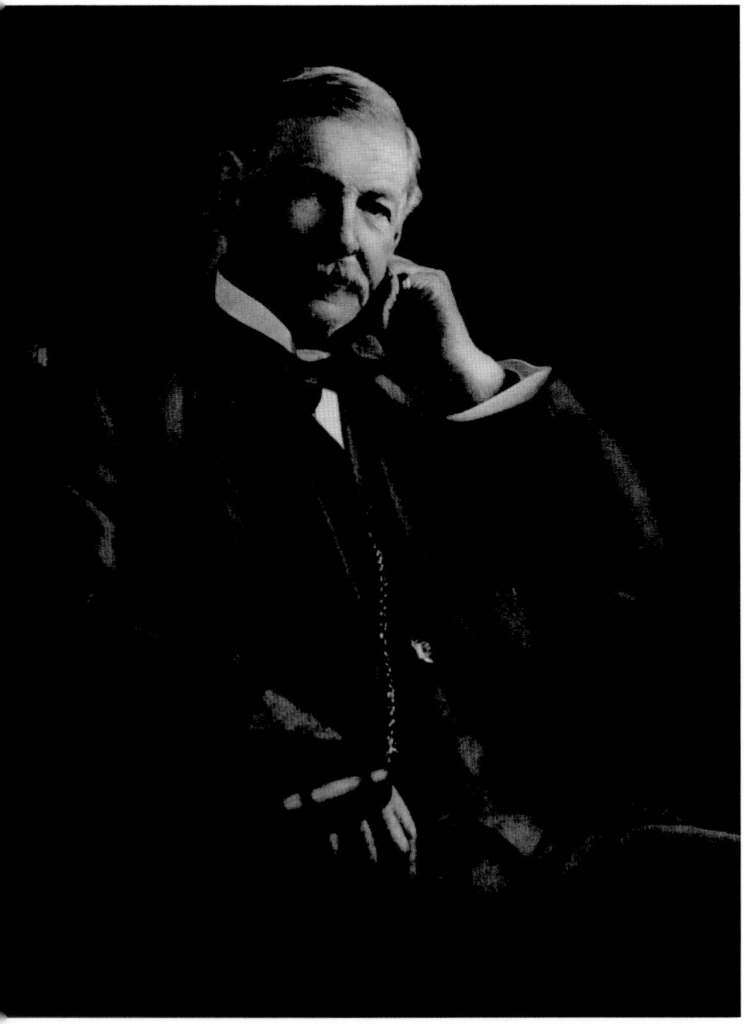

Whitaker Keesey
Born in 1848 in Ohio, Whitaker Keesey's first shock was when his father left home in 1851 and was never seen again. He had little schooling and had to work on a farm, which he hated. At 16, he apprenticed to a baker, a move that later stood him in good stead. He arrived in 1867 in Fort Davis as a baker with the troops sent to garrison the fort after the Civil War.

He worked hard and prospered. "With the coming of the railroad and the influx of cattlemen and settlers after 1880, Keesey & Co. became the largest mercantile establishment in the entire Trans-Pecos region," according to the *History of Jeff Davis County* by Lucy Jacobson and Mildred Bloys. From the elegant, well-dressed figure posing for a photograph, there is no indication of earlier hardships.

Louis Forchheimer (OPPOSITE PAGE)
Louis Forchheimer was born in Germany and arrived in New York in 1907, aged 18.

He worked for some years in the wholesale dry goods business before arriving in Alpine in 1921, where he started what was to become one of the best-known stores in the whole region.

Located on Holland Avenue, Forchheimer's Department Store sold a variety of merchandise, which changed as the needs of the community changed. Initially, the demand was for agricultural and ranching supplies. As Sul Ross State University grew and Alpine changed, the clients' needs changed and so did the store merchandise.

In 1976, the Forchheimer family sold the store, which retained its name, before closing down in the mid-1980s. After more than 50 years of successful retailing, the Forchheimers generously gave back to the community through the Paul Forchheimer Business Award and through strong support for Sul Ross State University and Big Bend National Park.

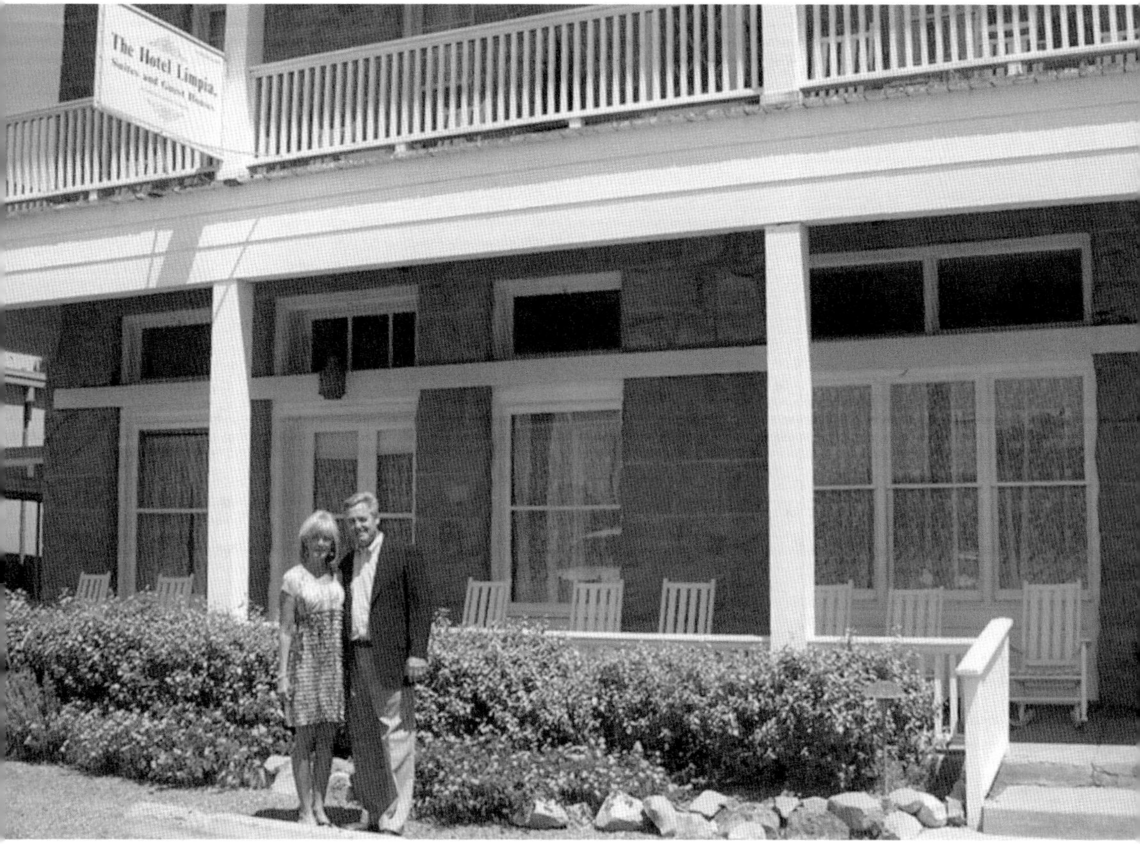

Lanna and Joe Duncan

In 1991, Lanna and Joe Duncan bought the Hotel Limpia in Fort Davis from Joe's parents. The couple married in 1983 in Fort Davis, and both families had roots in the region. With this move into the hotel business, they embarked on a course that, within 20 years, would make them the principal hoteliers in the region, owning three major hotels, one motel, six guesthouses, and one delicatessen. But even for these tireless hard workers, family concerns arose in 2011 when they sold the Hotel Limpia in order to spend more time with their son, Malcolm. The call of family had particular resonance for them since they always treated their staff like family, a major reason for their business success. (Photograph by Caleb Jagger.)

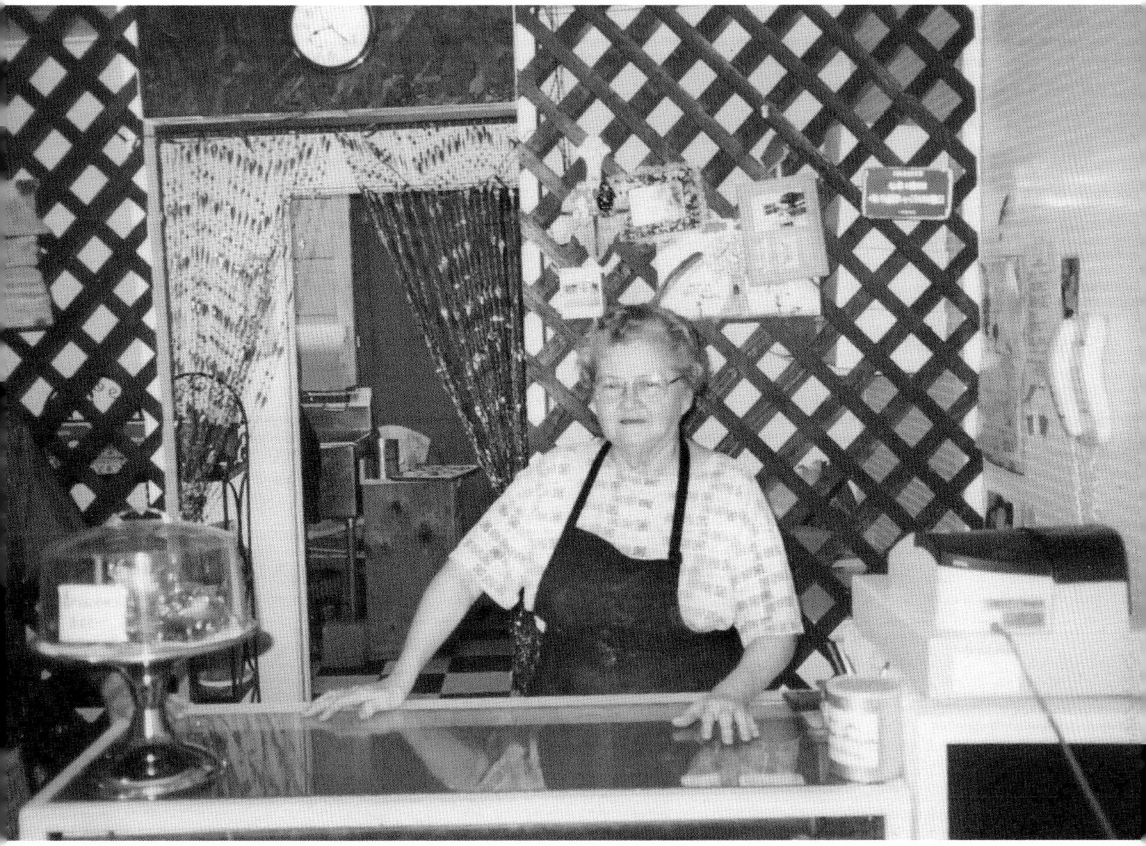

Shirley Rooney

Not long before she sold her Marathon bakery named Shirley's Burnt Biscuit Bakery, Shirley Rooney was surprised when two German tourists walked in saying they had read about her in a German travel guide. A strategic location, an effervescent character as baker, and a popular list of baked goods (loaves, biscuits, donuts, fried pies, and cookies) were the reasons for her fame.

All this happened after Shirley had retired in 1998 from her previous job as baker in the Holland Hotel, at age 64. Work at her own bakery started at 3:00 a.m., and the bakery opened to the public at 5:00 a.m. Favorable press notice started to appear in *Texas Monthly* and other magazines. Finally, Shirley sold out in 2006, now having more time to spend with her three daughters, Beckie, Francine, and Betty Jo. (Courtesy of Shirley Rooney.)

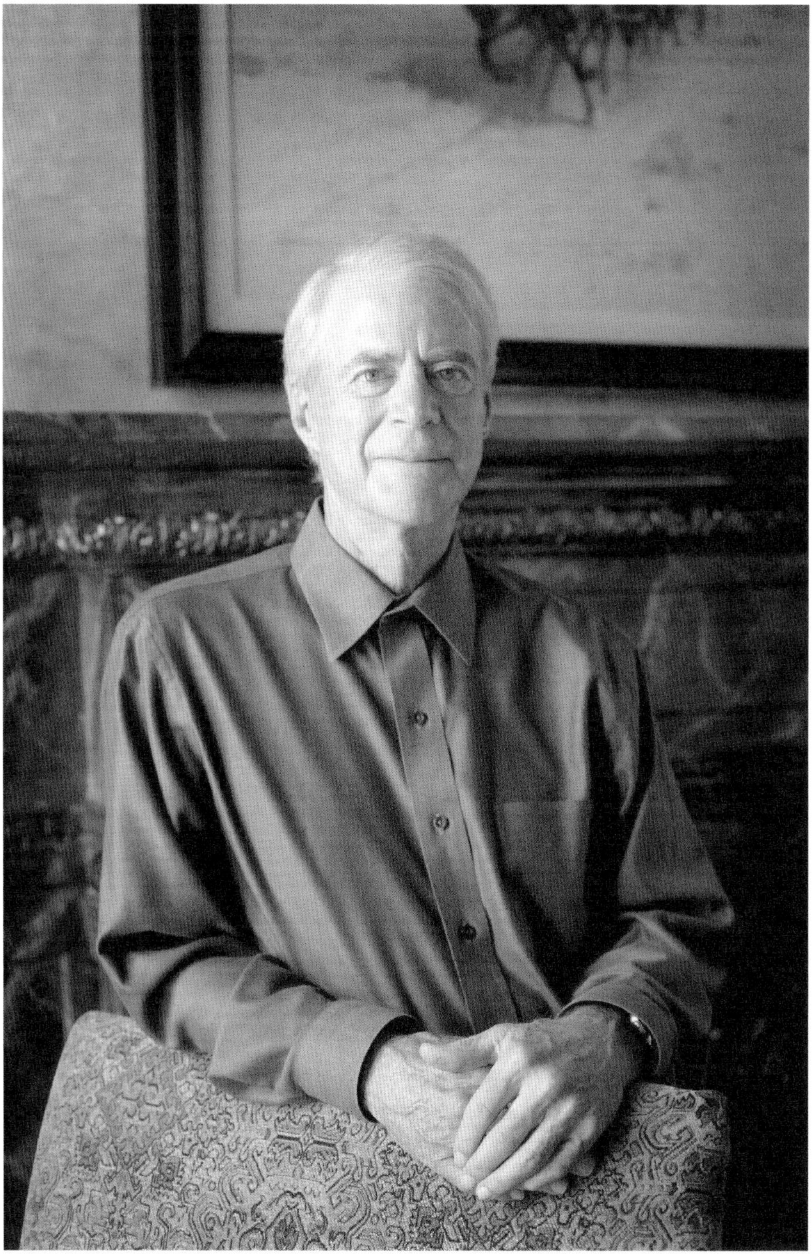

J.P. Bryan

Thirty-some years ago, oilman J.P. Bryan passed through Marathon and saw a "For Sale" sign outside an old building. Bryan was looking for a house for his family to stay in when visiting his nearby ranch. He had stumbled on the historic Gage Hotel, built in 1927 by Alfred Gage, one of Marathon's earliest ranching pioneers. The Gage Hotel has, since the addition of a new wing, become a destination of choice for visitors, catering to many weddings and reunions. It is also a touch of luxury for visitors on their way to Big Bend National Park. For Bryan, who is prominent in the Texas Historical Commission, the hotel is a fitting repository for part of his huge collection of Western artifacts, including the head of a white buffalo, which adorns the Gage bar. (Photograph by James H. Evans.)

90

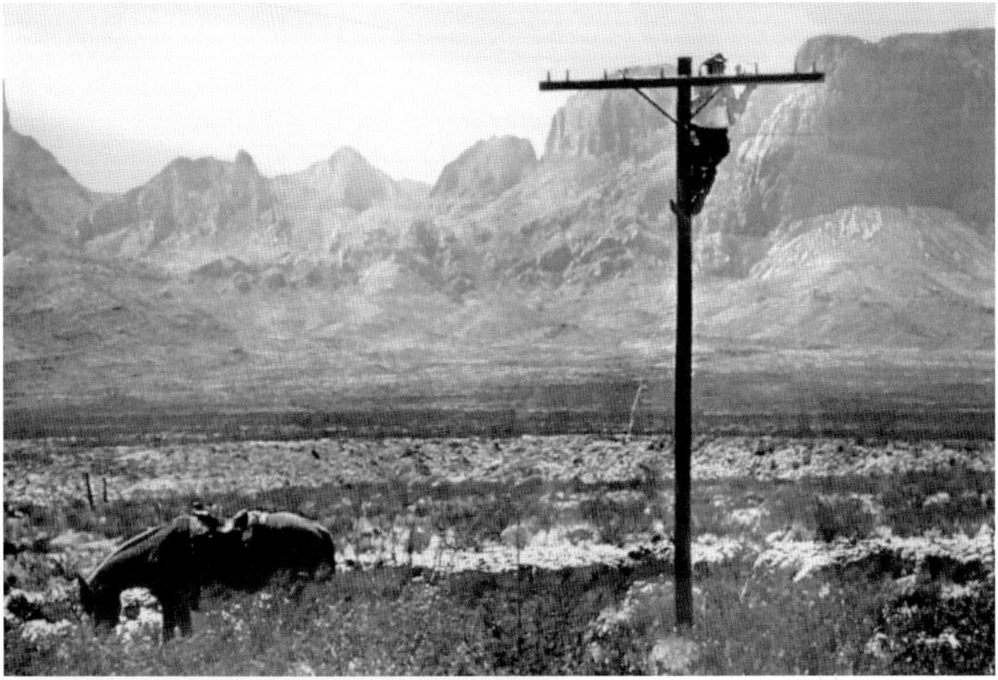

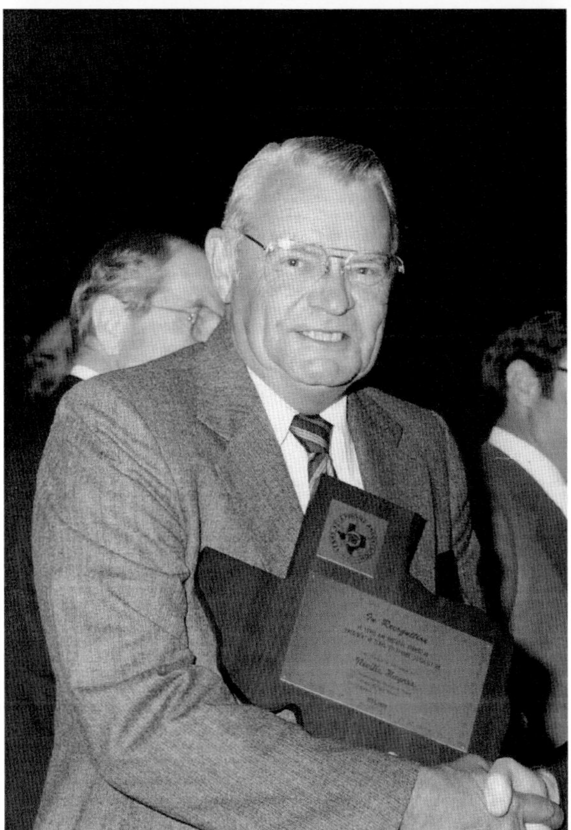

Neville Haynes
During the drought of the 1950s, local rancher Neville Haynes started to look at other business ventures. At that time, telephone communication was done on private lines owned by ranchers, often with lines strung on fence posts. The Big Bend Telephone Company was founded in 1960 with six telephones and one exchange. Despite the distances and rugged terrain that required travel on horseback to maintain lines, as seen above, the company obtained loans and grew, purchasing neighboring telephone exchanges during the 1970s and installing dial service.

Neville Haynes, who received numerous industry awards, pictured at left, stepped down in 1980. His son Jeff continued the innovations, installing the first fiber-optic route to Presidio, the longest in the nation by any independent telephone company. In 2005, the company became an Internet provider and, soon afterwards, implemented satellite radios. (Both, courtesy of Big Bend Telephone.)

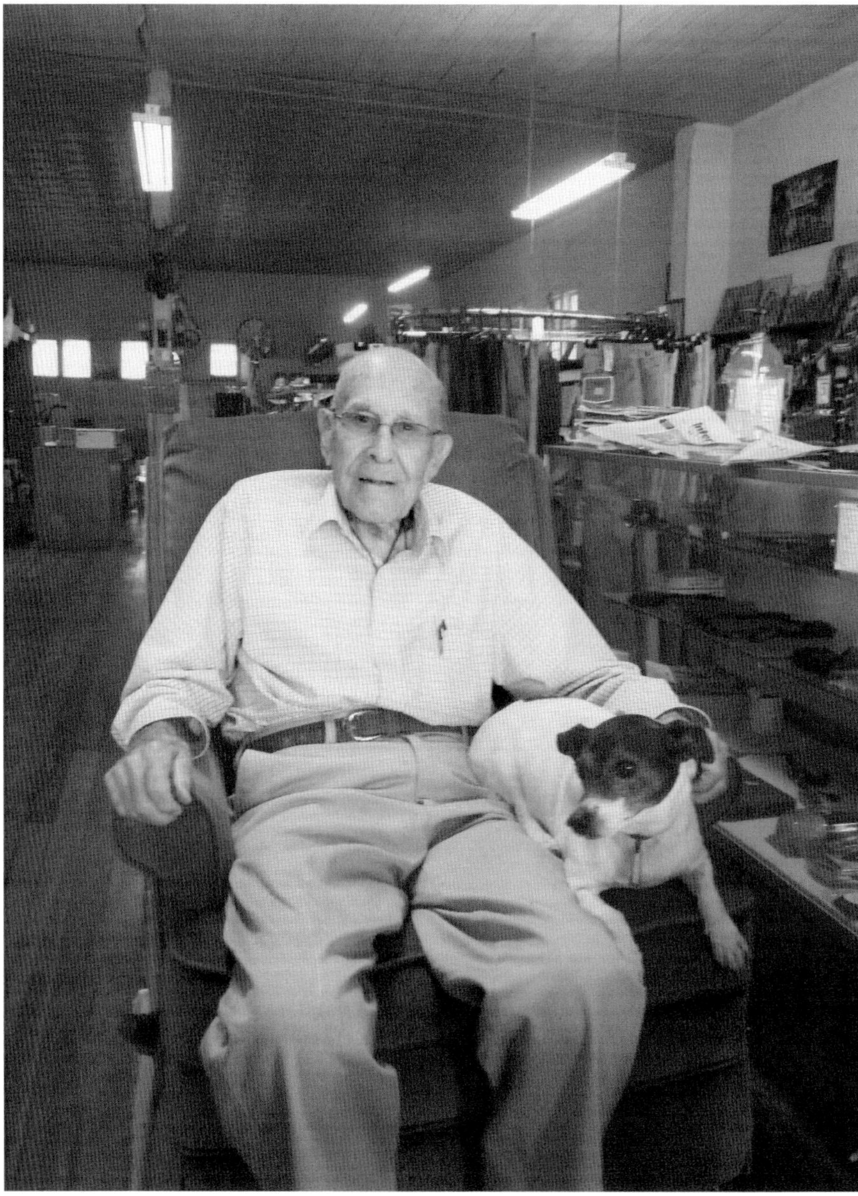

Edmundo Nieto
Sitting in a comfortable armchair, with his dog beside him, in the front of Miguel Nieto's Department Store, which has been his life's work, 93-year-old Edmundo Nieto exudes good humor as he vigorously answers questions about his life.

Edmundo went to a Presidio school run by nuns and then on to St. Edward's University in Austin, graduating in 1941 with a degree in business administration. He spent the war years as a sergeant in the artillery, serving in Europe.

He married Socorro Herrerra in 1946, and they had four sons. One is an architect, and another is a medical doctor, which makes Edmundo proud. In Presidio, his son Mario helps him run the store, and his other son Carlos is active in civic affairs. "Education is the key to success," he says, "No one can take it from you." (Author's collection.)

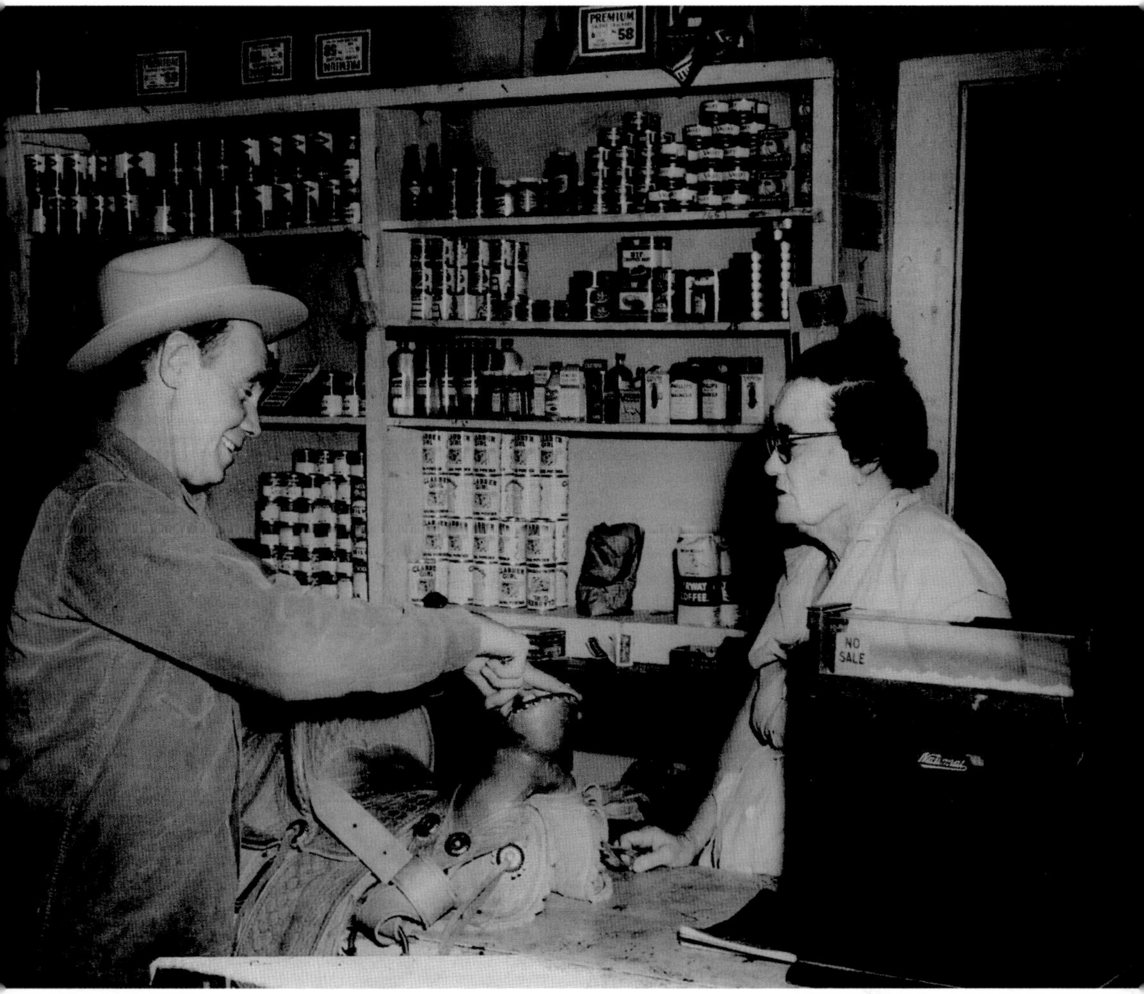

Maggy Smith

"One tough, pistol-packing lady" is how Bill Ivey, whose father owned the Lajitas store, describes Maggy Smith, operator of the stores at Hot Springs, San Vicente, and Lajitas. She was born in 1895, came to Big Bend in 1914, and married M.R. Hay, by whom she had six children.

Hay died in 1921, and Maggy married Henry Smith shortly afterwards. By 1940, they were at the Daniels Ranch near Boquillas and ran the mail service from Marathon to Hot Springs, where J.O. Langford presided. Smith died in 1942, and Maggy was on her own. She was well-equipped by temperament to take care of herself, and the National Park Service invited her to operate the post office and store at Hot Springs in the new Big Bend National Park.

For the next 20 years, her work at three different local stores gave her a reputation for single-minded toughness and fairness, laced with occasional heartwarming acts of compassion. It would not have been easy for a woman on her own in the culture of those days to be in the public eye as a storekeeper and to prosper.

Stores along the border at that time acted as much as a meeting place for folks crossing the border as a place to buy merchandise. Maggy did more than just sell goods. She acted as interpreter, midwife, and dealt with rattlesnake bites. She earned income from the lucrative cross-border candle wax trade at night, when the Mexican Customs inspectors were off-duty. Over 20 years, she earned the respect of all in the area. She died in 1965, aged 70.

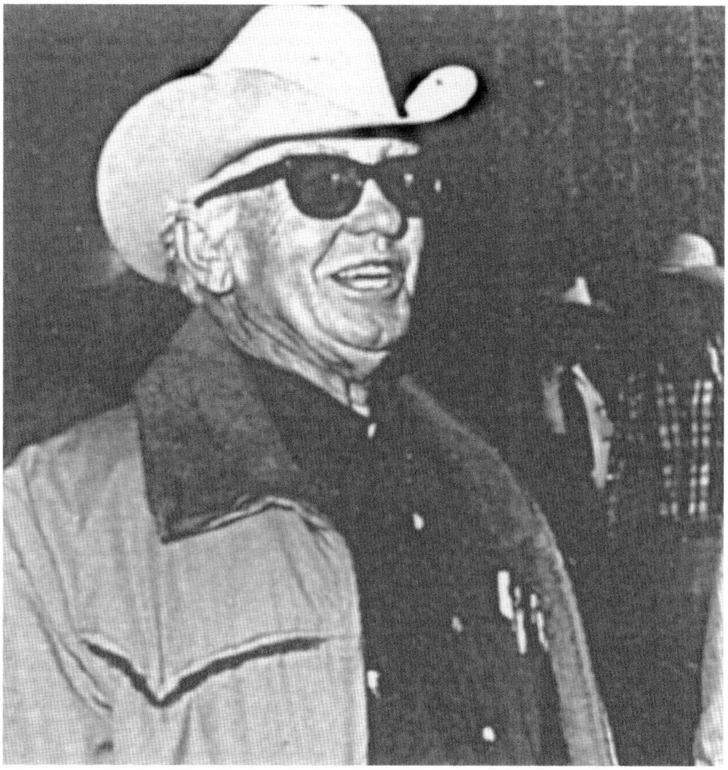

Rex Gordon Ivey

Born in 1910 near Lometa, Texas, Rex Gordon Ivey first came to Lajitas in the 1920s and gained the nickname "Skunk Ivey" due to his occupation as a trapper. In the 1930s, he got involved in the freight business and, in 1942, he bought the Lajitas Trading Post.

In those days, the trading post was the hub of the region, serving both sides of the border. Rex presided over this international hubbub of gossip and trade but took pains to update his enterprise by installing the area's first gas pump and, in 1963, the first telephone. Rex was also known for community barbecues, the largest of which drew 2,500 people, eating potato salad prepared in a bathtub, until his wife, Kitty, said, "Enough!"

Rex's younger son, Bill, grew up speaking Spanish at the trading post. When the trading post was sold in 1977, father and son together bought Terlingua ghost town, which became the family legacy for the future.

The candelilla wax business was a thriving enterprise in those times. The candelilla bush grew prolifically in Mexico, where it was harvested, and the wax was separated. The product was then carried across the Rio Grande on mule back and sold to entrepreneurs who arranged onward transportation to US markets.

Rex Ivey loved cars and he loved to drive excessively fast. He fed animals (dogs and javelinas) with food from the trunk, and horseshoes were welded onto the front. The car also acted as his office, and he spent a lot of time in it. Sometimes it could be seen with a mountain lion strapped to the hood.

In addition to the wild entrepreneurial and independent streak, Rex Ivey served the community well as county commissioner for 20 years. He also gave generously and privately and was a remarkable storyteller. His elder son, Rex III, died in an accident, but his younger son, Bill, continued the Ivey legacy in Terlingua ghost town. Bill delivered a fitting testimonial to his father, who died in 2001, aged 90: "He lived the life of the Old West and found the Last Frontier." (Courtesy of *Lajitas Sun*.)

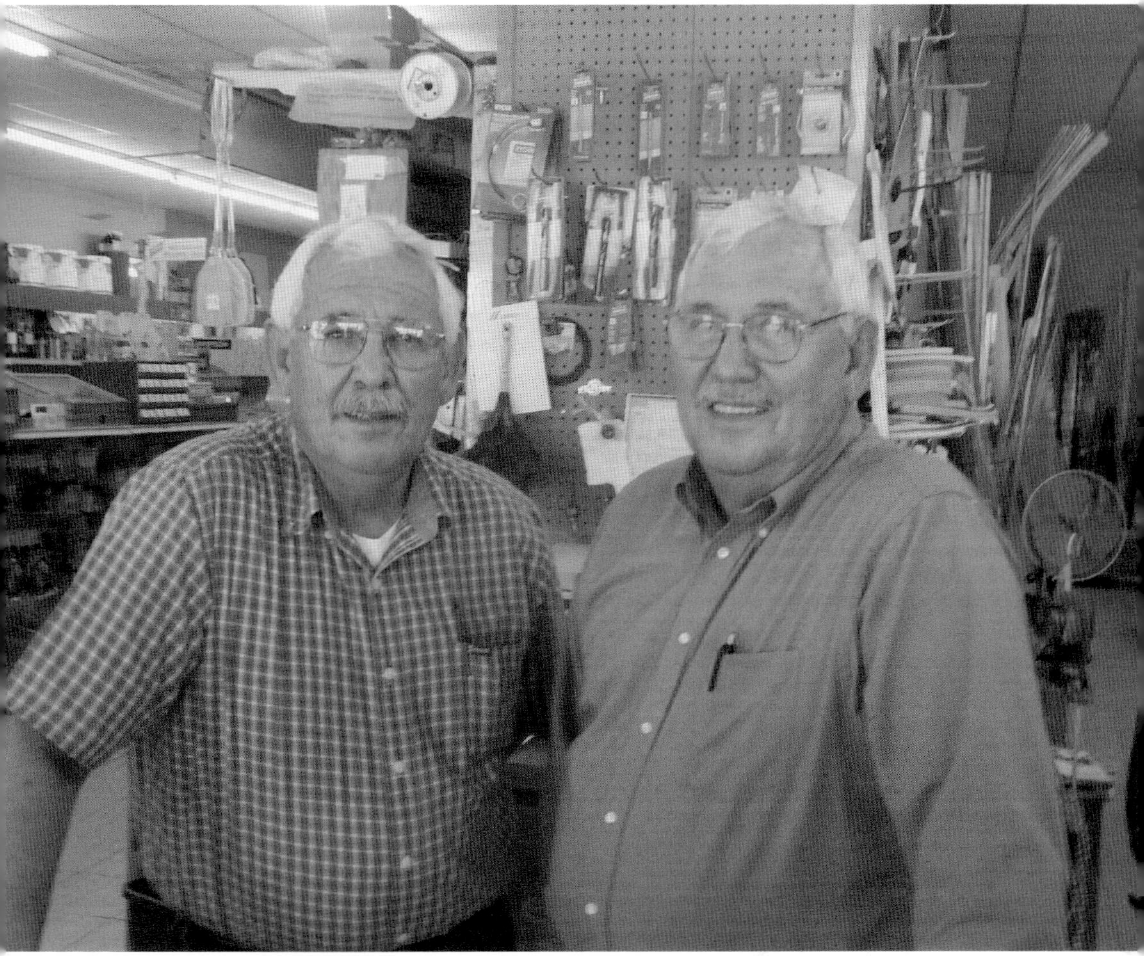

The Armandariz Family

When the Mexican Revolution started in 1910, the Armandariz family got ready to leave Ojinaga, Chihuahua. First, the girls and mother left while the boys, Luis and Carlos, stayed to guard the ranch. Then, the whole family was reunited in Presidio, where they built a store and started a new life.

Of the 11 children in the family, the twins Carlos and Luis and one sister were sent to New Jersey, where an aunt resided. Carlos (left) and Luis (right) attended a Catholic day school, graduating in 1962, followed by St. Michael's College in Santa Fe, New Mexico. With a business degree, Luis got a legal-administrative job in the US Army. Carlos served in Vietnam and came back to Presidio to mind the store.

In 1974, Luis started work with Texas Parks and Wildlife, a career that would last until 2006. While his wife, Rebecca, a dentist, practiced in Ojinaga, Luis was superintendent at Fort Leaton State Historical Site and, later, of the newly opened Big Bend Ranch State Park. After retirement, he joined his twin behind the counter in the family hardware store, The Presidio Lumber Yard. (Author's collection.)

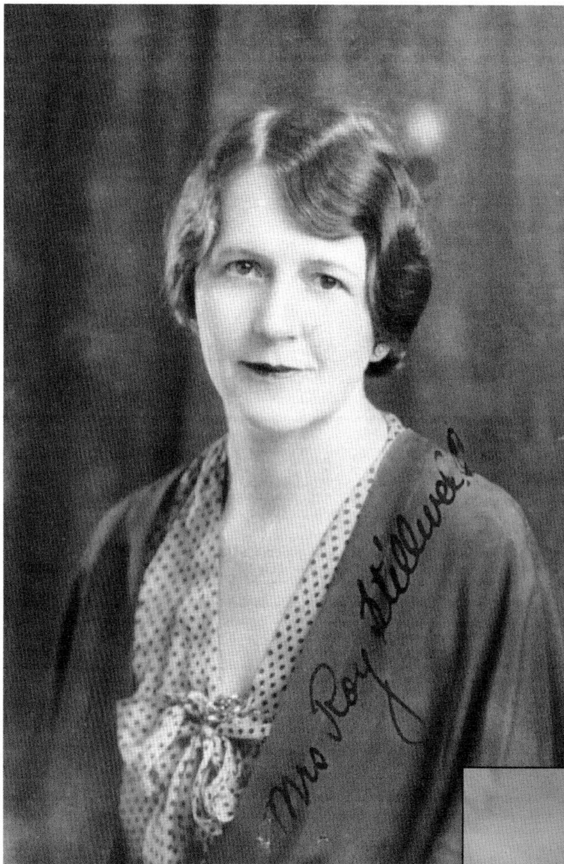

Hallie Crawford

Hallie Crawford was born in Waco, Texas, in 1897. Her family homesteaded in New Mexico in 1907 for three years, and Hallie attended a one-room school, located three miles away.

The family moved to Alpine, and Hallie entered the sixth grade at Alpine High School. She later gained a teaching certificate at Alpine Summer Normal School, before taking her first teaching job in Presidio. In 1918, she married Marathon rancher Roy Stillwell, who was twice her age, and learned how to shoot and herd cattle. During this period, she had three children, Dadie, Roy, and Guy.

After Roy's death in 1948, she moved to Alpine, where she wrote three books. She was elected justice of the peace for 20 years, and she became a chili cook-off judge and a tourist attraction herself. She died two months short of her 100th birthday, the teacher turned cowgirl.

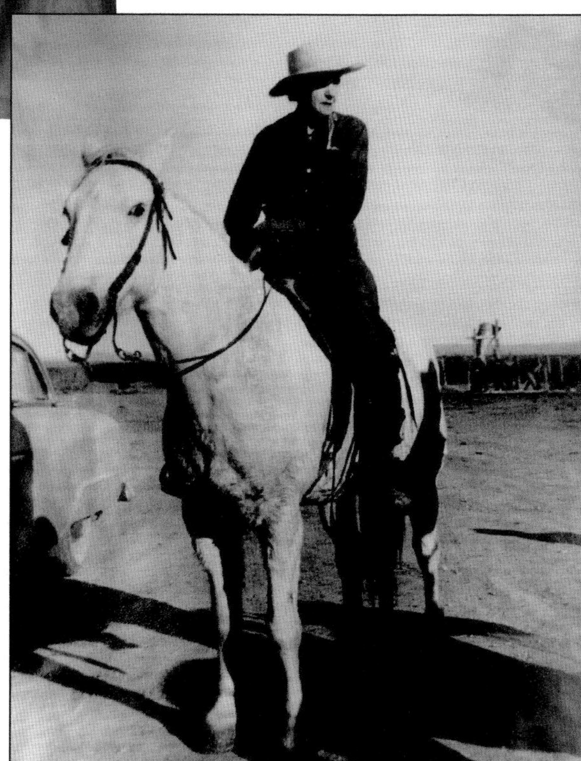

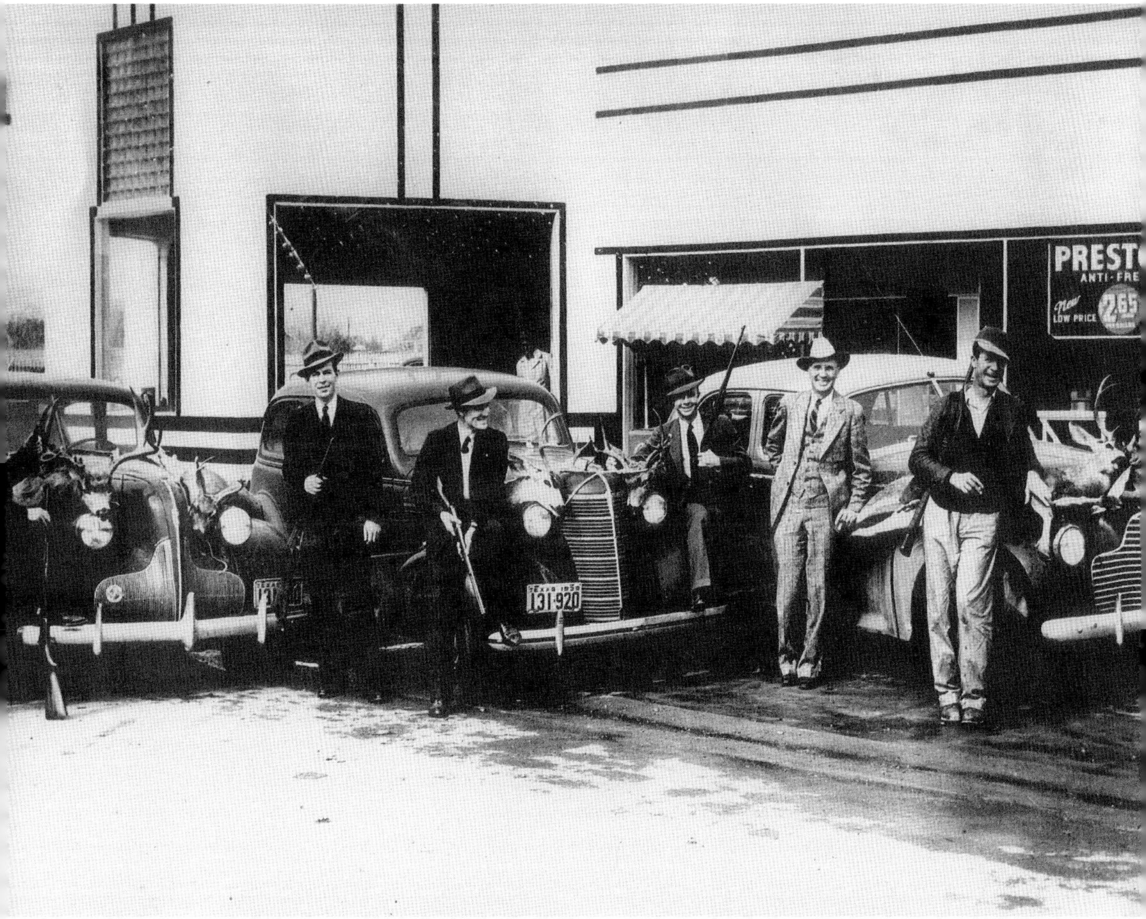

Jim Casner

Jim Casner, at 21 years old, headed West through Alpine in 1909 to seek a cure in Arizona for his tuberculosis. Cured at a sanitarium, he came back to Alpine in 1914 and, three years later, married Una Jackson, whom he met there on his way out. He also got into the automobile dealership business. The couple moved to El Paso in 1917, where they adopted a daughter, Una Joy, and Casner worked with his grandfather in the auto distributorship trade.

The family moved back to Alpine in 1933, and Casner developed the Casner Motor Company for 30 years, expanding to neighboring towns and gaining awards. His astute wife helped in testing other business ideas, like an innovative lechuguilla processing plant in the 1950s and a long-lasting, profitable candelilla wax business from the 1950s to the 1970s. He was a keen Rotarian and a city council member; he worked hard to promote Big Bend National Park and was named an honorary ranger. He died in 1983, aged 95; he had a long and busy life for someone who had tuberculosis.

The picture shows Casner (in the light suit) and friends posing in front of their vehicles like Al Capone after a successful deer-hunting trip. Their trophies are spread on the car hoods.

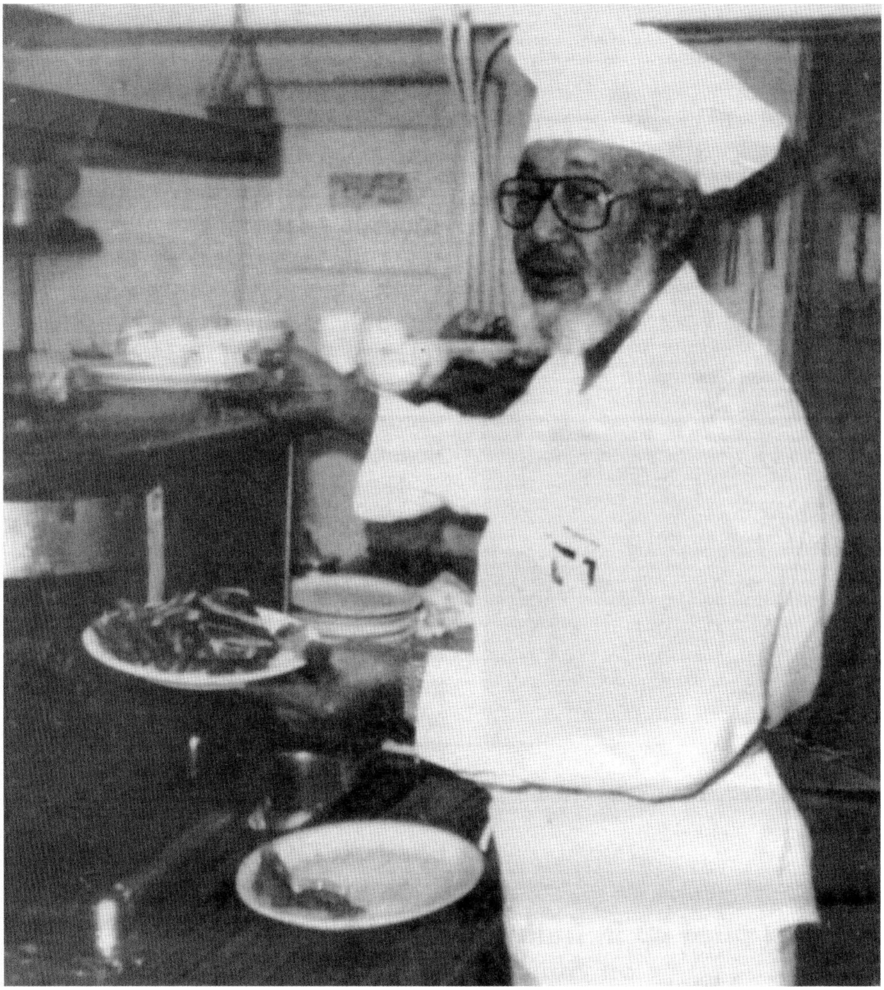

Lewis Gordon

Few people in Alpine know the location of the Morgan School, which opened its doors as a church and a school in 1929 to serve Alpine's black community. The founder of the school was Morgan Gordon, a descendant of a former slave, who arrived from Del Rio with his wife, Rita, who was half Seminole Indian. The school had eight students, including Lewis Gordon, the youngest of Morgan Gordon's six children. It functioned until the 1950s, when the students were transferred to nearby Centennial School.

Lewis Gordon was born in 1937, attended the Morgan School for black students (pictured here), and then left to work in the Holland Hotel kitchen, where he acquired an interest in cooking. He enlisted in the US Army in 1955 and was assigned to the Quartermaster School. He was honorably discharged in 1958, earning an Army Good Conduct Medal as well as a General Equivalency Diploma. On resuming civilian life, he went back to work as a chef, which was now his career.

In September 1965, he married Maria Vella Martinez, and together, they had five children, all of whom attended college. Donna, the fourth child, went on to earn her master's degree and teaches at Houston Community College. Meanwhile, Lewis pursued his cooking career at the Ponderosa Restaurant until he was in a position to purchase it for himself. He continued to work for another 13 years as owner-chef. Resplendent in a chef's white apron and hat, he became known for his enchiladas and liver and bacon. Today, Lewis is comforted by the success of his children and by his own achievements of owning a popular restaurant. (Courtesy of Lewis Gordon.)

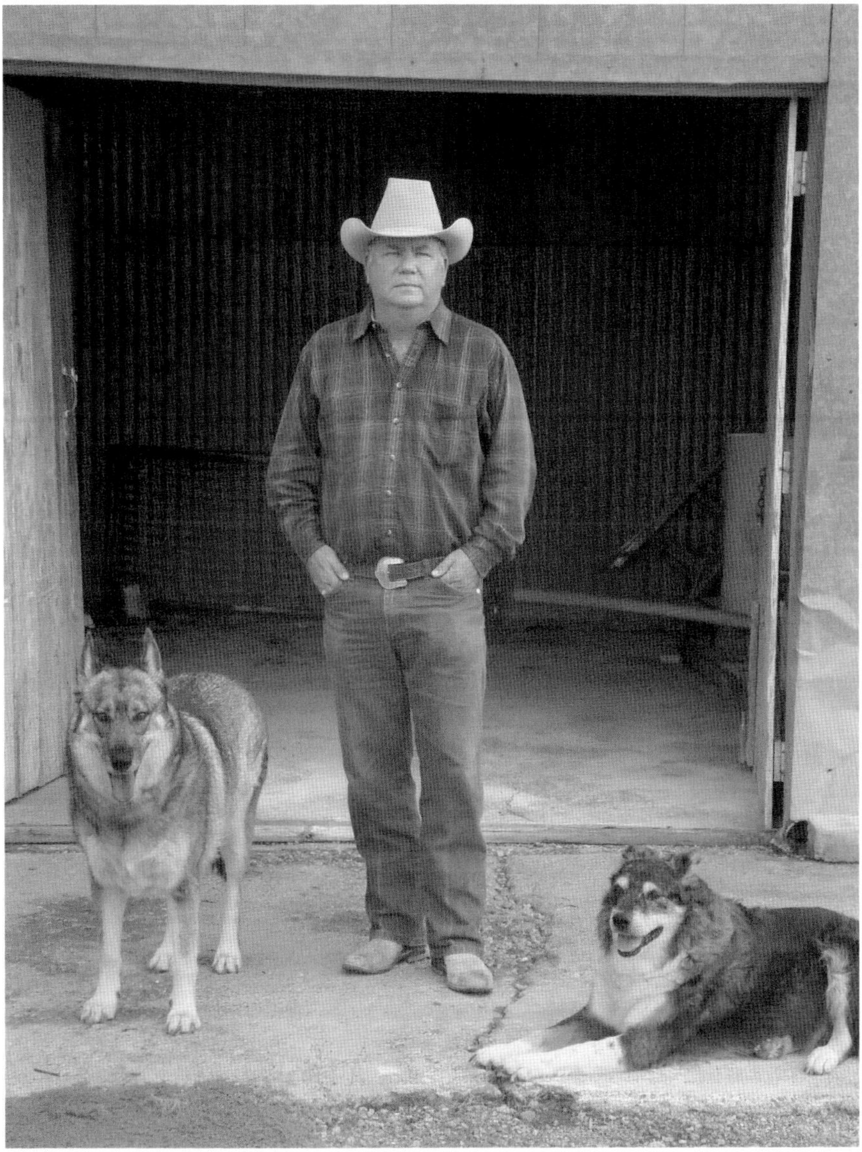

Terry Bishop

Terry Bishop's father, Bill, came to Presidio in 1965 to farm cotton along the Rio Grande. The business changed to growing cantaloupes, honeydew melons, and onions. At the peak, 2,000 acres were being farmed by 40 full-time workers.

However, US immigration law changed. By the time Terry took over in 1999, production of produce was no longer possible, and the challenge was to save the family land. A 10-year fight to change the Texas water law was finally won, enabling Terry to sell his water rights to Valley farmers downstream and retain the land.

Meanwhile, Terry's 40-year friendship with famed local artist and visionary A. Kelly Pruitt ended with Pruitt's death in 2009. Deeply influenced by Pruitt's legacy and vision, Terry undertook a move into sustainable agriculture to preserve the history of this land, known as La Junta de los Rios ("the confluence of the rivers"). (Author's collection.)

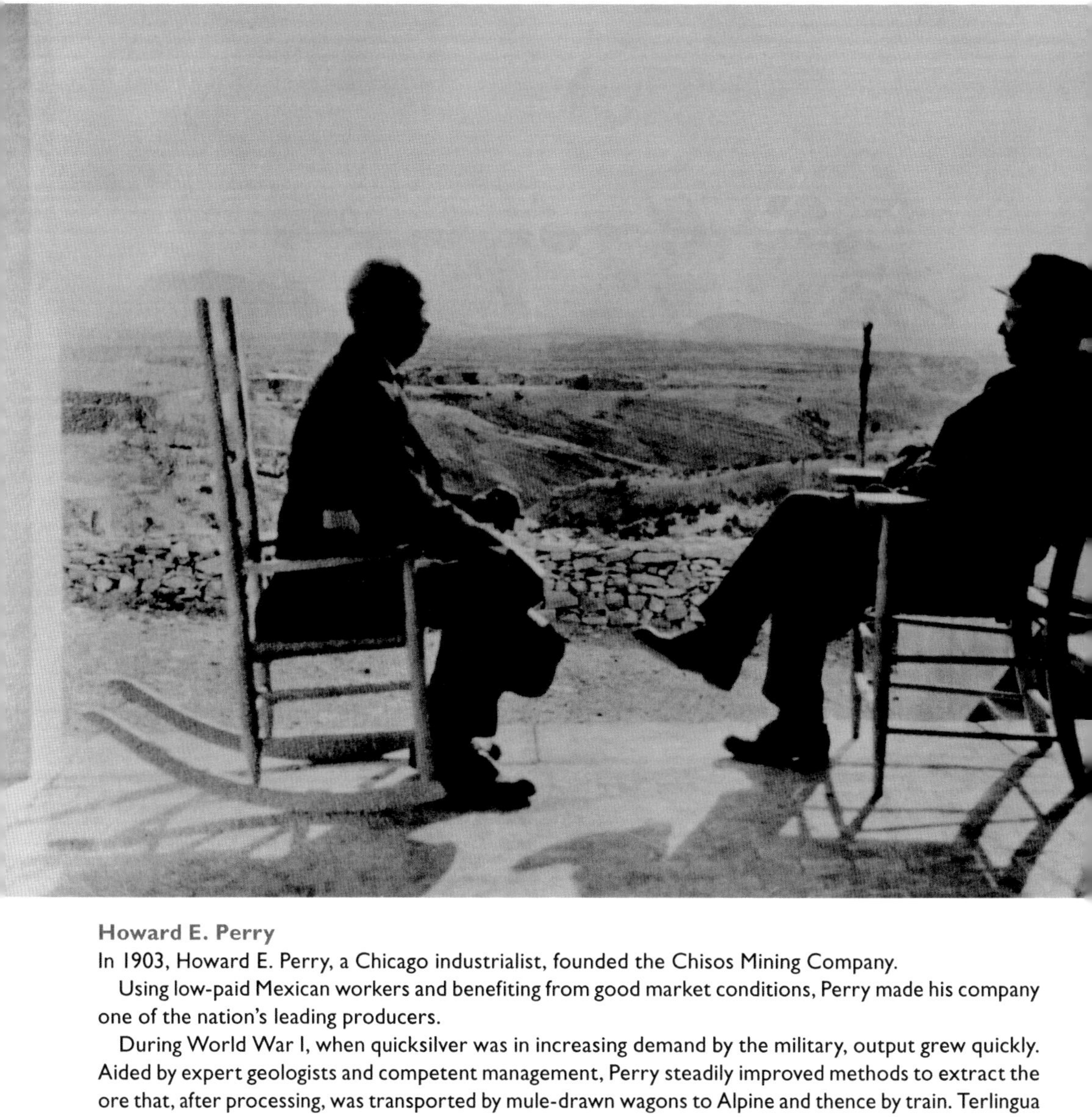

Howard E. Perry

In 1903, Howard E. Perry, a Chicago industrialist, founded the Chisos Mining Company.

Using low-paid Mexican workers and benefiting from good market conditions, Perry made his company one of the nation's leading producers.

During World War I, when quicksilver was in increasing demand by the military, output grew quickly. Aided by expert geologists and competent management, Perry steadily improved methods to extract the ore that, after processing, was transported by mule-drawn wagons to Alpine and thence by train. Terlingua grew to 1,000 inhabitants with a company store, hotel, chapel, telephone service, and a doctor.

Demand for quicksilver dropped after World War I, and the mine went into a long decline, ending in bankruptcy in 1942. Howard Perry, shown here on the right, died in 1944 and left a mixed reputation as a feudal exploiter and visionary industrialist.

CHAPTER SEVEN

Professional and Public Service

Mayors, justices of the peace, lawyers, doctors, military, sheriffs, and commissioners are all included in this section. The career of David Alloway, whose tragic and ironic death shocked many, is described here because he worked for a state agency, Texas Parks and Wildlife.

Politicians have little more credibility here than anywhere else these days. Pete P. Gallego, however, deserves a mention because of his 21 years of service in the Texas House of Representatives. Among other benefits he obtained for the area, the $110 million in funds for upgrading and extending Sul Ross buildings stand out.

The military presence in Fort Davis successfully challenged the "Indian menace," as it was then called, under a farsighted commander, Colonel Grierson, and his black troops named Buffalo Soldiers by the Indians. Lieutenant Flipper, the first black officer to graduate from West Point, served at Fort Davis and fared less well. He was convicted of making a false statement regarding some missing funds. President Clinton pardoned him 117 years later.

Though separated by about 100 years, two attorneys share the same style of courtroom tactics. Wigfall Van Sickle came to Alpine in 1885 to teach school but decided to become a lawyer. He had a knack of swaying juries in criminal cases, sometimes with the most unlikely tactics. Attorney Mike Barclay passed the bar in 1958, gained a solid reputation in Dallas, and then moved to Alpine in 1984. His oratorical flair, perfected after 54 years in the profession, worked equally well for his clients in West Texas.

Alpine and the region have been well served over the years by several doctors, whose patients spoke highly of them. Dr. Malone Hill stands out; he was a small man but held strong opinions. A gifted surgeon, he established a clinic in Alpine and gave generously to the community, which he served for 42 years. Doc Edwards, the Marfa veterinarian, is known for his almost 50 years of service, his expertise, and sense of humor, not least of which is the title of his book "Up to my Armpits: Adventures of a West Texas Veterinarian."

Fritz Kahl, mayor of Marfa, came to the area in 1943 as a pilot instructor. A large man with a fine voice, he energetically promoted Marfa during his two terms as mayor (1992–1998). He organized the first International Soaring Meet in the United States at Marfa's airport and brought jobs to the area. At age 79, he acted in a local production of *Our Town*.

Captain Matlack's foray into Mexico in 1919 to rescue two hostages is the stuff of legend. Other public servants, like Valenzuela and Howard, were less successful and died in the line of duty. By contrast, Justice of the Peace Fred Granado of Fort Davis administers judgments peacefully and appears to be the most popular man in town.

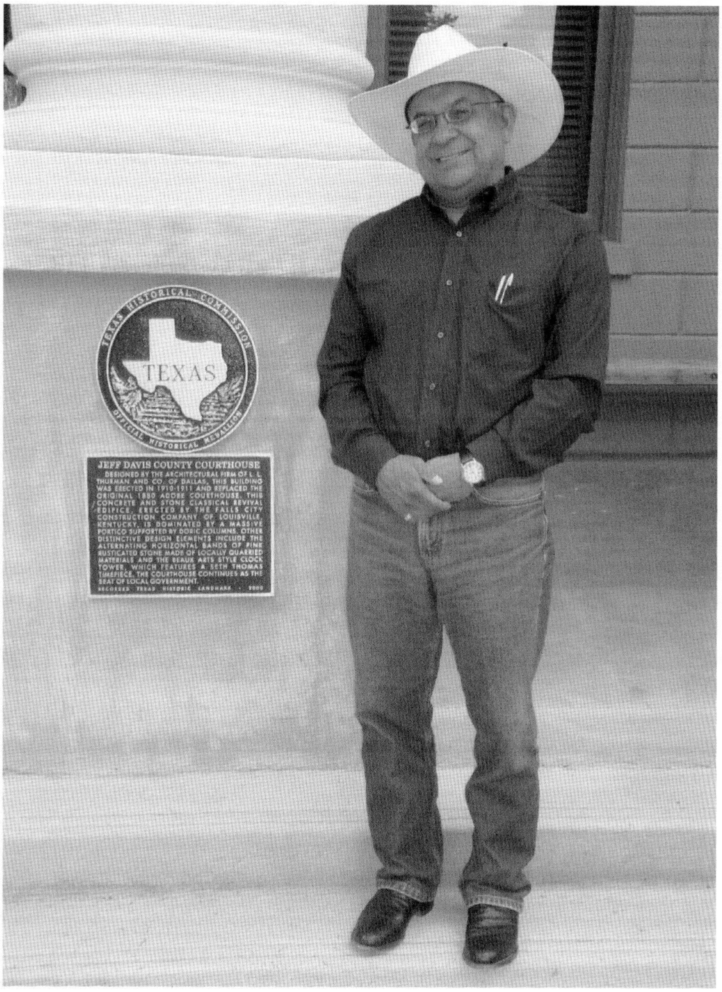

Fred Granado

Born in Fort Davis in 1954, Fred Granado was the youngest of three sons of Fred and Sulema Granado, whose forebears arrived in town in the late 1880s. Of his growing-up years, he has only the following good things to say: "It was a wonderful childhood and school experience." School segregation was over, and Hispanic kids could advance beyond the fifth grade.

After high school, he attended Sul Ross State University in Alpine, majoring in speech with a minor in Spanish. He already had a job doing maintenance at the Jeff Davis County Courthouse but, when a second job arose in Fort Davis at the Hotel Limpia, he jumped at it and quit Sul Ross before graduation. Income was paramount.

For 29 years, he toiled as a maintenance man, janitor, and jailor until 2003, when he thought to run for county commissioner. However, the justice of the peace job came up, and he ran for that office instead and was elected in a runoff. He has three sons by his wife, Olga, whom he married in 1986, and he talks about them with impish humor from behind his large desk.

For a man with a job that requires administering justice, he is remarkably popular. "Lovely, lovely person" is a comment heard around town when talking about Fred Granado, justice of the peace. When asked what is good about his job, he says, "Being in Fort Davis, and being able to walk to work. Small is good, and the community is wonderful." These sentiments come from a person who is legally blind. (Author's collection.)

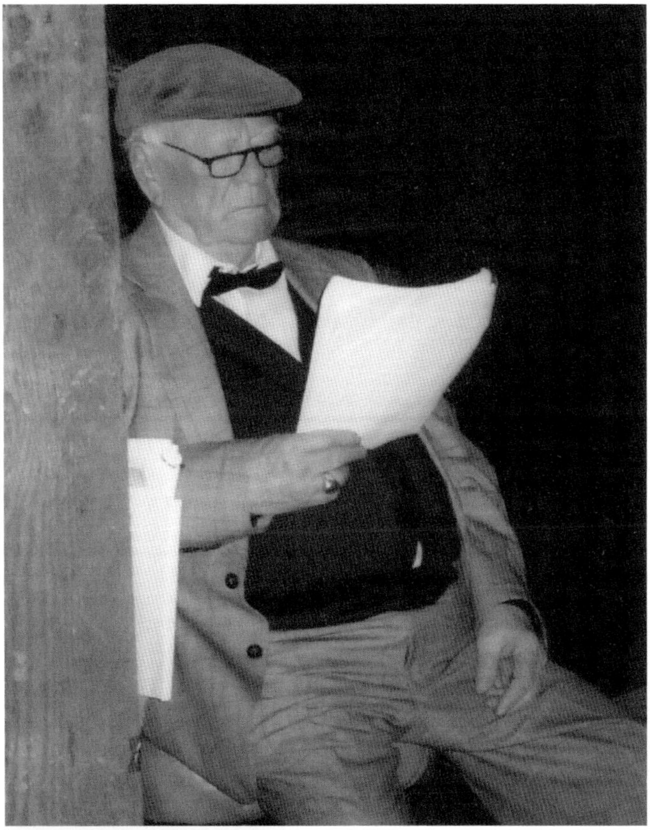

Fritz Kahl
Fritz Kahl arrived at burgeoning Marfa Airfield in 1943 to instruct trainee pilots. Later, he ran Marfa's airport for 22 years. He was twice elected mayor (1992–1998) and was responsible for bringing job-providing, but controversial, tomato farms to the area. He married Georgie Lee Evans, a rancher's daughter, in 1944. At age 79, he acted in *Our Town*, utilizing his deep voice and commanding presence. He died in 2004, aged 82. (Courtesy of Georgia Lee Kahl.)

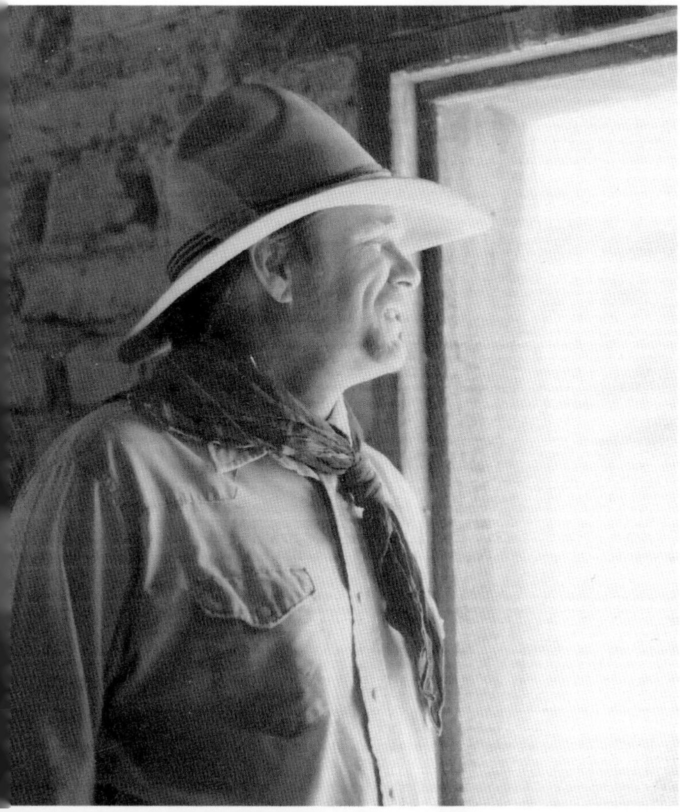

David Alloway
David Alloway's natural affinity with the desert was evident when he guided bus tours around the Big Bend Ranch State Park. He later started popular wilderness survival courses and wrote a best-selling book. Leaving Texas Parks and Wildlife Department to start his own business, he injured his foot but delayed going to the hospital until too late. He died of a severe infection exacerbated by diabetes on March 3, 2003, aged 45. (Courtesy of the Alloway family.)

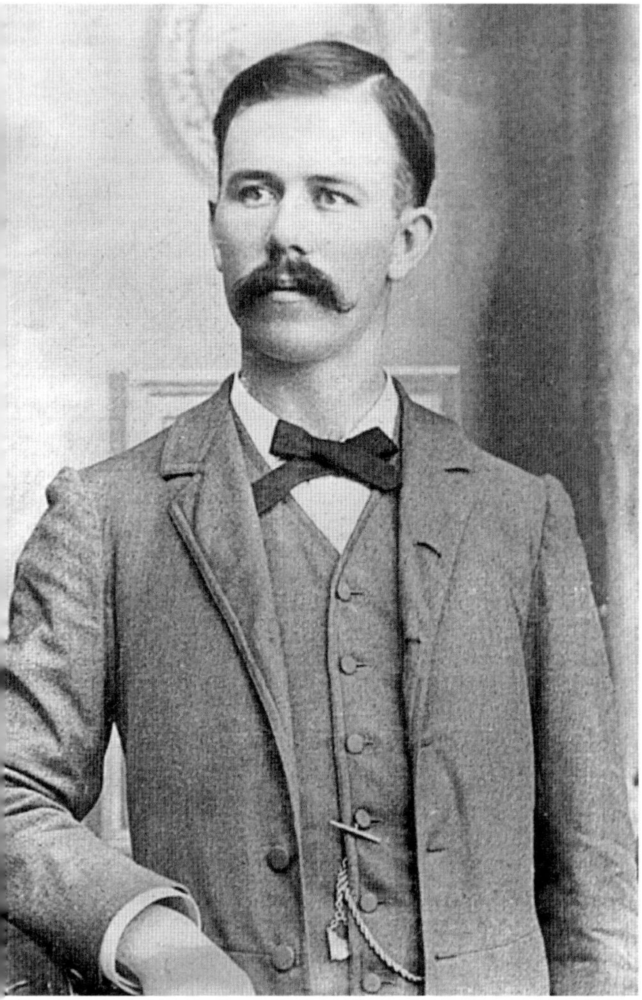

Wigfall Van Sickle

Wigfall Van Sickle arrived in Alpine in 1885 to teach school. While teaching, he studied law and gained admission to the Texas bar. He was appointed county judge of Brewster County and was twice elected to the state legislature. His oratorical skill and brazen tactics won him unexpected courtroom victories, even using chopped onions to induce tears by his client and sway the jury's judgment.

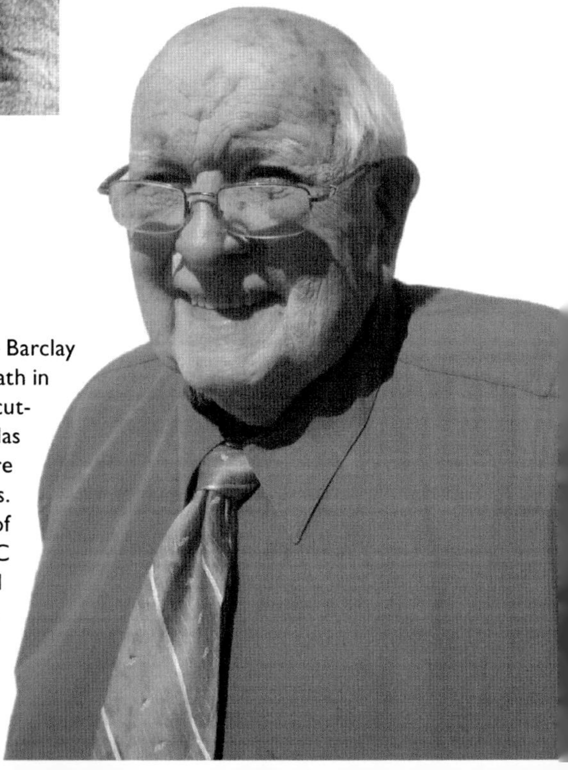

Mike Barclay

About 100 years after Van Sickle, Mike Barclay practiced law for 54 years until his death in 2013 at age 83. He learned about the cut-and-thrust of courtroom sparring in Dallas in the 1960s. He was an impressive figure with his bulky stature and ever-alert eyes. An admirer of the courtroom style of Rumpole of the Bailey, from the BBC series of the same name, Barclay used courtroom theatrics to his advantage. (Author's collection.)

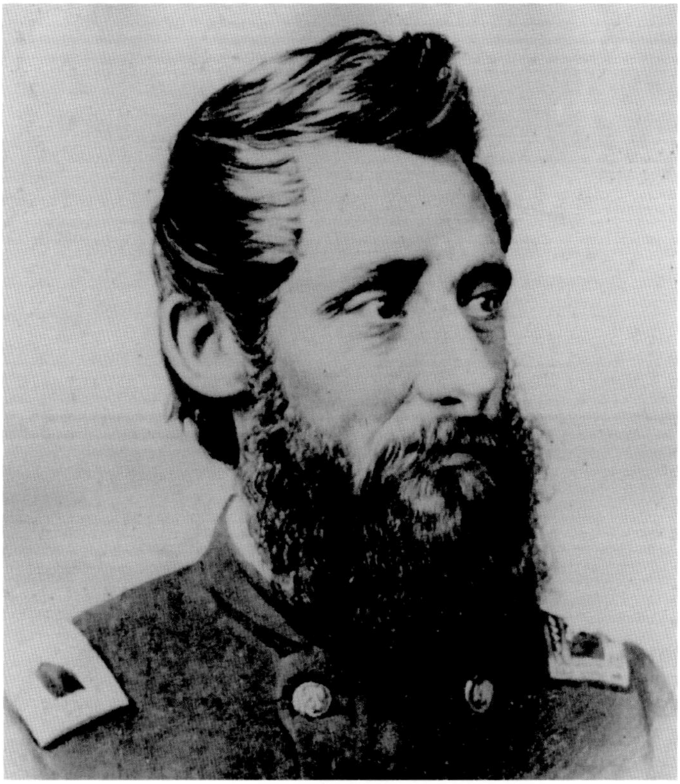

Benjamin Henry Grierson

Benjamin Henry Grierson was born in Pittsburgh in 1826 and was raised in Ohio. At age of eight, he suffered a near-fatal accident when a horse kicked him. He later became a music teacher and bandleader in Illinois. There, in 1854, he married Alice Kirk; the couple had seven children, four of whom survived to adulthood.

The horse accident and the early career in music notwithstanding, Grierson joined the 6th Illinois Cavalry when the Civil War broke out. Promoted to colonel of the regiment, in 1863, he led a successful raid behind the defenses of Vicksburg from LaGrange, Tennessee, to Baton Rouge, Louisiana. Toward the war's end, he had some resounding victories while leading two cavalry brigades, making him a Union hero and causing his promotion to the rank of brevet major general.

After the war, Grierson decided to remain in the regular Army and was appointed colonel with the responsibility of organizing the 10th US Cavalry, composed of black enlisted men and white officers. He had no West Point training, making him suspect to fellow officers, and his superior officer, General Sheridan, did not share his loyalty to his black troops. On top of those traits, some despised his evenhanded treatment toward Native Americans.

In 1878, he was posted to the Pecos District of West Texas, with the main task of stopping Indian raids against local settlers and travelers along the westward routes. His strategy against Victorio, the Apache chief, was to place his Buffalo soldiers at water sources and intercept the Indians when they approached. Two successful engagements at Quitman's Canyon and Rattlesnake Springs in 1880 validated this policy.

Victorio was forced into Mexico, where on October 14, 1880, at Tres Castillos in Chihuahua, he was killed by a Mexican Army detachment. Grierson moved his headquarters to Fort Davis in 1882. He paid tribute to his black troops' role in the campaign, complimenting their "genuine pluck and earnest activity." The music teacher had become a successful military commander. (Photograph by Kansas State Historical Society.)

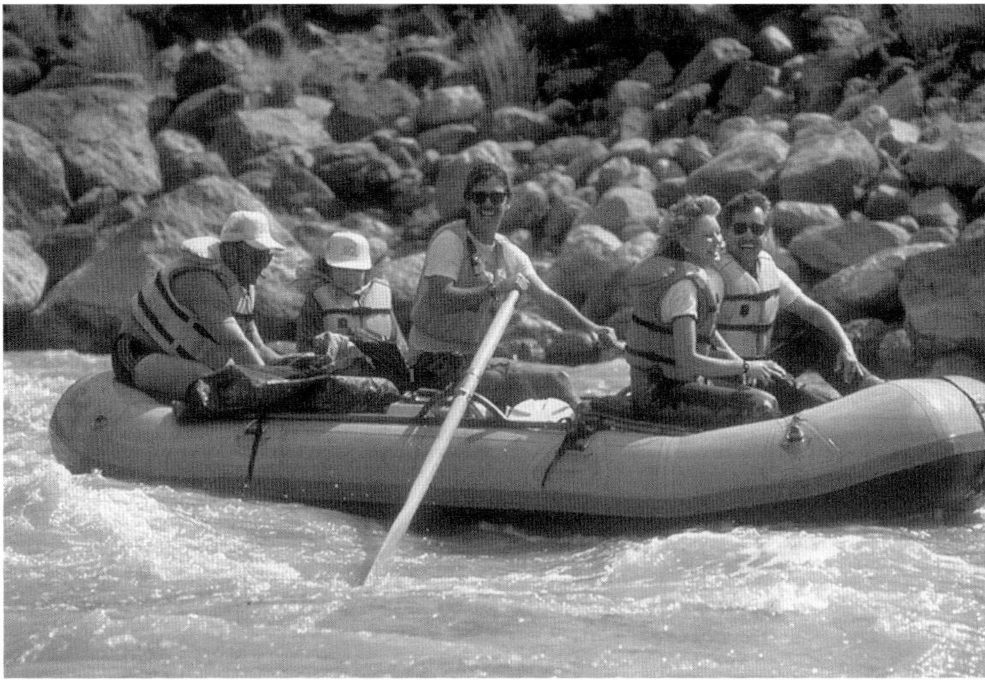

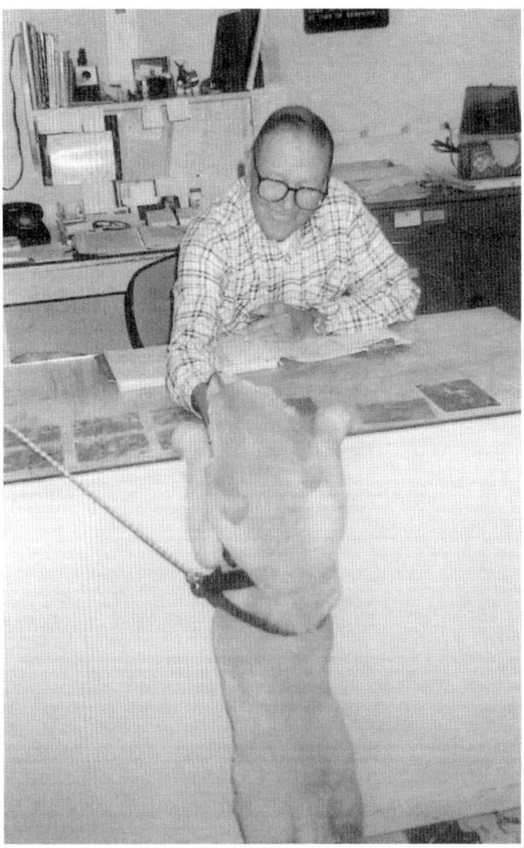

Mike Davidson
Following a 140-mile descent of the Rio Grande in the mid-1970s, Mike Davidson was hooked on river rafting. In 1976, with Steve Harris, he started Far Flung Adventures, the area's first river rafting company. Today, Mike Davidson is executive director of the area's tourism group, Visit Big Bend; director of the Trans-Pecos Water Trust; and a member of the Alpine City Council and of the Pinché Gringos band. (Courtesy of Texas Department of Transportation.)

C.W. "Charlie" Edwards
For someone who, over almost 50 years of practice, had been "stomped on, kicked, run over, gored, scratched, and bitten" by his patients, C.W. "Charlie" Edwards retained a sense of humor. He dedicated his memoir *Up to My Armpits* (2002) to his wife, daughters, and "all those cows I treated." Coming to Marfa in 1953 after war service, he stayed for 56 years, becoming a vital figure to the area's ranchers.

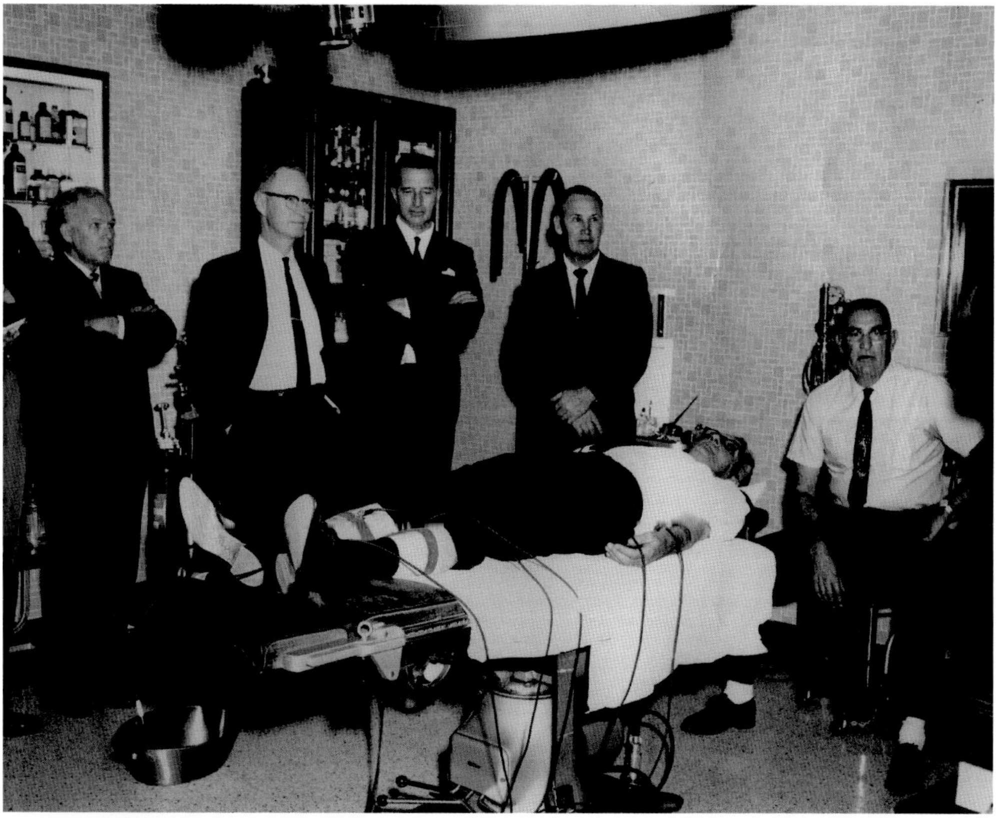

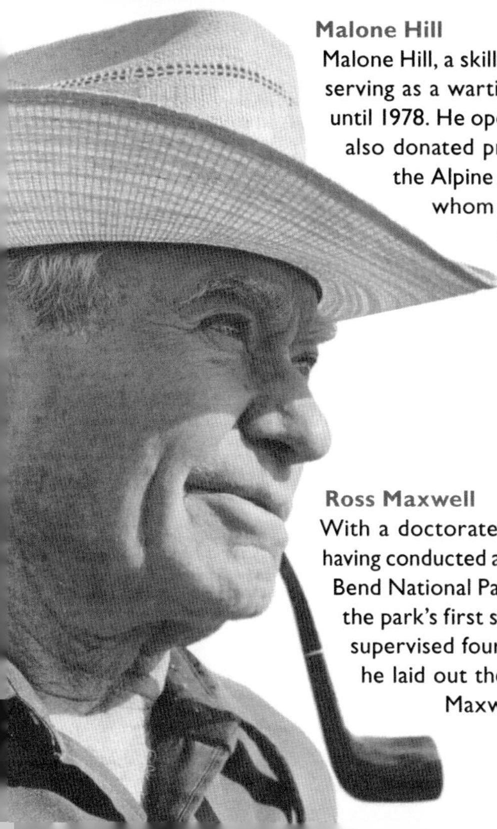

Malone Hill

Malone Hill, a skillful young surgeon, arrived in Alpine in 1937. After serving as a wartime surgeon, he returned to Alpine for 42 years until 1978. He opened a small clinic with his colleague Dr. Jeter and also donated property to the people of Alpine, which became the Alpine Public Library. He married Frances Morelock, by whom he had two sons. Here he is pictured (far left) observing a patient.

Ross Maxwell

With a doctorate in geology from Northwestern University and having conducted a geological survey in what was soon to become Big Bend National Park, Ross Maxwell was a good choice to be named the park's first superintendent. He served from 1944 to 1952. He supervised four employees (today's total is just under 100), and he laid out the route of the most scenic road in the park, the Maxwell Scenic Drive. (Photograph by Blair Pittman.)

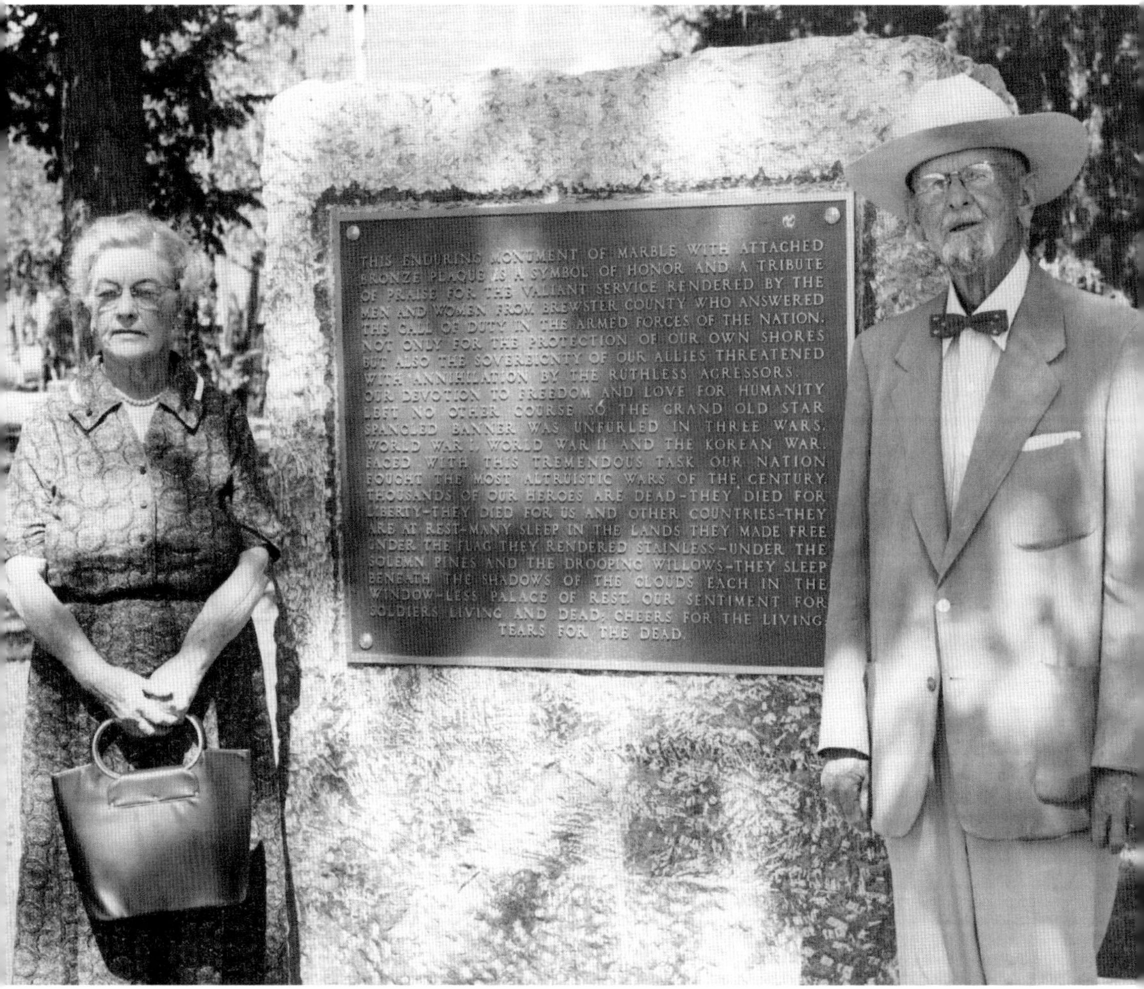

Dr. Benjamin Franklin Berkeley

Dr. Benjamin Franklin Berkeley arrived in Alpine at the turn of the 20th century. He immediately opened a medical practice and was subsequently appointed doctor on the Southern Pacific Railroad. In 1906, he helped establish a new bank, Alpine State Bank and later served as president.

On other fronts, he established the Alpine Commercial Club, which became the Alpine Chamber of Commerce. He was Alpine's first mayor (1917). As such, he oversaw an extensive list of civic improvements (water, sewer, and street paving) and all new projects. He served eight years as state senator. He was an early and effective supporter of the Big Bend National Park idea.

He married Clara Dugat, pictured here, in 1903, who bore him two children. After quitting public life, ever active, he got involved in numerous community groups, like the Rotary Club, the Big Bend Museum, and the Mitre Peak Girl Scout Camp. Even in his eighties, he would take morning strolls through downtown Alpine, wearing an old-fashioned frock coat, ready to chat with anyone. A large stone block outside the Alpine Chamber of Commerce building serves as a testimonial to this tireless community leader.

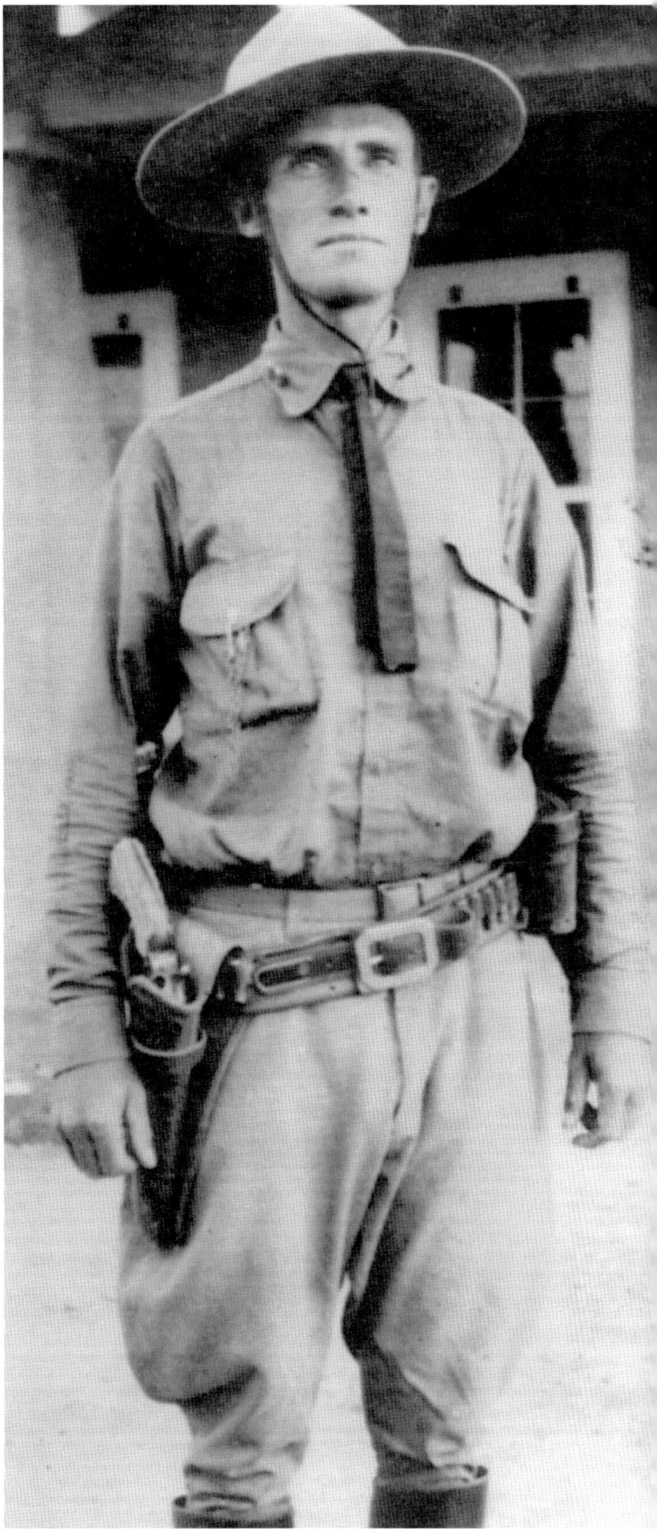

Captain Matlack

The year 1919 was a busy one along the Mexican border. The Mexican Revolution was still in full swing and violent incidents along the border were common. Aerial patrols by DeHaviland biplanes routinely flew along the border, lending support to the cavalry on the ground. In August 1919, one plane went off course and crash-landed in Mexico. It is probable that the navigator followed the Rio Conchos believing it to be the Rio Grande, thereby flying into Mexico instead of alongside it.

A ransom note from local Mexican bandit Jesus Rentéria, who had a steel hook in place of his left hand, was received shortly afterwards by a storekeeper, Mr. Kilpatrick, at Candelaria on the United States side of the border. Fifteen-thousand dollars was demanded for the safe return of the two American flyers, Peterson and Davis. When word of the demand was received by local ranchers at their annual camp meeting at Bloys Encampment near Fort Davis, the amount was raised within five minutes from five ranchers.

Captain Matlack, from the military post at Camp Marfa, was designated to take the ransom money, hand it over, and secure the release of the two airmen. The following day, early in the morning, Captain Matlack crossed the Rio Grande at Candelaria to the Mexican village of San Antonio del Bravo, the meeting place for the handover.

Matlack gave half the sum, and Peterson was released and got on the back of Matlack's horse for the trip to the river. Coming back for Davis, however, Matlack overheard in the darkness some bandits talking about killing the gringos, indicating they were not going to honor the second part of the handover. So anticipating this move, instead of handing over the second half of the ransom, he pulled a gun on them while Davis jumped on the back of his horse. Together, they recrossed the Rio Grande to the United States side. His alert ears and quick thinking saved $7,500. (Courtesy of Glenn Justice.)

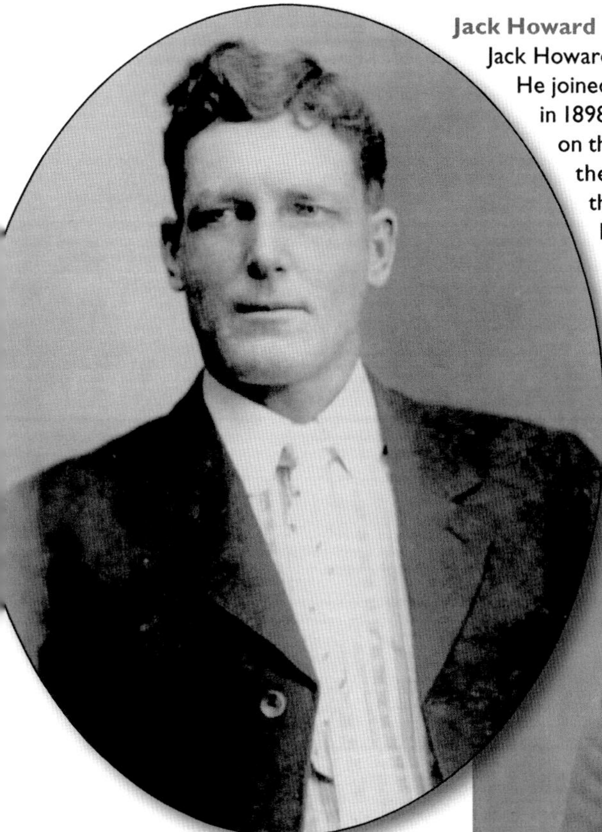

Jack Howard
Jack Howard, titled English immigrant, came to Texas in 1882. He joined Roosevelt's Rough Riders and saw action in Cuba in 1898. Later, he became a mounted inspector of customs on the Mexican border. For 12 years, Howard patrolled the border. With his partner Sitters, he captured the notorious Mexican outlaw Chico Cano in 1913. Escorting Cano in handcuffs, Howard's patrol was ambushed, and Howard was shot. He died two days later. (Courtesy of Glenn Justice.)

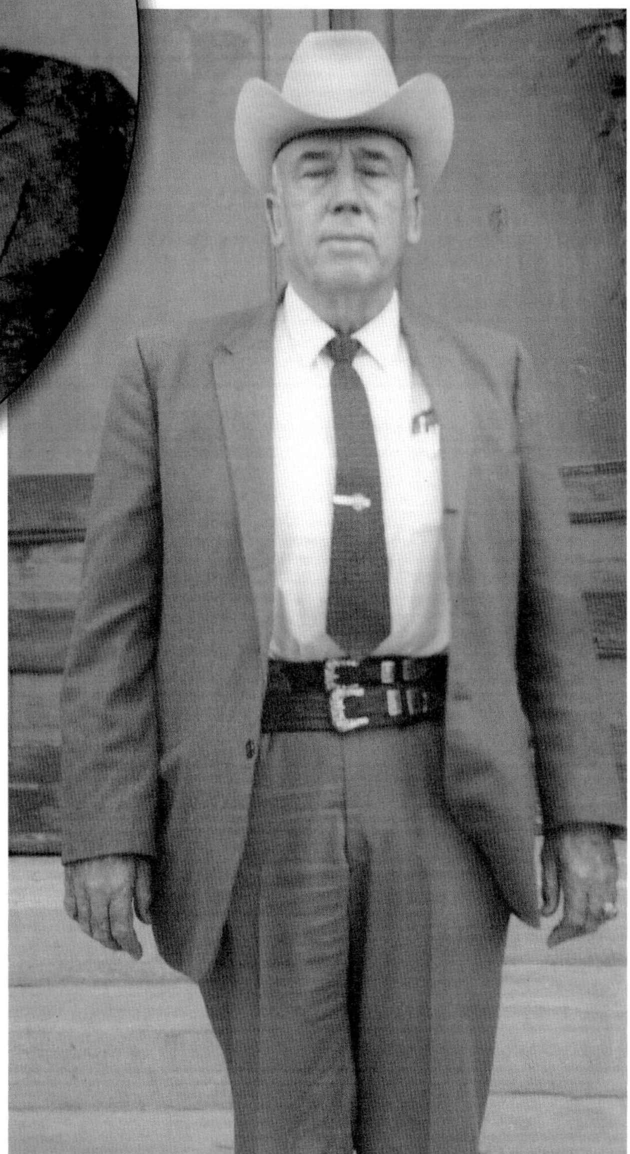

Arthur Hill
He started work on a horse and ended in a vehicle. Arthur Hill (born in 1909) served 33 years in the Texas Department of Public Safety; 27 of those years were as a Texas Ranger, a record. He did not agree with some of the changes taking place within the Texas Rangers, but he enforced them and abided by them as long as he was a ranger.

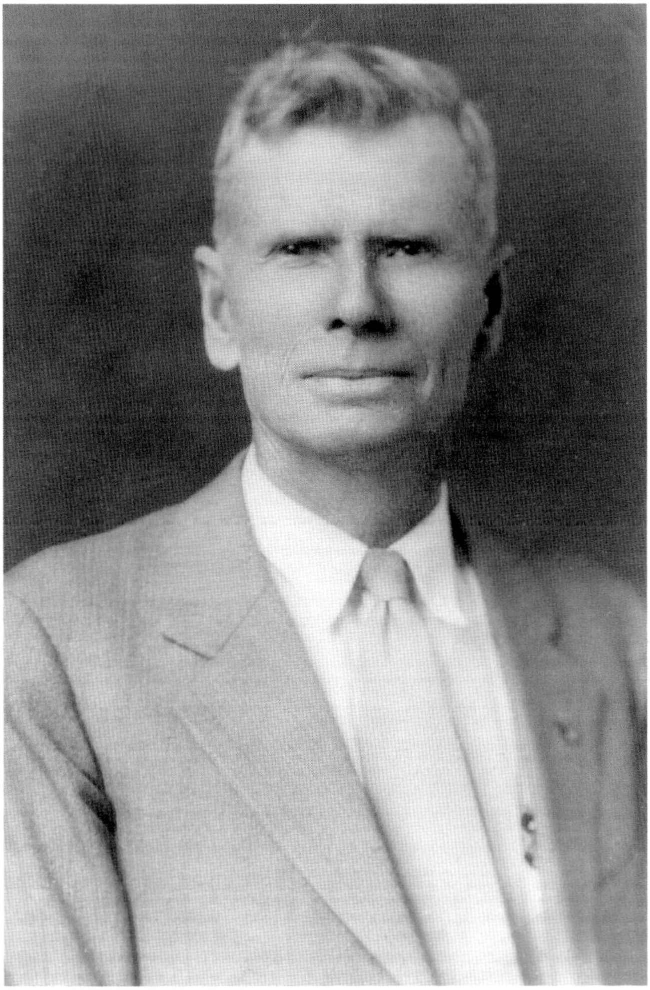

E.E. Townsend

E.E. Townsend once stated, "When I first drifted into the Alpine country back in the early nineties of the last century, I found a lot of good fellows scattered around here. Alpine was a little 'Cowtown' spraddled across the railroad tracks as uncertain in conformity as a pair of ragged overalls." This facility with words is one reason that E.E. Townsend was successful as a proponent of the Big Bend National Park.

Born in Colorado County, Texas, in 1871, the third of eight children, Townsend was mainly homeschooled. At age 17, he joined the Texas Rangers stating he was 21. Two years later, he enlisted in the US Customs Service as a mounted inspector based in Presidio, which gave him a firsthand experience of the territory. In 1895, he met and married Alice "Allie" Jones, with whom he rode on horseback over 1,000 miles before their daughter, Margaret, was born.

After a second stint with the Texas Rangers, he resigned and took a job as ranch manager for 16 years. He moved to Alpine in 1916, was elected sheriff of Brewster County for three terms, and then as state representative in 1932. It was in this capacity that he was able to help realize his dream, stated when he was a customs inspector, of "saving the wilderness from civilization."

Within two years, the Texas legislature voted to set aside land for a future Texas state park along the Rio Grande, first named Texas Canyons State Park, later Big Bend State Park. Townsend next worked with Fort Worth publisher Amon Carter to promote the Big Bend National Park, which finally opened to the public in 1944, earning Townsend the accolade of "father of the Big Bend."

Felix Valenzuela

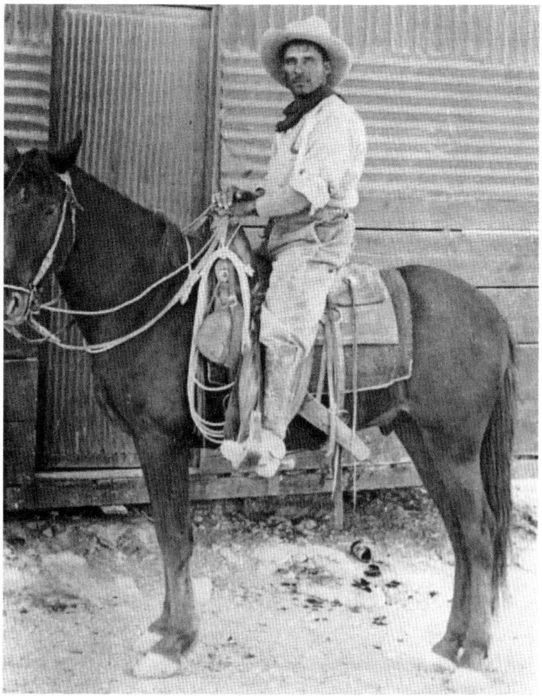

Felix Valenzuela, employee at the Chisos Mine and Brewster County constable, was traveling with Justice of the Peace R.L. Cartlidge, manager of the mine, on June 19, 1938. They stopped a car they suspected of carrying illegal liquor, and the car driver shot 56-year-old Valenzuela and then escaped into Mexico. It was unusual in those days for a Hispanic to be in law enforcement. In 1998, a resolution to honor the memory of Felix was passed by Brewster County.

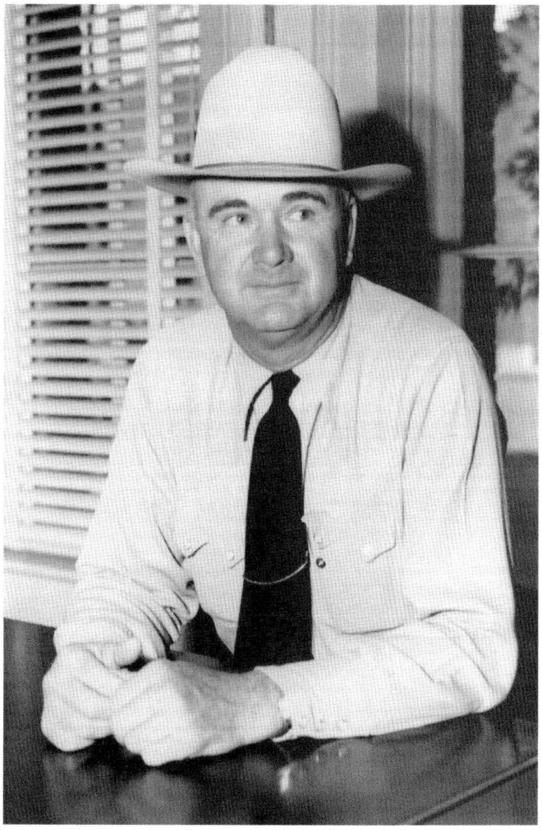

Jim Skinner

Jim Skinner arrived in Brewster County in 1940. He married Lanell Sansom and they had one son, Jim S. Skinner II. He was the longest tenured sheriff in Brewster County's history (1949–1965). A man known for sticking to his word, he is remembered also for enforcing his own laws. Young men who persisted in wearing their hats at dances were removed from the dance floor to jail. During the Vietnam War years, his calm demeanor took care of potentially violent cases, and he also sometimes revealed a compassionate side.

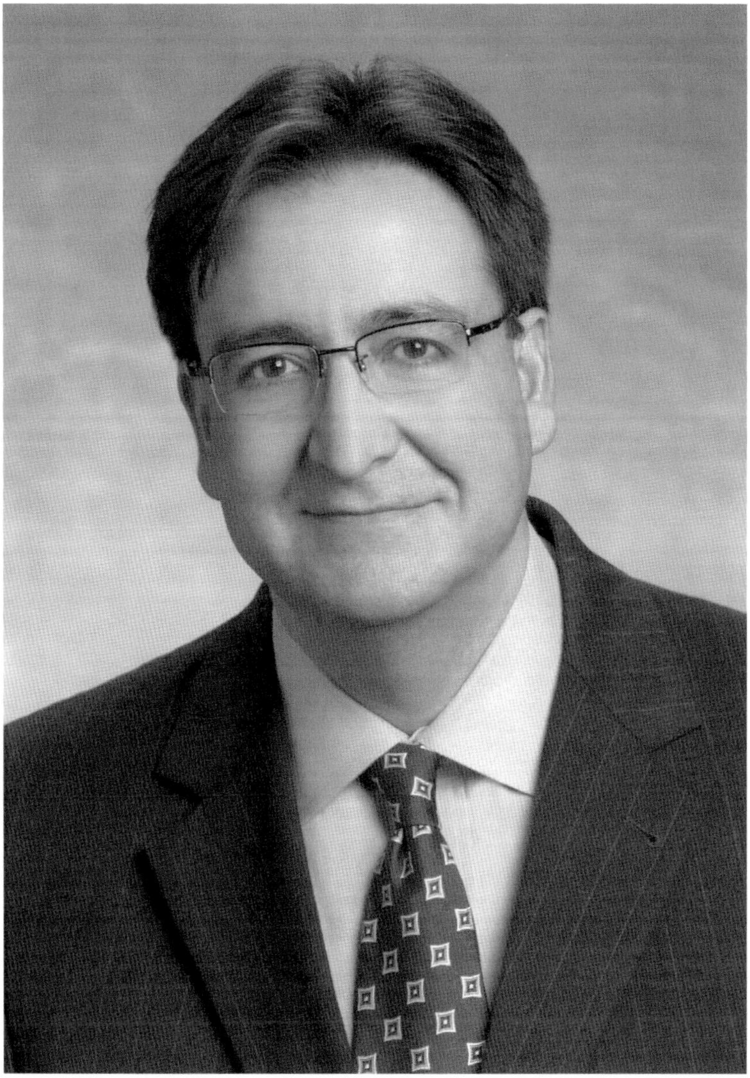

The Gallego Family

The Gallego family has lived in Alpine since the first years of the 20th century; it is a large family, and none is better known. The family's achievements include starting (in 1934) and operating for many years the popular Green Café on Alpine's south side, breaking through the school discrimination barrier, and producing the area's most successful state politician, who is now a Congressman in Washington, DC, for Texas's 23rd Congressional District.

When Pete A. Gallego Jr. returned from World War II, he found his hometown little changed. Old prejudices prevailed, and the Hispanic population was the loser. Determined to change discrimination against Hispanics in the school system, a feeling shared equally by his wife, Elena, Pete got elected to the school board in 1959. By 1970, after a period of harassment, desegregation was ended.

Born in 1961, Pete P. Gallego (pictured), the youngest of three children, grew up in Alpine. In 1982, he gained his bachelor's in political science from Sul Ross and, in 1985, he received his doctorate of law degree in Austin. Since 1991, he served in the Texas House of Representatives. Among other achievements benefitting Alpine, he was responsible for obtaining $110 million for improvements to Sul Ross.

He married Maria Elena Ramon in 1991, and they have a son named Nicholas.

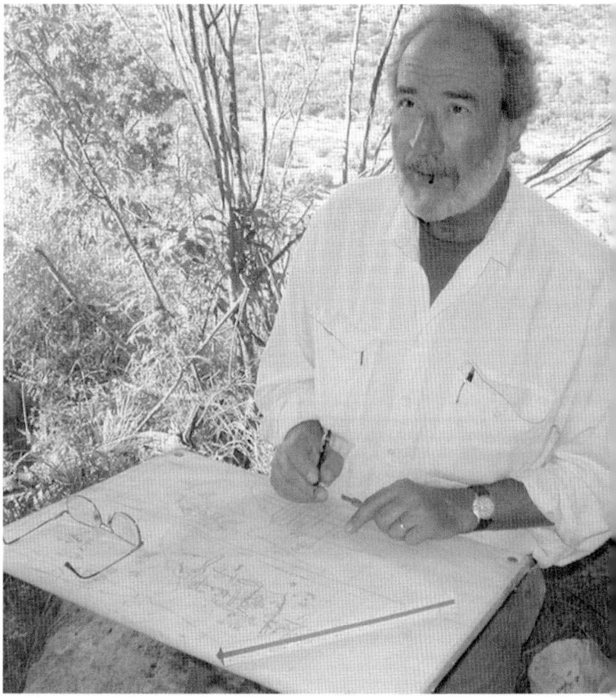

Robert J. Mallouf
Archeological research and preservation work over 40 years has been the professional career achievement of Robert J. Mallouf. Having studied in Austin, Berkeley, and Cairo, Egypt, he later became Texas State Archeologist from 1981 to 1995 and, subsequently, director of Center of Big Bend Studies and assistant professor of anthropology at Sul Ross State University.

He has authored numerous professional publications and received several Texas awards, including the Texas Award for Historic Preservation. Among the local sites where he has made scientific exploration are the Tall Rock Shelter, the Wolf Den Cave, and the Lykes-Duncan Site, the oldest (8,500–9,000 BC) known in the region. Mallouf and his son Parker reside in Alpine. (Both, courtesy of Center for Big Bend Studies, Sul Ross State University.)

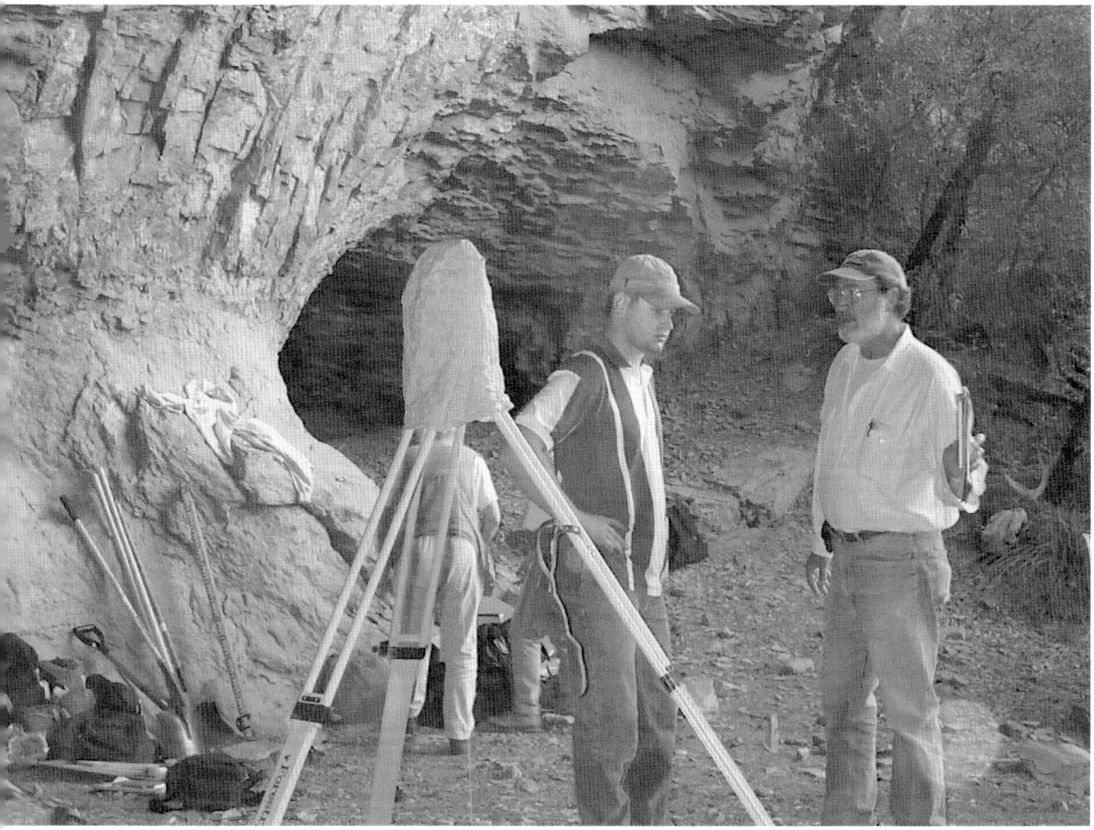

CHAPTER EIGHT

Others

Perhaps it is the frontier mentality or the wide open spaces, or living on the Mexican border, but the Big Bend and Davis Mountains region sure breeds some characters. Where else would the residents elect a beer-drinking goat as mayor? Where else would a whole population turn out for the burial of an elderly woman who traveled the roads of the region with a burro, sleeping at night by the side of the road?

Victorio, the Apache Mescalero Indian chief, caused the US military a few problems for a while until driven into Mexico, where he was killed by a Mexican army detachment. A complimentary epitaph adorns the wall of the museum in Fort Davis, the headquarters of the troops pursuing him, and states the followings: "The greatest commander, white or red, who roamed these plains."

Volunteerism is active in the region and not just the Relay for Life annual event for cancer survivors. Individuals, often shunning publicity, apply themselves to situations that are important to them, like helping Mexican neighbors (Cynta de Narvaez, Teda Neill), feeding the hungry (Lupe Rubio), or keeping Alpine clean and green (Edie Elfring). The husband-wife team of Hal and Mary Flanders, having retired to Alpine, both made a huge difference as volunteers. Hal focused on recycling; Mary founded a food cooperative.

Age seems to be no setback to achievement here. Pilot George Vose, at age 91, is still licensed to fly, and the clear skies around Alpine are a constant encouragement to climb onboard his plane and take off. By contrast, many years earlier, a young black woman named Carrie Miller arrived in Fort Davis as nanny to a family from Houston vacationing in West Texas. When she died in 1954, her previous employers, the affluent families of Fort Davis, packed the church at her memorial service, acknowledging that she had "standards beyond compare."

Thanks to a local rancher who formed a semiprofessional team and built a jewel of a field to play on, baseball gained Alpine recognition in the 1940s and the 1950s. The all-too-short life of the Alpine Cowboys is the sort of story to warm the heart and is admirably recalled in D.G. Stout's book *The Amazing Tale of Mr. Herbert and His Fabulous Alpine Cowboys Baseball Club.* A young player on the team, Norm Cash, went on to play for 17 years in the major leagues, winning the American League batting title in 1961 and hitting a career total of 377 home runs.

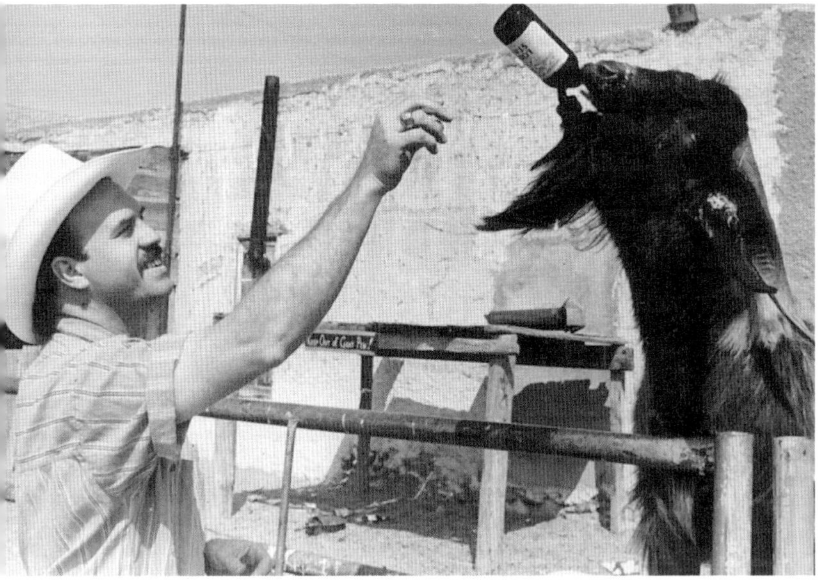

Clay Henry
In the old Lajitas Trading Post, Clay Henry, a goat residing in a pen outside the store, fit right in. Named mayor of Lajitas by the local residents, Clay Henry, pictured here with Bill Ivey, loved Lone Star beer, which he would drink straight from the bottle.

In 2003, tragedy struck. A visitor who was upset that the goat was drinking on a Sunday castrated Clay Henry. (Courtesy of Bill Ivey.)

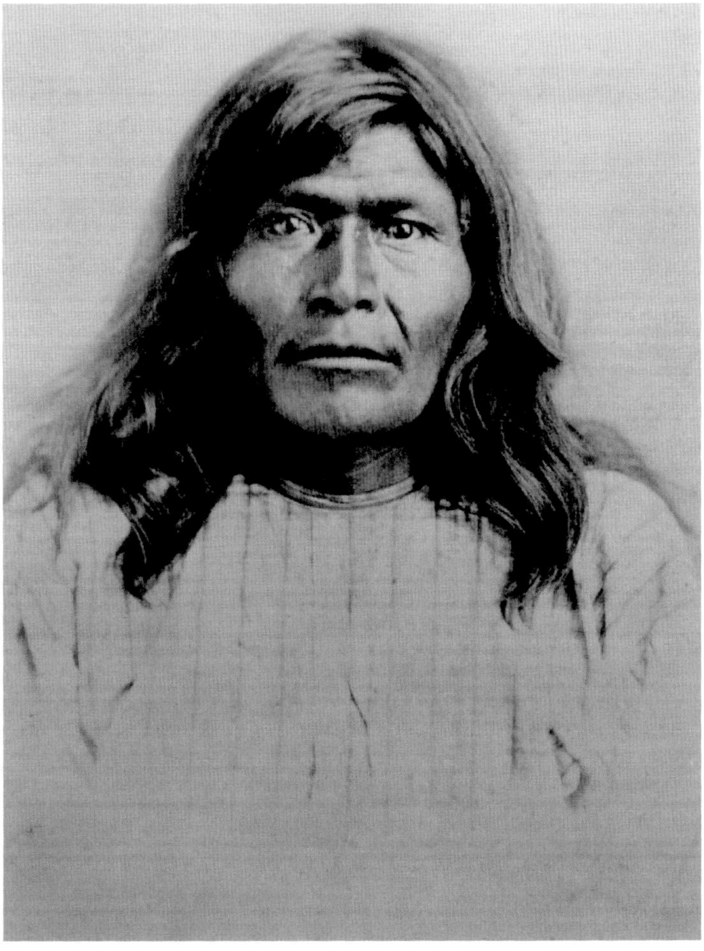

Victorio
In the late 1870s, the Mescalero and Apache Indians coming off their reservation in Arizona, led by Victorio, were keeping Colonel Grierson's troops busy. Gradually, Victorio was forced across the Rio Grande to Mexico, where, in 1880, he was killed at Tres Castillos, Chihuahua. An epitaph in the museum at Fort Davis National Historic Site pays tribute to him as follows: "The greatest commander, white or red, who roamed these plains." (W.W. Mills, El Paso politician.) This image is believed to be of Victorio; however, the identification is uncertain. (Courtesy of Anthropological Archives, Smithsonian Institution.)

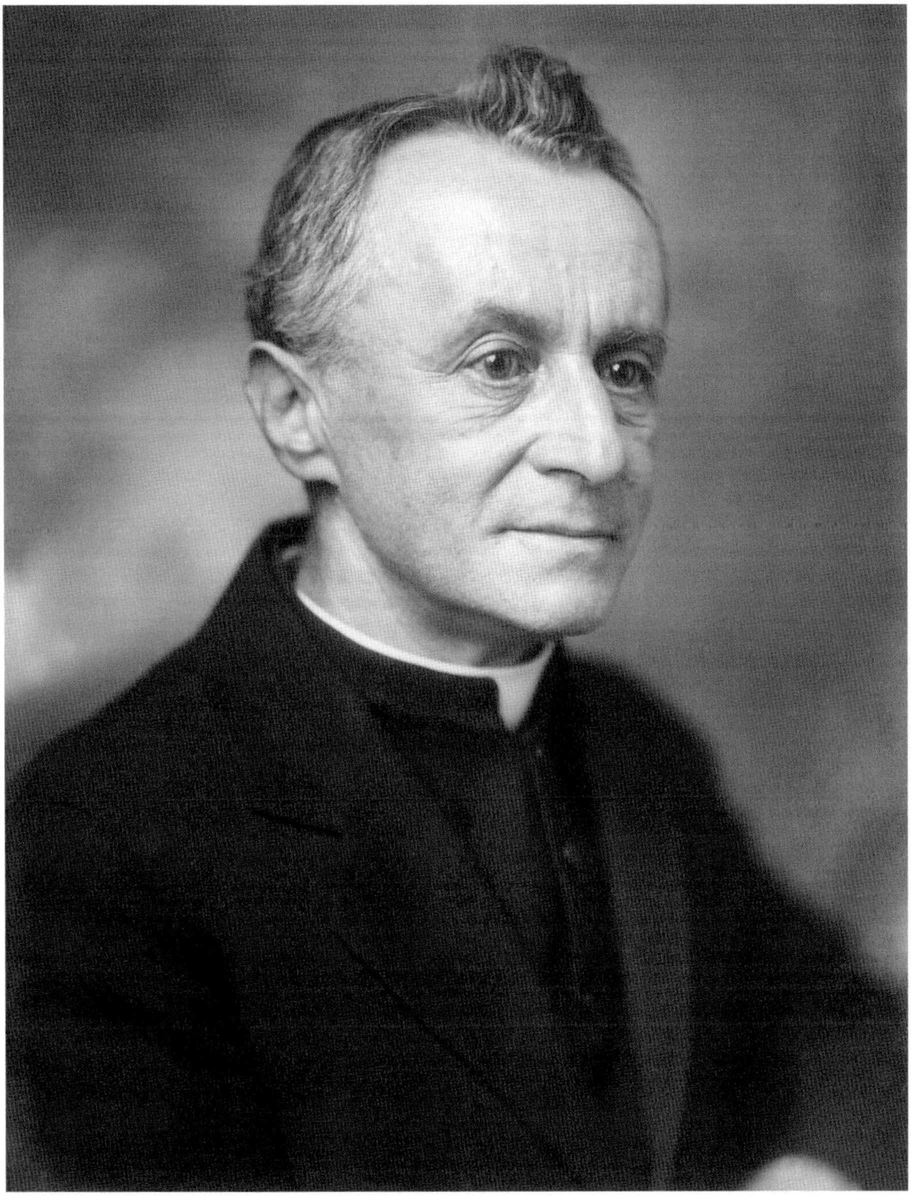

Nicholas Brocadus Eeken

Nicholas Brocadus Eeken, who was born in Holland, arrived in the United States in 1887 and was ordained in the Carmelite Order. Seeking a dryer climate, he came to Fort Davis in late 1895. His territory as a circuit priest encompassed 17,800 miles, and he covered it by mule, on horseback, by buggy and, finally, in a Model T Ford.

For 37 years, he administered St. Joseph's Catholic Church in Fort Davis. He moved to a retirement home in El Paso in 1932 but, missing the familiarity of Fort Davis, returned to lodgings there. The county had to pay toward his lodging expenses since he had given his life savings of $4,000 toward the construction cost of St. Joseph's.

He died in 1941. The small community of Brogardo, near Balmorhea, is named after this diligent and gentle priest.

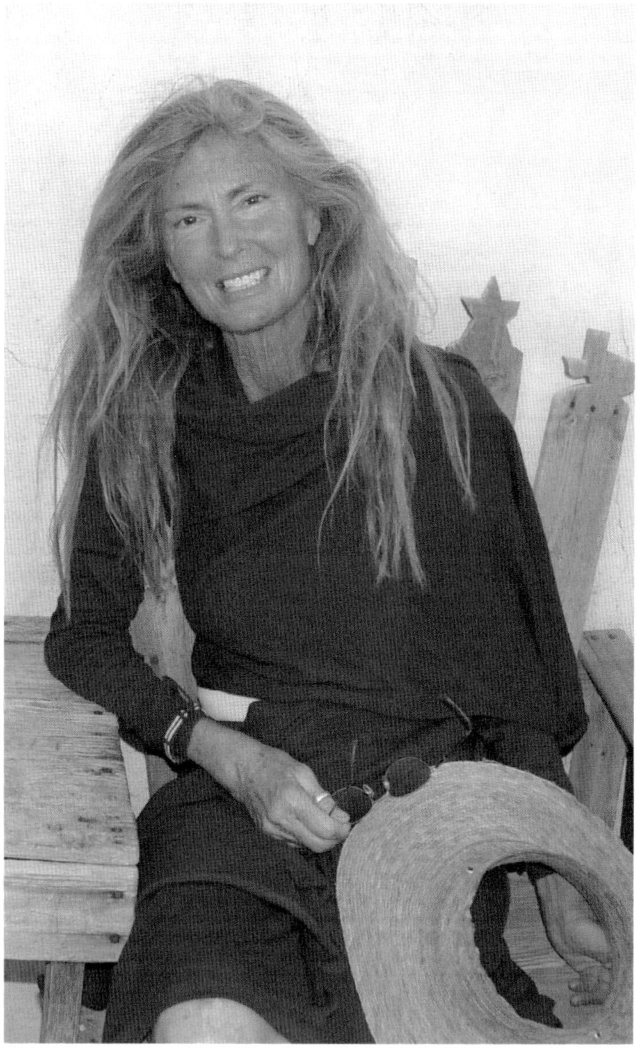

Cynta de Narvaez

Leaving the socialite life in Manhattan in 1978, Cynta sent herself to St. John's College in Santa Fe where she graduated in the great books program in 1983. Next, she learned how to be a river guide in the Grand Canyon and other Western rivers, including the Rio Grande (1991). She broke off to gain a second degree in quaternary studies (four sciences) in Arizona, before returning to Terlingua for good in 1996.

Since then, in addition to being a local guide, she has acted as the historian of Terlingua ghost town. Drawing memories from the elderly Hispanic families, she staged two miners' reunions, in 2005 and 2008, bringing together descendants of those who had worked in the Terlingua mine when it was active in the early 1900s.

She often crossed the Rio Grande into Mexico, knowing the shared affinity of people living on both banks of the river. Following the closing of the unofficial border crossings to the Mexican villages, and their disastrous loss of tourism income, she started teaching the Mexican women to earn alternative income through quilting, including supplying sewing machines. Enormously time consuming in view of the lengthy travel time needed to reach these villages, Cynta de Narvaez persevered. She brought back quilts to sell in Alpine, and the villagers benefitted. Now, surprisingly, one of the villages, Boquillas, is accessible again by boat from the Big Bend National Park. (Photograph by Sue Rife, Rife Photography.)

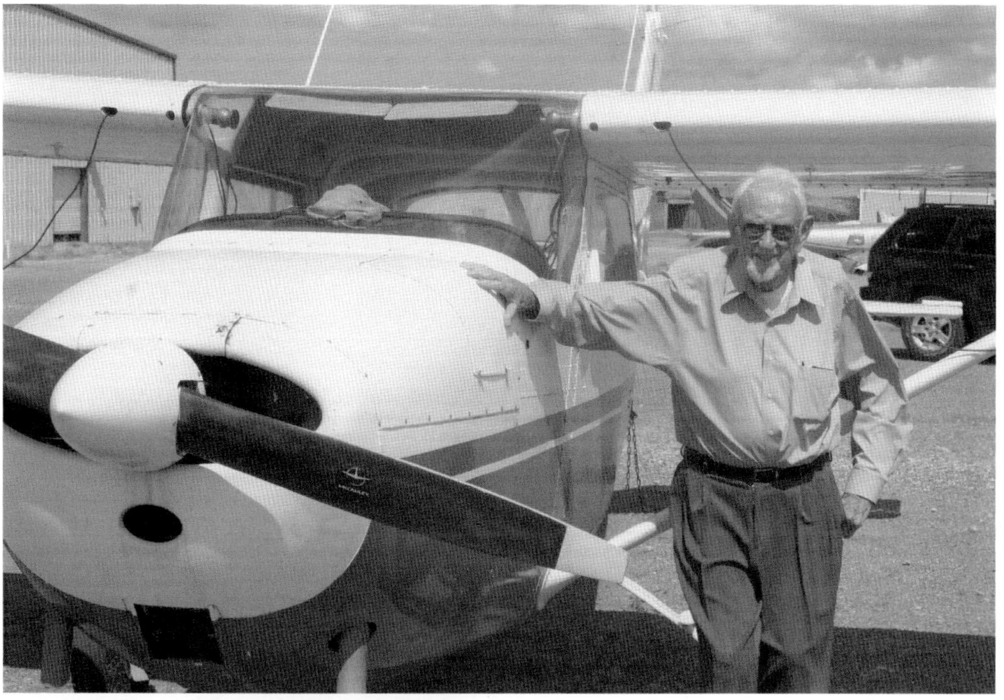

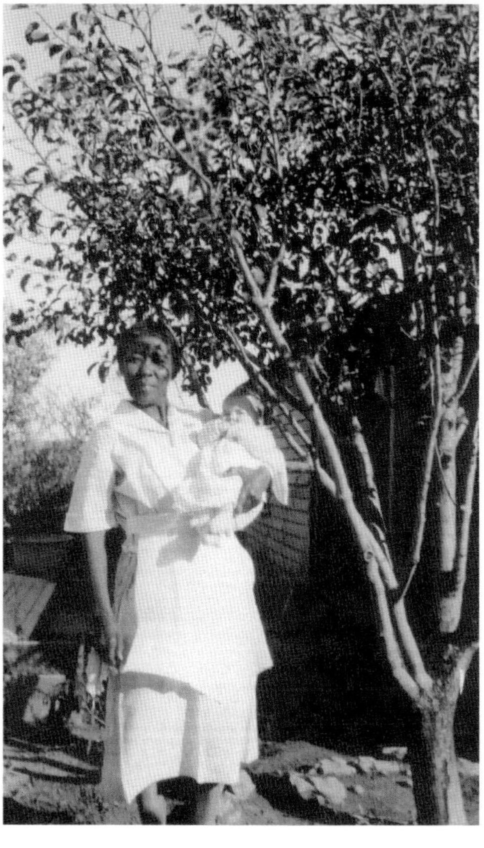

George Vose

George Vose took his first flight in 1937 in Maine. In 1943, he obtained a pilot instructor's license. His chosen career field was in bone metabolism, but his passion was flying. Moving to Denton, Texas, he tested 2,500 students for private and commercial flying; he moved further west to Alpine in 1976 and continues to fly, aged 91. To-date he has flown in excess of 24,000 hours, all on propeller craft. (Photograph by Harlan Gardner.)

Carrie Montgomery

Carrie Montgomery, a black nursemaid, arrived in Fort Davis in the late 1870s at the age of 14. She brought with her standards from the Old South and was employed by many prominent local families. Between 1906 and 1908, she taught at the Mexican school in Fort Davis. When she died in 1954, the Baptist church was filled with white families, who had come to show love and respect for a fine woman. (Courtesy of Kimball Miller.)

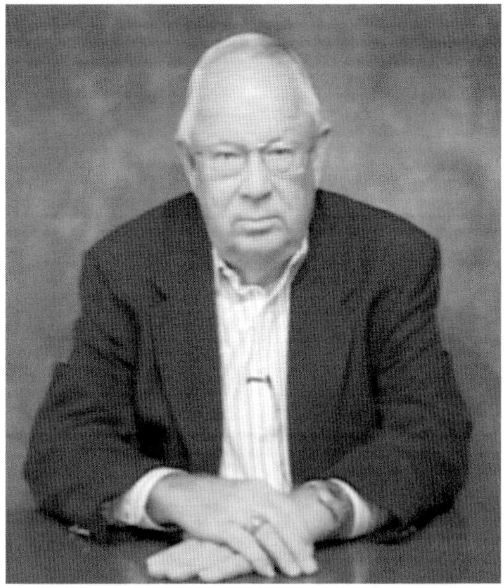

Travis Roberts

Travis Roberts from Marathon (born in 1937) graduated from Texas A&M University with a bachelor's degree in civil engineering and started a career as a consulting engineer and land surveyor. Aided by the invaluable resources of the archives at Sul Ross, he is also the region's preeminent historian. He serves on innumerable academic, preservation, and tourism boards and was named Volunteer of the Year in 2010 by the Texas Historical Association. (Courtesy of Travis Roberts.)

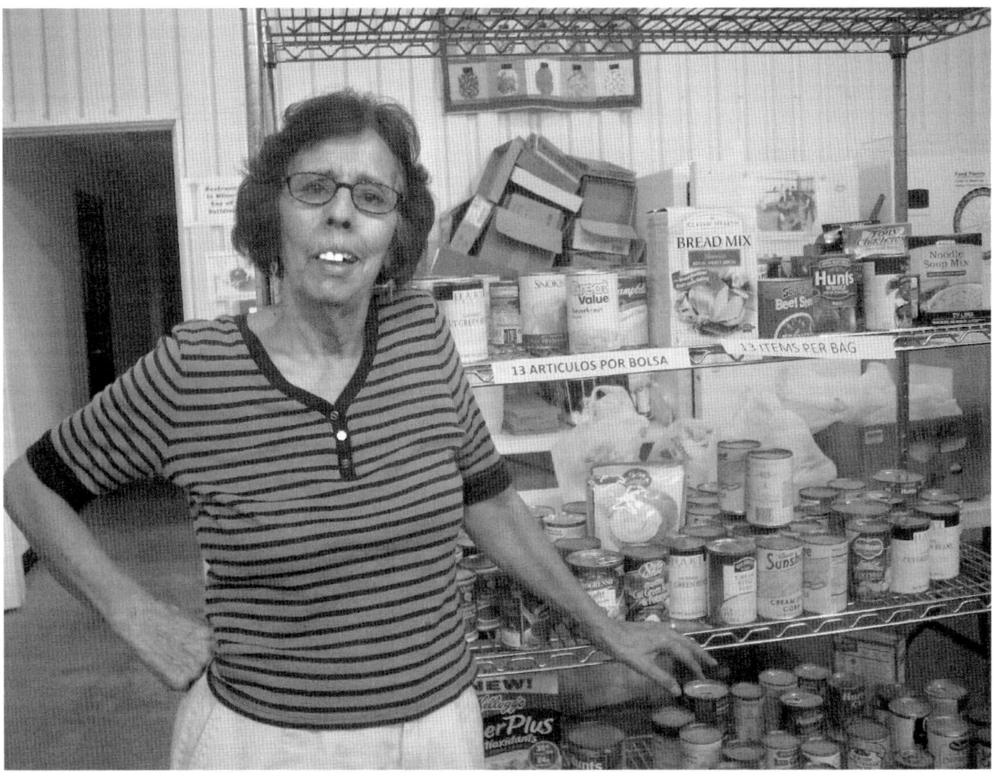

Lupe Granado

Lupe Granado grew up in Fort Davis and graduated from high school in 1968. She married Robert Rubio in 1972 and bore two sons, Jeremiah and Robert.

Twice honored as Volunteer of the Year by the chamber of commerce, she works with the Food Pantry, providing 200 to 300 meals weekly. "I like being with people" she says, and it only needs one look at her cheerful face to confirm this. (Photograph by Brenda Bell.)

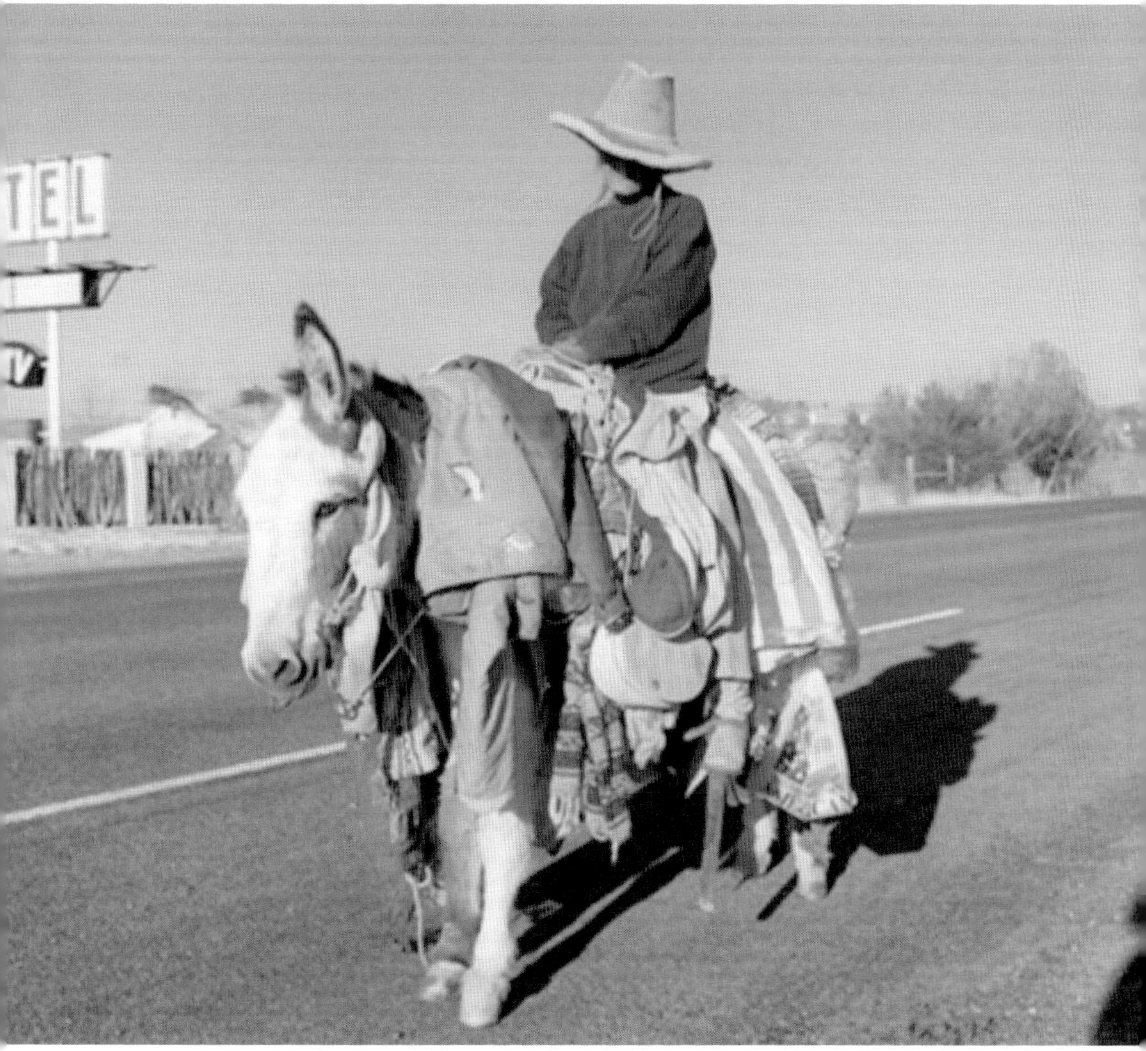

The Burro Lady
Terlingua residents have long had a reputation for independence and individuality, admired or suspect according to the observer. When a funeral took place in Terlingua's rocky, rustic cemetery in 2007, which attracted 100 persons, there had to be a reason.

The reason was the deceased, Judy Majers or "The Burro Lady," who had traveled the roads of West Texas for 10 years with solitary determination on her burro, earning her the admiration of Terlingua residents. She lived rough, throwing a tarp on the ground to sleep upon after tending to her burro. She resisted most attempts to start a conversation. She seemed determinedly solitary, valuing her privacy and independence. But who was she, and why was she on this solitary trek?

Her name was Judy Majers, and she died, aged 65, of natural causes. She was outside, near her burro, close to Sierra Blanca, at the extreme edge of her circuit. At her funeral, her five children, living in four different states, turned up. One, her oldest, who lives in California, shook his head, saying, "I've been looking for her for five years, and now I've found her."

Why she followed this lifestyle, no one ever found out. She was very sparing with words and usually indicated a strong preference to be left alone. The community respected this, even the state highway patrolmen, who checked that she was alright and then moved on. (Photograph by James H. Evans.)

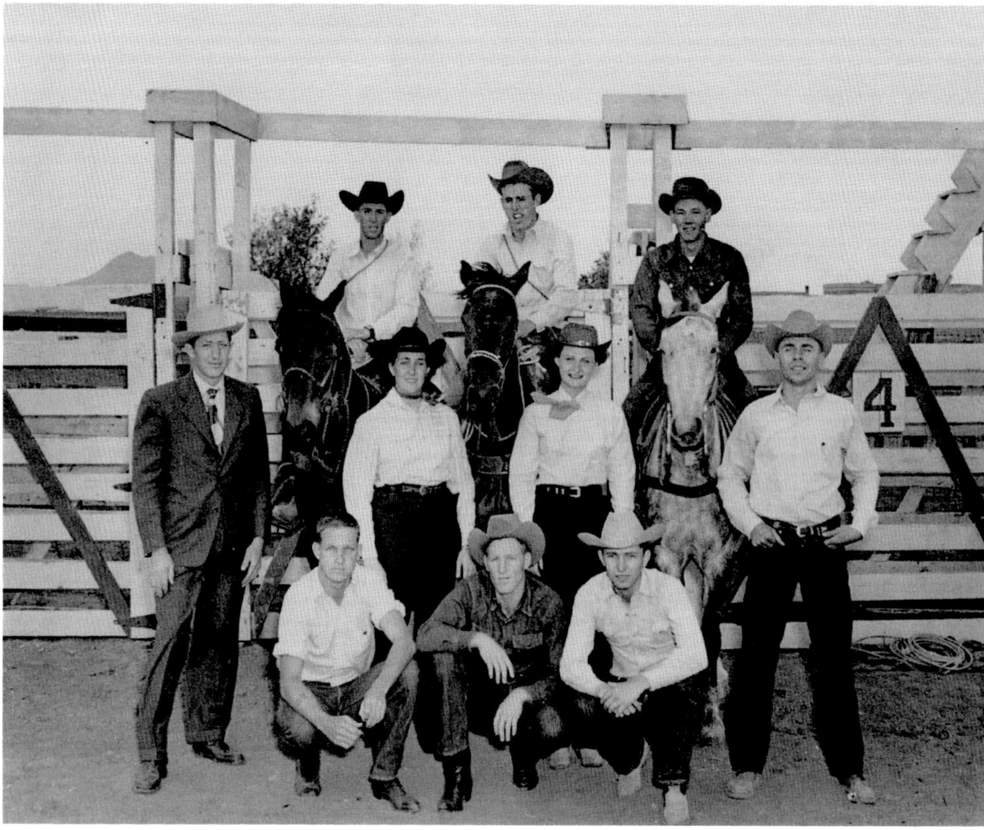

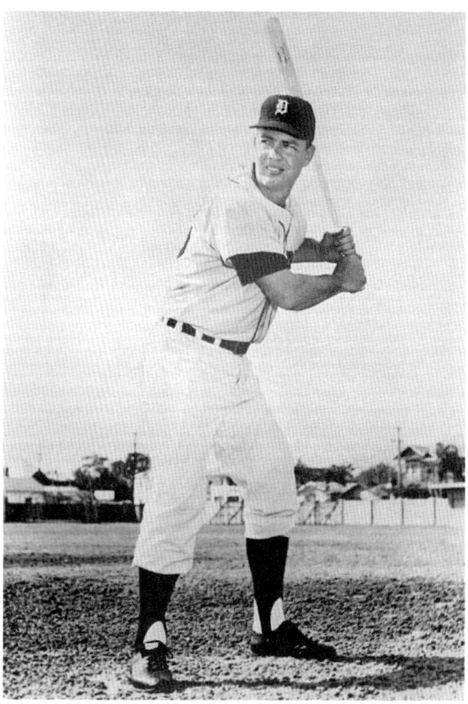

Harley May
At the first College National Rodeo in 1949, Harley May, at center in the back row, won the cowboy title, and also helped the Sul Ross team win. Over the next four years, Sul Ross and Harley May dominated the National Intercollegiate Rodeo Association. Graduating in 1951 with a bachelor's in science in range animal science, he turned professional, winning three World Champion Professional Cowboy titles. Altogether, he won 44 saddles and more than 200 buckles.

Norm Cash
Born in 1934 in Justiceburg, Texas, Norm Cash came to Sul Ross with a football scholarship in 1953. He could have played professional football but turned it down. Starting with the Chicago Bears, followed by the Cleveland Indians and the Detroit Tigers (1960), over 17 years in Major League baseball he hit 377 home runs. He was posthumously inducted into the Texas Sports Hall of Fame in 2002.

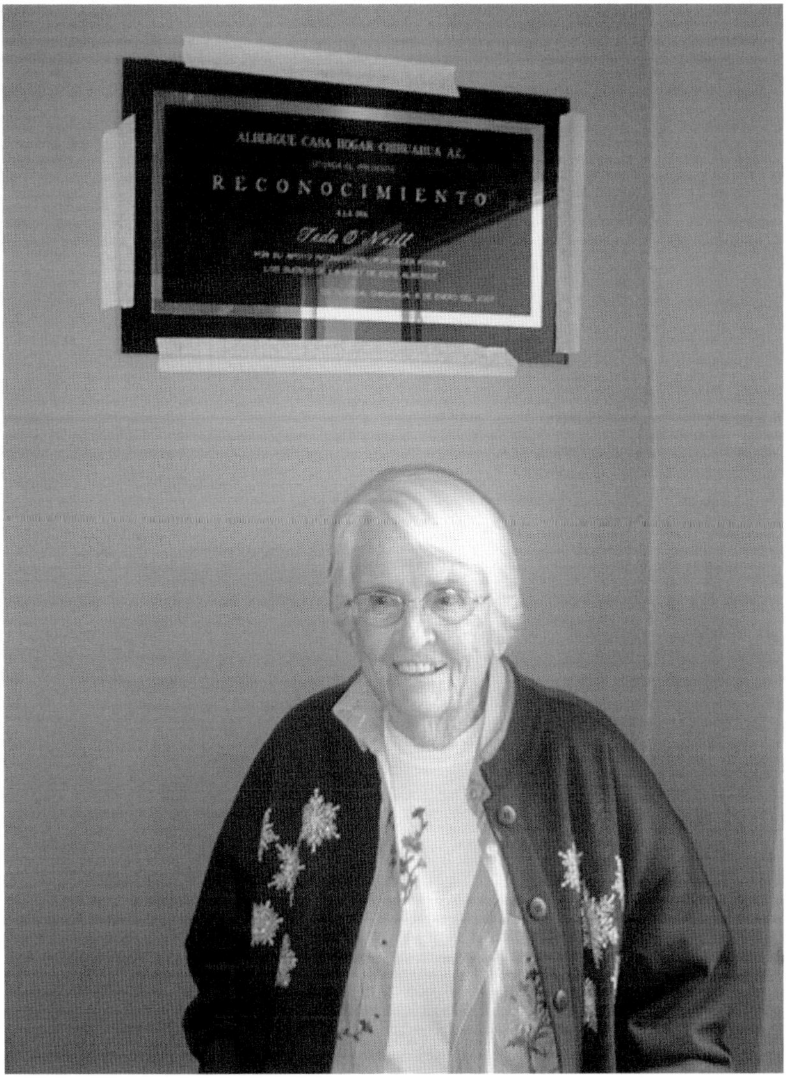

Teda Neill

In the summer of 2012, the youthful occupants of Casa Hogar, an orphanage for children in Ojinaga, Mexico, just across the border from Presidio, Texas, got ready for a party. The person they were honoring came from Texas for the event. Her name was Teda Neill, and she was 100 years old. In addition to the 40 Mexican youngsters, there were Ojinaga residents, the president of Ojinaga, and a contingent of supporters from Texas who had made this cross-border cooperation work.

Ten years ago, Casa Hogar (meaning "House of Shelter"), which was for children abandoned on the streets, was in poor condition. Roofs leaked, kids slept two to a bed, and the place was not clean. But a group of Texans from the Big Bend and Davis Mountains region, spearheaded by Victoria and Wes Bannister, with the willing participation of Teda Neill, started a support program of fundraising together with practical assistance, working through a binational board, which in time led to this remarkable transition.

At that party, presents were opened, speeches were made, and a mariachi band played while a big spread of food was laid out. Throughout it all, Teda Neill smiled, opened presents, and drew the Mexican youngsters close to her. (Author's collection.)

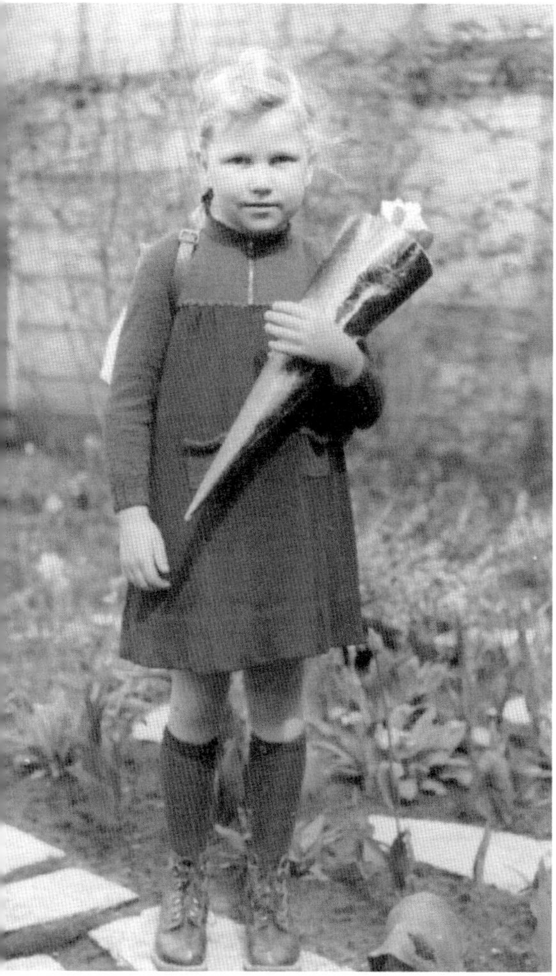

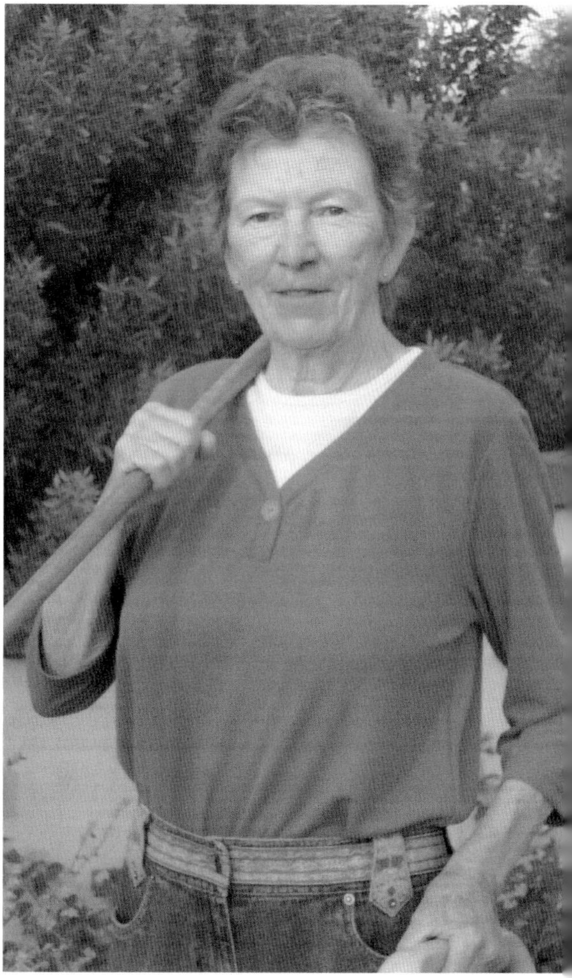

Edie Siebert Elfring

Edie Siebert was born on the tiny German island of Fehmarn in the Baltic Sea; she was often hungry but was at least wild and free. As a six-year-old, she first attended school, pictured here, in 1950. She wrote about those days in her memoir *Faraway, the Candle Softly Flickers*.

She came to the United States in 1968, worked many jobs, and then met and married Steve Elfring in St. Louis in 1981. They settled down south of Alpine in 2001. Since then, Edie has—unasked and unpaid—methodically picked up trash, weeded, pruned, and watered Alpine's three public gardens, as well as volunteering regularly at the Fort Davis Animal Shelter. In between, she participates in the Native Plant and Texas Master Naturalist Societies. (Left, courtesy of Edie Elfring; right, author's collection.)

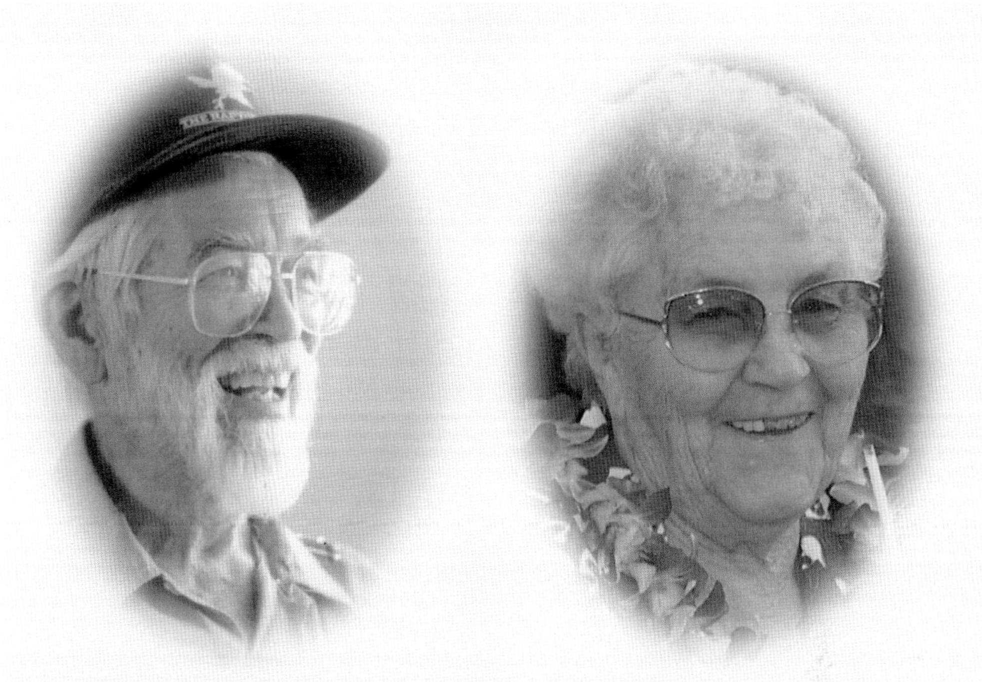

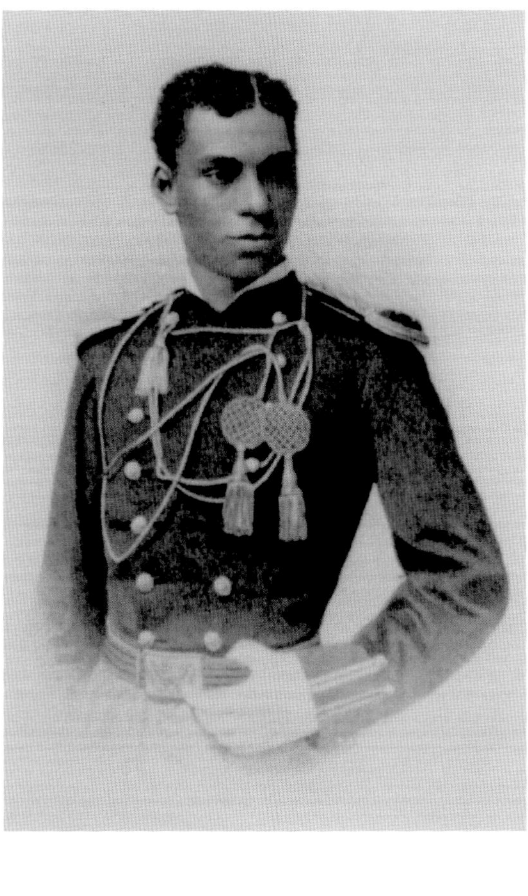

Hal and Mary Flanders
After a career as a telephone engineer, Hal Flanders retired in 1972 to Alpine with his wife, Mary. Hal saw the need for a recycling plant. He saw his dream come true when the Alpine City Council voted to make recycling permanent and named the site after him.

Mary, meanwhile, started a food cooperative that lasted for many, many years and became the largest in the area. (Photograph by Susan Penney.)

Henry O. Flipper
In 1877, Henry O. Flipper, aged 21, became the first black graduate of the United States Military Academy at West Point. He was assigned to the 10th US Cavalry at Fort Davis. In 1881, Flipper, in charge of the post's accounts, was court-martialed on a general charge when funds went missing and was cashiered. He subsequently led a successful civilian life as an engineer. He died in 1940. With the passage of time came changing attitudes. In 1999, President Clinton posthumously pardoned Flipper. (Photograph by United States Military Academy, West Point.)

INDEX

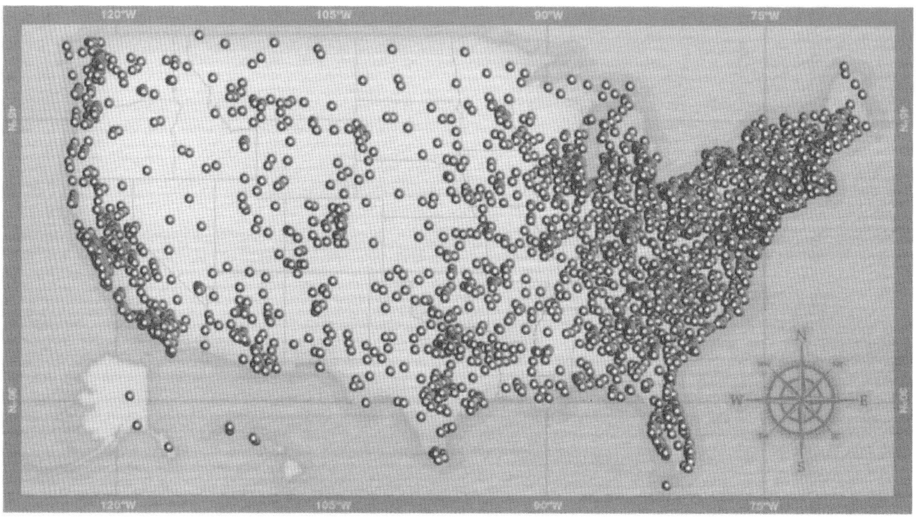